CIVIL DISOBEDIENCE
IN AMERICA

CIVIL DISOBEDIENCE IN AMERICA

A Documentary History
edited by
DAVID R. WEBER

CORNELL UNIVERSITY PRESS *Ithaca and London*

for NOEL PERRIN and
     DOUGLAS N. ARCHIBALD

*Our great error as a people is, that we put an idolatrous trust
in our free institutions; as if these, by some magic power,
must secure our rights, however we enslave ourselves to evil
passions. We need to learn that the forms of liberty are not its
essence; that whilst the letter of a free constitution is preserved
its spirit may be lost; that even its wisest provisions and most
guarded powers may be made weapons of tyranny.*
    —William Ellery Channing, "Spiritual Freedom" (1830)

Contents

VII. Epilogue

Preface

One purpose of this volume is to counter the widespread impression that the history of civil disobedience in the United States before the Vietnam period has only two figures of lasting interest, Henry David Thoreau and Martin Luther King. On the contrary: the advocates of civil disobedience in our history have been numerous, influential, and extraordinarily varied—in their group identities, their professions, their religious affiliations, their values and objectives. Women and men, blacks and whites, they include academic philosophers, congressmen, college presidents, laborers, genteel farmers, writers, and ministers of many denominations.

Their arguments are nearly as diverse as their backgrounds. Some were committed to nonviolence; others—including Thoreau (much literary history to the contrary notwithstanding) —were not. Some regarded going to jail as an integral part of the disobedient act; others—including Thoreau (despite his celebrated imprisonment)—did not. Some engaged in ad hominem attack and vituperation; others were careful to avoid extraneous grounds of offense. Many reached their disobedience reluctantly and with great regret; a few relished the role of iconoclast, radical, or combatant. Most ran at least some risk of incurring prosecution, fines, and imprisonment; some were indicted and a few jailed. Several of the ministers were dismissed from their churches or otherwise rejected by less principled or more moderate parishioners. Taken together, their essays, poems, sermons, speeches, and other writings make up a rich national heritage of conscientious dissent.

Within this diversity several themes reappear more or less continually. Despite the wide range of arguments and concerns, one is struck, for instance, by the prevalence in these documents of a certain sort of moderation, even of conservatism. Without precise historical definition such labels are not very satisfactory; but I want to emphasize how much feeling most of these disobedients have for much of American life, how far they are from being a collection of alienated iconoclasts or romantic visionaries. Two, for instance (Francis Wayland of Brown and John William Ward of Amherst), are college presidents, and I might have included others, such as Oberlin's James Fairchild. And if one profession tends to dominate the collection, it is the ministry—Baptists, Unitarians, transcendentalists, orthodox Congregationalists, Universalists. I hope the reader will sense how reluctant most of these people are to break the law, how seriously they take the possible objections to their position. Most of them believe that their mission is more nearly a self-sacrificing restoration of the law than a subversion of it. So they know very well that they need to have persuasive answers to the questions that are always asked of them: if authority—especially in a democratic society—is not based on the law of the land, what is it based on? And who is to determine it?

Since there are so many statements to choose from, I have been under some constraint from limitations of space. In deciding what to include I have been concerned first of all with articulated moral argument and advocacy rather than with narrative. Indeed, in some cases (William Ellery Channing's "Lecture on War," for example) the development of a rationale for civil disobedience does not seem to have been followed by actual illegal acts. (That Channing was not a lawbreaker, despite his principles, was due not to any hypocrisy but simply to the historical chance that he was not placed in personal conflict with a statute that compelled his resistance.) I have included these pieces nonetheless, both for their intrinsic interest and because some were widely known publications that were available to later disobedients and may well have influenced them. They are part of our theoretical tradition in any case, and perhaps, in the broad sense, of the practical one as well.

Second, I have tried to select documents and passages in which the persuasive language still works, documents that read well. In that sense the book has as much to do with literary history and the history of rhetoric as with the intellectual and social history of conscientious violations of the law. Thus the reader will find some fiction, poetry, and drama represented here as well as essays, sermons, and speeches.

One other principle of inclusion is worth noting. Some readers will perhaps feel that such pieces as Thomas Wentworth

Higginson's *Massachusetts in Mourning* and Thoreau's "Slavery in Massachusetts" pass in their full-blown militancy beyond civil disobedience into some other category of resistance to government, perhaps even into revolution. But our political history is more protean than such clean terminology suggests. Despite their rhetoric, Higginson and Thoreau are not revolutionaries: they do not aim—at least not here—at the transfer of governmental power or the reorganization of society in accordance with different economic or political principles. To both of them revolution is much more a moral than a political conception. That they embrace some forms of violence does indeed separate them in an important way from such gentler disobedients as John Greenleaf Whittier, but it does not necessarily mean that their disobedience has become something else. As other pieces in the volume will also show, the decision to disobey the law in the name of conscience and the choice of method by which to disobey it are distinguishable. Moreover, the choice of means is often provisional; one may be prepared philosophically for violence but be thankful that events do not call it forth. Such a position is not identical with that of a disobedient whose nonviolence is absolute, but neither does it seem so remote as to be altogether in a separate realm.

In any case, as the General Introduction will help to make clear, the documents that follow do not represent quite the full range of America's history of civil disobedience, even if one were to insist on a narrower definition of the term. The early part of that history includes several decades of opposition by Quakers, Baptists, and other dissenters from the establishmentarian church laws of the Massachusetts Bay Colony; from this period the reader will find here only a part of Isaac Backus's "Appeal to the Public for Religious Liberty," which appeared perhaps a century after the dissenters began to disobey the Puritan requirement that all parish residents pay a tax in support of the ministers of the (Congregational) Standing Order. Many nineteenth-century advocates of civil disobedience are also missing from these pages. (To have included them all—especially from the period 1850–1854, when public declamation against the Fugitive Slave Law of 1850 was at its height—would have required several volumes.) And the reader will see at once that the disobedients of our own time have been relatively neglected. Since so many of these contemporary voices have already been anthologized, I have chosen to include from the modern civil rights movement and the Vietnam period only a few classic pieces and a couple of others that seem particularly suggestive in relation to earlier ones.

At many points in the preparation of this collection I have been assisted and encouraged by the resourceful and generous efforts of colleagues and friends. My largest debt is to Richard Ward Day, of the Montclair-Kimberley Academy, and Alan H. Vrooman, John B. Heath, and Henry F. Bedford, all of the Phillips Exeter Academy, who made it possible for me to have a year free for scholarly work. Mr. Bedford has also been an acute and helpful critic of the draft of the General Introduction and some of the headnotes. I am also grateful for the cooperation and assistance of the staffs of several libraries; I thank especially Frances F. Gates of the New Hampshire State Library and Mary Lee Worboys and Edouard Desrochers of the Phillips Exeter Academy Library. Bernice B. Nichols of the Swarthmore College Peace Collection, Donald S. Harrington of The Community Church of New York, and Robert E. Anderson, Jr., of the Southern Regional Council have been more than courteous in helping me to secure access to documents that are not readily available. My father, Louis A. Weber, and Michael A. Schiffman have skillfully simplified the task of obtaining documents and securing permissions. Horace S. Peck, literary sleuth extraordinaire, has given me a gloss on a difficult reference in one of the texts and has otherwise provided moral support. My wife, Ilona Weber, has been patient in many ways, not least in her willingness to share the labor of verifying transcribed textual material. Finally it is a pleasure to record my gratitude to Jervis Anderson, Albert Bigelow, William Sloane Coffin, Jr., Michael Ferber, Margaret Finch, Charlotte E. Keyes, Haynes Trébor, and John William Ward for their cordial willingness to provide information and good cheer in precise, unstinting correspondence.

DAVID R. WEBER

Exeter, New Hampshire

CIVIL DISOBEDIENCE IN AMERICA

General Introduction

The potential for civil disobedience lies deep in the mainstream of American attitudes and thought. "The Judeo-Christian religion," Harrop Freeman observes, "has always maintained the duty to obey God speaking through conscience as superior to any civil law. . . . Touch where you will American thought and you will find this same emphasis on conscience." [1] But it is one thing to say that the concept of the rights and obligations of conscience is sanctioned by much of our religious tradition; it would be quite another to imply that civil disobedience has generally had a consensual support in our society. Many Americans have held attitudes or ideas that might have led them into conscientious lawbreaking; but most have had other, contradictory ideas and values—as well as strong practical motives —that have led them to avoid or oppose it. Sometimes their refusal to break the law has made their professions of religious conviction seem hypocritical. John Richardson, a Baptist minister in mid–nineteenth-century Massachusetts, thought that the distance between their religious theory and their secular practice did little credit to the supporters of the Fugitive Slave Law of 1850:

> Near that month of 1850, in which the Constitutional Convention was assembled in Faneuil Hall to urge submission to the Fugitive Slave Law and discountenance the doctrine of the higher law, addressed by the Curtises, the Halletts, the Choates and the Henshaws,* I was sitting in one of the school rooms of this town listening to a class who were reading a section which inculcated the sentiment that God's law should be obeyed and man's disobeyed when the latter required a conduct contrary to the former. The subject of the narrative was a Roman Christian, commended because he would not violate the laws of his Master, Jesus Christ, to practice obedience to a law of his country. The textbook from which this

---

*Supreme Court Justice Benjamin Robbins Curtis, U.S. Commissioner George Ticknor Curtis, District Attorney Benjamin Franklin Hallett, former Senator Rufus Choate, and former Secretary of the Navy David Henshaw were prominent figures in Massachusetts law and politics who supported Daniel Webster's advocacy of the Compromise of 1850.—Ed.

class were reading is in extensive use in the schools of this Commonwealth. Why do not the conductors of the Faneuil Hall meeting raise a crusade against the instruction of the children in Massachusetts? If all the principles promulgated in the convention are truthful, the books which our children read should be expelled from their schools. The religious ideas, the sentiments of the Bible that have worked in our educational system ought, according to the wisdom of those who plead for submission to an iniquitous law, to be expurgated from every page on which the youth of our land cast their eye. Do these men know what they are doing?[2]

Whether or not the men he names were, as Richardson believed, at best confused about their own ideas and motives, for many other Americans—Christian theologians as well as ordinary citizens—conscience itself has flatly forbidden lawbreaking, "conscientious" or otherwise. So civil disobedience has remained the province of what has arguably been a "wise minority" (in Thoreau's famous phrase); in any case this minority has usually been small. Yet it has been a felt presence in American thought and life out of all proportion to its numbers. The issues it has raised seem to have become a characteristic and revealing part of American intellectual and moral experience.

The history of American civil disobedience falls into three broad and generally distinct traditions. The first is opposition, mainly by individual dissenters in the seventeenth and eighteenth centuries, to legal violations of the principle of religious liberty; the second is disobedience, mainly in the nineteenth century and among many twentieth-century war resisters, to statutes that seemed to implicate individual citizens in immoral actions; the third is the use of mass civil disobedience as a tactic to achieve social or legal change, mainly in the civil rights movement of the 1950s and 1960s. Each of these traditions has its own characteristic forms, its own internal logic, and its own problems.

A good many of these traits and difficulties are discussed in the documents themselves and described in the headnotes. These introductory remarks will seek to characterize the three main varieties of American civil disobedience, to consider the major issues that have been present in the debate from the beginning, and to assess some of the implications of this history for our contemporary political life.

The first of the three traditions was a continuing part of the life of the Massachusetts Bay Colony, where dissenters against the orthodox (Congregational) Standing Order, mainly Quakers and then Baptists as well, were hanged, banished, or whipped. Later they were fined, imprisoned, or distrained (that is, their goods were seized and sold to raise the money they had refused to pay in taxes for the support of orthodox ministers). They seem to have produced for several decades no manifesto or discourse suitable for inclusion here. But their spirit is suggested by the Quaker John Tucker's statement to the Bristol (Massachusetts) County Court at the session of 1702–1703. The town of Dartmouth, he said, far from complying with the legal requirement to choose and support an orthodox minister, "doth absolutely refuse to do what the law in that case Requires."[3]

By the mid–eighteenth century the dissenters' lot had improved somewhat. The physical ferocity of the penalties meted out to them had declined, but the milder punishments were severe enough: one woman in Raynham, Massachusetts, was jailed for thirteen months when she refused to pay a tax of nine pence.[4] Through a series of laws passed in 1727 and the years following, an Anglican, Baptist, or Quaker could obtain exemption from church taxes by filing "an annual certificate signed by his minister and a committee of respectable lay members of his church attesting that he was 'conscientiously' of their persuasion."[5] This attempt at statutory accommodation was fatally undermined, however, by a combination of factors: social prejudice against the dissenters, with its resulting bitterness; the readiness of parish tax assessors to deny the validity of many certificates by exploiting legal technicalities, so that the dissenters' revenue wouldn't be lost to the orthodox community; and finally, the dissenters' sense (partly as a result of these pressures) that the mere requirement of the certificate itself was a violation of religious liberty, since it granted to the civil authority the power to sanction spiritual choices and to penalize unacceptable religious views.[6]

So the new laws did not bring the disobedience to an end. Instead the Baptists, frustrated by continuing harassment after decades of more or less patient suffering, felt driven to new measures. The manifesto of their new mode of resistance was Isaac Backus's "Appeal to the Public for Religious Liberty," which in its strategies is perhaps the nearest thing in our earlier history to an anticipation of the mass civil disobedience advocated in the twentieth century by A. Philip Randolph and Martin Luther King. In its central principle, however, Backus's pamphlet looks back rather than forward: for him what is at stake is still religious freedom implemented by separation of church and state.[7]

American civil disobedience begins, then, with resistance to specifically religious persecution or harassment, rather than with opposition to injustice conceived in broader or more secular terms. In its tenacious defense of the right to determine freely the forms and content of one's own religious practice, this tradition looks back to the religious martyrs of the Bible. It had numerous advocates and practitioners in the two centuries before religious disestablishment was fully achieved.

This earlier tradition served and in some sense fostered its successors, since religious experience, religious commitments, and religious logic remained central to American civil disobedience. Throughout the ante bellum period Protestant ministers advocated (and opposed) civil disobedience in sermons based on biblical texts; and disobedience as recent as Dr. King's and the Berrigans' is of course informed by Christian faith and passion. In one crucial respect, however, the early tradition had little help to offer subsequent disobedients: the resistance of Baptists and Quakers to religious taxes had scrupulously avoided any challenge to secular authority in most of its provinces; it had been merely an attempt to exempt religious worship from the realm of that authority. These early disobedients were, William McLoughlin observes, "radicals only in religion; their social and political views were virtually identical with their neighbors', and on moral issues . . . they were decidedly conservative."[8] So the newer strain of disobedience had in an important way a more delicate task; Jonathan Mayhew, John Woolman, and William Ellery Channing had carried the prohibitions and prescriptions of Christian revelation onto new ground. The challenge now was to vindicate the rights of the individual conscience in some secular areas without undermining the authority of human government generally. Those ministers who sought to extend the doctrine of religious liberty and obligation into social and political behavior were angrily challenged on the ground that they were now "preaching politics." Laymen who made the same arguments were accused of anarchy. This issue has been a live one ever since; so in considering the principal defenses developed by nineteenth-century disobedients, we shall anticipate as well some aspects of the twentieth-century debate.

Throughout much of our history, then, the advocates of civil disobedience have been accused of holding principles that lead straight to disorder, anarchy, or subversion, or at best to violations of law in support of less admirable causes than those of religious liberty, racial and sexual justice, and peace. The disobedients have generally replied to this charge in two ways. First, they have argued that the prediction is false, that it is only the "wise minority" that will brave legal and social sanctions in the name of conscience; they have suggested further that their own effort to maintain the connection between law and justice by opposing unjust legislation will do more in the long run to foster reverence for law than will the inflexible authoritarianism of their opponents. The latter, they have argued, will breed cynicism about the moral dimension of the law and thus, however paradoxically, will itself ultimately foster lawlessness. Second, they have simply maintained that the moral imperative under which they act transcends all concern for consequences. The abolition of slavery, Thoreau said, is one of those cases "in which a people, as well as an individual, must do justice, cost what it may. . . . This people must cease to hold slaves, and to make war on Mexico, though it cost them their existence as a people."[9]

The first of these positions has not always held true. One need not consider here the whole range of American lawlessness that has had nothing to do with conscientious motives or moral principles, since such behavior would presumably have taken place whether the society had had its advocates of civil disobedience or not. But more complicated instances have occurred: certainly Jeb Magruder's Watergate testimony (see the Epilogue) is one fulfillment of the antidisobedients' predictions. An earlier case —and a more difficult one theoretically—is that of Amos Kendall, Andrew Jackson's postmaster general, who upheld the refusal of southern postmasters to deliver abolitionist literature. "We owe an obligation to the laws," Kendall stated publicly, "but we owe a higher one to the communities in which we live, and if the former be perverted to destroy the latter, it is patriotism to disregard them." [10]

The second defense—that consequences should not be consulted in matters of overriding principle—is still less satisfactory, since it lends itself to a potentially dangerous level of romantic abstraction. To borrow terms from Richard Hofstadter, disobedients who hold their actions to be above a consideration of consequences have scorned "the rational calculus of tactical probabilities"; their "claims for therapy or sanctification . . . rest upon an arbitrary assumption of success." [11] For two reasons, however, the argument of the disobedients is less sinister than that of the advocates of "revolutionary" violence whom Hofstadter discusses. The first is simply that the risks of immediate harm are much smaller and less grave in the disobedients' case; the second is that their position is based upon a metaphysical optimism that they affirmed in innocence and good faith. In the nineteenth century they simply took for granted that since a benign devine providence ultimately determined the nature and course of human history, any truly conscientious action could not fail to have generally beneficial consequences. This was a central element in their world view, not an easy rationalization or a mask for self-indulgence. (Most of their nineteenth-century opponents in fact shared this premise, while drawing different conclusions from it.) [12] Even if to us this perspective is no longer available, our grimmer sense of history ought not to impose a too hasty judgment of their personal choices.

In any case, today's disobedients are likely to be diffident about consequences. Perhaps all that they can really say on this score is that even if they contribute to a decline in respect for the law—even if they do make it more likely that the sort of confused lawbreaking done by Magruder will take place—the gains of their disobedience in upholding moral principles and social justice are worth that price; that the tawdrier forms of "conscientious" disobedience are more fairly viewed as the responsibility of their perpetrators than as the unintended consequence of other disobedience; and that opposition to civil disobedience runs its own risks of abuse, as the history of Nazi Germany and My Lai have clearly shown.

Another recurrent issue that disobedients have had to face from early on is the relation of their lawbreaking to violence. It is widely assumed that this problem has had a single solution—that nonviolence is a necessary aspect of civil disobedience—but the assumption is arbitrary and unhistorical. It has led among other things to a view of Thoreau which misrepresents him by making his civil disobedience far more similar to Gandhi's and King's than it actually is. Among nineteenth-century disobedients John Greenleaf Whittier is actually a much closer parallel: "the destruction of one human life," Whittier said categorically, "would be too great a price to pay for any social or political change." [13] Whittier generally held to this absolute nonviolence even during the turmoil over the Fugitive Slave Law; and many other nineteenth-century disobedients—Nathaniel Hall is an example—joined him in this stand. Their position is remote, however, from the one espoused by some others. Thomas Wentworth Higginson is perhaps the most overt exponent in this volume of a willingness to adopt physical violence as an aspect of his disobedience, but Theodore Parker and Thoreau embrace the same logic. Even so cautious a contemporary of theirs as Frederic Henry Hedge, who described himself as "ecclesiastically conservative, though intellectually radical," [14] wrote to a friend after the fugitive slave Anthony Burns had been surrendered to the authorities in 1854:

> To my feelings it would have been much more satisfactory if some demonstration, however ineffectual had been made & even if some lives had been sacrificed in the cause of freedom. Until that is the case I am convinced there will be no end to the surrender of fugitives.
> I think that some of those people who talked so big at Faneuil Hall should have proved their zeal by their acts. . . . The antislavery men in Boston ought to have been long ago organized & armed for such exigencies. . . . What provokes me most is the unhesitating alacrity with which the Boston &

Massachusetts companies of militia came forward at call to enforce the law of bondage—not one resignation of office. And then the legal pretence, & the foolish talk 'The law must be obeyed' as if it were not better for law and order that there should be a mob in a just cause than that the universal sense of justice should be outraged by the execution of an unrighteous law. . . .[15]

Similarly Wendell Phillips, despite his long association with William Lloyd Garrison, argued in 1852 that fugitive slaves could legitimately use violence to prevent their recapture; his position is, he notes, "a new measure in the antislavery enterprise."[16] Phillips spoke for those abolitionists who were theoretically committed to nonviolence but who discovered under the pressure of events that their deepest feelings actually lay elsewhere and thus reluctantly came to accept the logic of a more militant position than they had wished to occupy.

Thoreau and Parker, however, had never adopted nonviolence as a positive principle to begin with. Even in "Resistance to Civil Government" ("Civil Disobedience"), written before the fugitive slave cases of the 1850s had clarified the ways in which violence might be morally justified, Thoreau had separated himself from "those who call themselves no-government men"— that is, from the radical nonresistants. And once the fugitive slave issue had been posed, Parker was quick to add firearms to the resources of his Bible.

Perhaps it will be objected that Thoreau, Parker, and Higginson had actually moved beyond civil disobedience into a form of revolution or at least of guerrilla warfare. It is true that Higginson and Parker were to be two of the Secret Six who raised funds for John Brown in the weeks before his attack on Harpers Ferry, and that some of the language of "Slavery in Massachusetts" and *Massachusetts in Mourning* has a paramilitary ring. Further, in the sermons in which Parker espouses civil disobedience he often appeals to the moral authority of the American Revolution. We may clarify this question, I think, by considering somewhat more closely the logic by which certain forms of violence justified themselves to these men.

They derived their ideas from two sources that seemed to them complementary: the Bible and the Anglo-American tradition of natural rights and natural law by which the American Revolution had been justified. Parker liked to make the fusion symbolically explicit. When he married the escaped slaves William and Ellen Craft, members of his parish, he concluded the ceremony on a dramatic note: "he put a Bible and a sword into William's hands and bade him use both with all his might." [17]

A cornerstone of this position was the conviction that life, liberty, and the pursuit of happiness—especially life and liberty —were values of fully equal authority. An implication of this view was that someone whose liberty was threatened by a slave-catcher had precisely the same right of capital self-defense as one menaced by a would-be murderer. It meant too that just as a fellow citizen should if necessary intervene forcibly to prevent a killing, so he should employ whatever force was necessary to frustrate an attempt to kidnap a fugitive slave. In both cases the aggressor had forfeited his own right to further life by threatening the inalienable natural rights of someone else. These views, Parker and the others thought, were sanctioned by both natural and revealed religion, as well as by their association with our successful revolution. But these ideas did not necessarily move beyond civil disobedience to general resistance or revolution. They were available to men who had no thought of a general overthrow of the government in power; they were accepted by some whose resistance to law remained steadily focused on what they saw as a single anomalous statute. When Higginson, Parker, and Thoreau spoke of revolution, they were articulating a conception that was more moral than political. In short, this way of thinking about violence lent itself very readily to militant theories of civil disobedience.

Nonviolence, then, has by no means always been a part of civil disobedience. (The reverse is also true, of course: much of the tradition of nonviolent thought and nonviolent direct action—demonstrations, boycotts, protests, petitions—has no concern with lawbreaking.) Similarly, some but hardly all American disobedients have viewed an acceptance of legal penalties as an indispensable part of their illegal action. For some, going to jail has been an important symbol of their allegiance to the overall rule of law in the society; it has been a way of making clear the limits of their quarrel, of saying that though one particular statute compels their disobedience, the authority of secular law in general remains intact and binding. "Where duty to God and man required us to refuse active obedience to such enactments," Whittier said, "we would submit, *as good citizens*, to the penalty incurred."[18] On this point, as on nonviolence, Thoreau and many others take a different stance. Despite his famous night in the Concord jail, Thoreau seems to have regarded imprisonment as a risk to be run rather than as a symbolic experience to be embraced on principle. It is true that he calls jail "the only house in a slave State in which a free man can abide with honor" and that he argues for mass jailgoing by "all just men" as a means of bringing injustice to a halt. But just as his characteristic note is individualistic and not that of a participant in a movement, so his usual position about imprisonment is that it is an inconvenience imposed by the state, not an integral part of the act of civil disobedience. The disobedient in Thoreau's view has all the right on *his* side; he is not bound to make conciliatory bows to state authority. All the evidence seems to indicate that if Sam Staples had not come after him, Thoreau would not have sought out the jailhouse. Even in his hope of catalyzing resistance in many others, it is the readiness to face imprisonment—that is, the lawbreaking itself—which he emphasizes as the effective moral force. And in any case his rationale for the dissident's presence in jail is quite different from Whittier's and Hall's. For them it is a guarantee that civil disobedience will not tend to foster a breakdown of law and order. For Thoreau, when it isn't simply a price the disobedient has to pay for his moral freedom, it is an aggressive tactic by which the state can be made to give up its support of slavery. Thoreau believed that Massachusetts, through its complicity in slavery, had forfeited its moral authority generally; his is a much more radical analysis than the emphasis of Whittier and Hall on reconciling civil disobedience with loyal citizenship. Thoreau would have been quick to say that his own behavior was also in the interests of true citizenship; but the role played by imprisonment in his thinking about civil disobedience has none of the social piety of more conservative disobedients.

The complexities of Thoreau's "Resistance to Civil Government" should help us to see that American civil disobedience has often been ambiguously rooted in two distinguishable motives: the impulse to free oneself from guilt or sin and the impulse to end some social evil, to reform or remake the world. These objectives have sometimes been so harmonious that the disobedient has had no need to distinguish between them: Thoreau's essay—many other instances could be cited, especially from the nineteenth century—is shaped by the assumption that to act with maximum personal principle and integrity is also necessarily to act with maximum beneficial effect upon the social and political world (though such action may well involve a high price, possibly even martyrdom, for the disobedients themselves). Thoreau refused to pay his poll tax not only because a man could "not without disgrace be associated" with the government but because conscientious action was "essentially revolutionary" and held out far greater promise of bringing northern complicity in slavery to an end than political practicality could do.

In the twentieth century civil disobedience has tended to be inspired less by a vision of individual innocence maintained in opposition to state decree than by a determination to influence the state and the society both—either to restrain them from doing evil or to lead them into a process of active regeneration. A. Philip Randolph's testimony before the Senate Armed Services Committee in 1948 is in this sense a major watershed in the history of American civil disobedience. In his advocacy of disobedience in response to segregation in the armed forces, Randolph makes use of the concept of a "higher law," but his ideas are cast in secular and political terms:

> In resorting to the principles of direct-action techniques of Gandhi, whose death was publicly mourned by many members of Congress and President Truman, Negroes will be serving a higher law than any passed by a national legislature in an era when racism spells our doom. . . . In refusing to accept compulsory military segregation, Negro youth will be serving their fellow men throughout the world.
>
> I feel qualified to make this claim because of a recent survey of American psychologists, sociologists and anthropologists. The survey revealed an overwhelming belief among these ex-

perts that enforced segregation on racial or religious lines has serious and detrimental psychological effects both on the segregated groups *and on those enforcing segregation*. . . . Negro youth have a moral obligation not to lend themselves as world-wide carriers of an evil and hellish doctrine.[19]

Nothing in this appeal to the authority of modern science, however, would hinder an alliance between secular and religious disobedients. (Indeed, when Adam Clayton Powell supported Randolph's position before the committee, he envisioned a national movement of draft resistance led in the black community by its thousands of Protestant ministers.) Men of many different persuasions could share too in Randolph's appeal to the other authority on which his disobedience is based: the conceptions of equality and freedom at the center of our national political tradition.

At several points Randolph anticipates the thinking of Martin Luther King, though for King it was "Christ [who] furnished the spirit and motivation, while Gandhi furnished the method."[20] Like King, Randolph looks to Gandhi for both practical and moral reasons; he sees in Gandhi's movement both an instance of success in the struggle of dispossessed groups against established power and a compelling example of moral superiority to the wielders of power. Randolph's tone, however, holds less love and more anger than King's. While King's emphasis is on the power of nonviolent direct action, as a manifestation of love, to bring about the "blessed community," Randolph's is on the tactical strength of organized direct action by blacks and on the psychological benefits for black people that will follow from their having seized an independent initiative to secure the dignity of equal status. In this sense his perspectives and tonalities are more in harmony with those of contemporary black activism than King's.

Both Randolph and King value civil disobedience chiefly for its promise of desirable social results; but this emphasis is still fully in harmony with the older one on personal innocence. In the last ten years, however, the two motives have been felt more and more to be distinct, or even to be in conflict with each other. John William Ward's piece (in Part VI), for example, makes no romantic assumptions about the identity of conscientious and effective action. Ward was moved to his action by a wish to bear personal witness against the war in Vietnam and also by frustration that conventional methods of protest had had no influence upon American policy, but he was under no illusion that civil disobedience would be effective where other means had failed. In Stokely Carmichael's "Black Power" (Part V), on the other hand, this division between conscience and consequence was approached from the other direction: his sense of the power of institutionalized wrong was so intense that it all but eliminated any feeling that individual guilt or character was at stake. The solitary citizen, who is all but powerless, can bear little personal responsibility for his government's actions. Carmichael's call for mass civil disobedience was a tactic by which, he hoped, the normally powerless radical or liberal citizenry could cripple the projects of those in authority. Though his program at first seems similar to Randolph's, Carmichael's ideas are in some ways nearer to the concepts of a revolutionist than to Randolph's willingness to suffer in a just cause. By 1966 Carmichael had little or no stake in nonviolence, even for strategic purposes; he assumed that the resister's moral advantage over the state was so great that no obligation of restraint remained. Personal innocence, in other words, could now be taken for granted. In a way, Carmichael revived the Thoreau of "Slavery in Massachusetts."

In 1971 Allard Lowenstein invoked a different sense of the practical probabilities to oppose civil disobedience, feeling that its effects were likely to be the reverse of what the disobedients wished. Since civil disobedience was too radical and threatening to be accepted by most Americans, he argued, actions like the Berrigans' raid on the Catonsville draft board would tend to discredit rather than to galvanize popular opposition to the war. The citizen conscientiously opposed to the war, then, had to face an excruciating dilemma: he could end his own complicity through tax refusal or other illegal action, but only at the cost of futility or worse; or he could hope to play some role in turning public feeling against the war through more acceptable, conventional means, all the while paying taxes that would purchase automatic weapons and napalm. If he chose the latter course, he would probably be haunted by the possibility that his deepest motive for remaining within the law was the ignoble one of protecting himself from the penalties of disobedience. If he chose the former, he risked fearful personal consequences with very little assurance that he would achieve anything more than the semimartyrdom of imprisonment.

This sort of approach to questions of personal political ethics is perhaps distinctively modern in its fundamental lack of faith that goodness or justice will ultimately prevail in human affairs. Civil disobedience has never been an easy choice, because it has generally entailed great personal risks and has often been deeply troubling philosophically, even for its advocates. But in the latter part of the twentieth century, virtually bereft of political heroes and dominated by images (and not just images) of institutionalized power, it is perhaps harder than ever to sustain a sufficient sense of the reality and power of the individual conscience, a sense that makes civil disobedience an act of moral force and promise, not just of frustration or desperation. The wish or willingness to bear moral witness even at large personal cost must now contend with a malaise to which Thoreau and his contemporaries were generally immune: the sense that "in the vast impersonality of twentieth-century society and government, it has become almost impossible for individuals to affect the grinding course of things."[21] In short, it seems harder now to hold to either of the assumptions that have historically been at the heart of civil disobedience.

What does such a history suggest for a continuation of the practice of civil disobedience in our own time, should further cases arise? In the absence of the cases themselves, it is hard to say: one's sense of the moral authority of many of these voices depends considerably on the circumstances that precipitated their disobedience. But several tentative conclusions seem to suggest themselves.

First, to evaluate civil disobedience in terms of its likely effectiveness—its public results—is both necessary and insufficient. If disobedience does foster contempt for law, if it is ineffectual in ending the injustice it resists, if it does alienate its advocates from the rest of the society and thus remove them from practical social and political debate, then there is a strong moral argument to be made against it. If, on the other hand, it retains the capacity to awaken a passive citizenry to a new sense of obligation and responsibility, then this argument works the other way. The problem is that the calculation of these probabilities is extremely difficult. The passionate witness of the Berrigans shocked and antagonized many people, but who can say how many? And who can say how many others were stirred by it into taking more conventional action that ultimately helped to get American soldiers and bombers out of Vietnam? In some cases—the civil rights movement is one—civil disobedience does seem clearly to have been tactically valuable. But in many others, utilitarian or prudential arguments will remain inconclusive, and the decision will have to be made on more private grounds.

Second, the history may suggest something about the style in which disobedience may best be affirmed when the decision has been made. William Sloane Coffin argues (see the Epilogue) that what separates Jeb Magruder's lawbreaking from that of more admirable conscientious disobedients is that while he acted in secret, hoping to circumvent and frustrate the law, the others acted publicly and submitted themselves to public judgment. Historically this distinction is a shaky one; many intensely conscientious disobedients have felt no obligation to make their actions public or to pay a legal price for them. As a prescription, however, Coffin's view may be perfectly appropriate.

In a sense Coffin's argument may serve as a foil to Thoreau. There is unquestionably in the unaccommodating Thoreauvian stance something exhilarating, something that calls one to acts of principle and courage. But his moral certainty also carries the risk of self-righteousness, of arrogance. Perhaps those who are drawn to him but who do not share his romantic assumptions can keep what is essential by modifying his style. Both as a practical and as a private matter, an acceptance of penalties as part of the disobedient act may strengthen that act's moral position. The penalty can serve not as a sign of fealty to the state but rather as a recognition by the disobedient of his own social accountability. It may be an appropriate concession to the chance of error or abuse; it may help to keep even the wise minority honest and self-critical.

The classic recent instance of disobedience in which these issues have been painfully alive is of course that of Daniel and

Philip Berrigan, who began in the public mode and then shifted to a fugitive style after their conviction. Morally this choice was, I think, reasonable and consistent; they had, like Thoreau, reached a point of categorical rejection of the government's moral authority. They must have felt that to submit meekly to its penalties would have been obsequious and masochistic, that it would have blunted the edge of their statement. Like Thoreau, Parker, and Higginson, they were engaged in moral revolution. Nonetheless, one may feel that as a practical matter their own cause would have been better served had they held steadily to a more conciliatory mode, one in which they accepted the government's authority to punish them even as they denied its right to do so. To act in the less antagonistic way reduces the chance that those who are undecided will switch the issue from the government's behavior to one's own. But such a calculation is always problematical. The Berrigans deliberately adopted their final mode of disobedience in the hope that the radical symbolism of their action would stimulate further resistance and in the faith that adequate social safeguards were inherent in their Christian roots, their Christian witness. If the experiment now seems not to have succeeded, that is not to say that in 1968 it was not worth trying.

A third use of history may be to show us the utility of the assumptions that have been lost to us. It is probably impossible for us to recover the sense of historical faith by which most of these disobedients were at least partly sustained. But their confident courage may remind us that our own chastened world view has its own liabilities—that to accept as inescapable a historical pessimism may be to engage in self-fulfilling prophecies. If so, then to give up altogether the idea of civil disobedience may be a choice with its own considerable risks; we may do better to keep the tradition in mind, however tentatively. And for private purposes we may wish to recall Thoreau's warning that there is "a sort of blood shed when the conscience is wounded. Through this wound a man's real manhood and immortality flow out, and he bleeds to an everlasting death. I see this blood flowing now." Despite the secularization of our society, it is perhaps here more than anywhere else that the roots of future disobedience lie dormant.

I ORIGINS

Your studies, I doubt not, you pursue, because I know you to be a studious youth; but, above all, preserve a sacred regard to your own honor and reputation. Your morals are worth all the sciences. Your conscience is the minister plenipotentiary of God Almighty in your breast. See to it that this minister never negotiates in vain. Attend to him in opposition to all the courts in the world.

—John Adams to John Quincy Adams, 1782

1. Edward Hart and others:
The Flushing Remonstrance (1657)

When militantly evangelical Baptists and Quakers came to New Netherland in the mid-1650s, they precipitated disobedience and confrontation in a community already charged with political, religious, and national tensions. The conflict was sharpest in Flushing, most of whose inhabitants were English settlers living as aliens under the Dutch colonial rule of the West India Company and its Calvinist governor, Peter Stuyvesant. Though the company wished, for the sake of the struggling colony's health, to encourage settlement through liberal policies of religious tolerance, still it gave official sanction only to Holland's established church, the Dutch Reformed. Though most other Protestants could worship without harassment, only the Reformed church could be sure of the right to hold "assemblies or conventicles." Even Lutherans were arrested and jailed by Stuyvesant for attempting to hold public services. The government also sought to support the Reformed church through a tax on all inhabitants. In Flushing this practice led to numerous instances of tax refusal.

To Stuyvesant the Quakers in particular were anathema. When he found that inhabitants of the colony's English towns were extending hospitality to them and even joining them in private meetings, he "issued a proclamation, which was printed on placards and posted in every town, declaring that any person entertaining a Quaker for a single night was to be fined 50 florins, of which one-half was to go to whoever informed the authorities."[1]

The townspeople of Flushing regarded this proclamation as a violation of religious freedom and as grossly inconsistent with the terms of their town patent, granted them in 1645 by Stuyvesant's predecessor, Governor Kieft; that document had specified their right "to have and enjoy liberty of conscience, according to the custom and manner of Holland, without molestation or disturbance from any magistrates, or any other ecclesiastical minister, that may pretend jurisdiction over them."[2]

This language was not without its ambiguities, however, and both the Dutch government and the West India Company had trouble reconciling their conflicting religious and political interests. On the one hand, the representatives of the Reformed church, both in Holland and in the colony, pressed them to limit the spread of unorthodox sects; on the other, the growth and prosperity of the colony were dependent on a climate of considerable religious freedom. In any case, "liberty of conscience, according to the custom and manner of Holland," did not extend to a license to oppose civil authority, and Stuyvesant was unmoved by the Remonstrance's reference to the town patent. The four signers who were town officials in Flushing were jailed and removed from office. One, Sheriff Tobias Feake, was given a choice between a heavy fine and banishment from the province; the others were freed after apologies, pleas for mercy, promises not to commit further offenses in the future, and the intercession of neighbors. These recantations under duress did not, however, alter the tolerance of many of the signers toward the Quakers. Several years later the same issues were raised in the case of John Bowne, who was arrested by Stuyvesant for inviting Quakers to worship in his home. Bowne tenaciously appealed to the West India Company, and was, after extraordinary efforts and considerable personal sacrifice, ultimately vindicated.

Reprinted from Haynes Trébor, *The Flushing Remonstrance: The Origin of Religious Freedom in America* (Flushing, N.Y., 1957), pp. 3–4, by permission of Haynes Trébor.

Right Honorable,

You have been pleased to send up unto us a certain prohibition or command that we should not receive or entertain any of those people called Quakers because they are supposed to be by some, seducers of the people. For our part we cannot condemn them in this case, neither can we stretch out our hands against them, to punish, banish or persecute them, for out of Christ God is a consuming fire, and it is a fearful thing to fall into the hands of the living God.

We desire therefore in this case not to judge least we be judged, neither to condemn least we be condemned, but rather let every man stand and fall to his own Master. Wee are bounde by the Law to doe good unto all men, especially to those of the household of faith. And though for the present we seem to be unsensible of the law and the Law giver, yet when death and the Law assault us, if wee have our advocate to seeke, who shall plead for us in this case of conscience betwixt God and our own souls; the powers of this world can neither attack us, neither excuse us, for if God justifye who can condemn and if God condemn there is none can justifye.

And for those jealousies and suspicions which some have of them, that they are destructive unto Magistracy and Minstereye, that can not bee, for the magistrate hath the sword in his hand and the minister hath the sword in his hand, as witnesse those two great examples which all magistrates and ministers are to follow, Moses and Christ, whom God raised up maintained and defended against all the enemies both of flesh and spirit; and therefore that which is of God will stand, and that which is of man will come to nothing. And as the Lord hath taught Moses or the civil power to give an outward liberty in the state by the law written in his heart designed for the good of all, and can truly judge who is good, who is evill, who is true and who is false, and can pass definitive sentence of life or death against that man which rises up against the fundamental law of the States General; soe he hath made his ministers a savor of life unto life, and a savor of death unto death.

The law of love, peace and liberty in the states extending to Jews, Turks, and Egyptians, as they are considered the sonnes of Adam, which is the glory of the outward state of Holland, soe love, peace and liberty, extending to all in Christ Jesus, condemns hatred, war and bondage. And because our Saviour saith it is impossible but that offenses will come, but woe unto him by whom they cometh, our desire is not to offend one of his little ones, in whatsoever form, name or title hee appears in, whether Presbyterian, Independent, Baptist or Quaker, but shall be glad to see anything of God in any of them, desiring to doe unto all men as wee desire all men should doe unto us, which is the true law both of Church and State; for our Saviour saith this is the law and the prophets.

Therefore if any of these said persons come in love unto us, we cannot in conscience lay violent hands upon them, but give them free egresse and regresse unto our Town, and houses, as God shall persuade our consciences. And in this we are true subjects both of Church and State, for we are bounde by the law of God and man to doe good unto all men and evil to noe man. And this is according to the patent and charter of our Towne,

given unto us in the name of the States General, which we are
not willing to infringe, and violate, but shall houlde to our patent and shall remaine, your humble subjects, the inhabitants of
Vlishing.

Written this 27th day of December, in the year 1657, by mee

EDWARD HART, *Clericus*

2. Jonathan Mayhew: "Discourse Concerning Unlimited Submission and Non-Resistance to the Higher Powers" (1750)

Jonathan Mayhew was from 1747 until his death in 1766 the conten-
tious, radically antiauthoritarian minister of Boston's West Church. In
theology he was one of the early Arminian forerunners of ante bellum
Unitarianism; in politics he raised a strenuous voice against the doctrine
of the divine right of kings and in favor of liberal, Lockean, Whig concepts of government. The legitimacy of secular authority, Mayhew
believed, is contingent on its success and good faith in advancing the
well-being and happiness of the people. He was not a highly original
theoretician but was a prominent, bold, and influential controversialist.

Mayhew was far from being a revolutionary by intention. "To his
dying day," his biographer Charles Akers points out, "he thought of
himself as a true Englishman, loyal—certainly more loyal than Governor Bernard—to the beloved though nebulous British constitution."[1]
Nonetheless, his "Discourse Concerning Unlimited Submission"
helped to establish potentially revolutionary ideas and attitudes in the
northern colonies. This impassioned, truculent sermon, Bernard Bailyn
has observed, "created for the extreme radical position on the subject of
civil disobedience a more attentive public audience than it had had before in America."[2]

Actually this sermon is not very consciously concerned with the individual citizen who has been confronted by a law he believes to be
unjust. Preaching on the anniversary of the death of Charles I, Mayhew
wants first of all to insist that the authority of a king or of any other
human government is limited; he wants to vindicate the right of the
people to overthrow a government that has become tyrannical.
Nonetheless, in its assertion that resistance to government is
sometimes a positive duty, and above all in its reserving to "the reason
and consciences of men" the decision whether or not the point of

unbearable injustice has been reached, Mayhew's sermon points the way toward acts of individual disobedience. Indeed, most of the logic of the sermon applies with equal force to single statutes that dismay private consciences. Mayhew had also defended civil disobedience more explicitly (if less memorably) in an unpublished sermon the previous year:

> It indeed is often a sin to transgress human laws; but not universally so. It is possible for human legislators who are sometimes wicked, and always fallible, to enact unrighteous laws; to enjoin things that are in their own nature unlawful; and to forbid things that are in their own nature good and commendable. Now when iniquity comes to be thus established by a law, it can not be any iniquity to transgress that law by which it is established. On the contrary, it is a sin not to transgress it. . . . It is universally better to obey God than Man, when the laws of God and Man clash and interfere one with another.[3]

✿ Reprinted from John Wingate Thornton, ed., *The Pulpit of the American Revolution; or, The Political Sermons of the Period of 1776* (Boston: Gould & Lincoln, 1860), pp. 73–74, 76–77, 78–79, 84–86.

Rulers have no authority from God to do mischief. . . . It is blasphemy to call tyrants and oppressors God's ministers. They are more properly "the messengers of Satan to buffet us." No rulers are properly God's ministers but such as are "just, ruling in the fear of God." When once magistrates act contrary to their office, and the end of their institution—when they rob and ruin the public, instead of being guardians of its peace and welfare—, they immediately cease to be the ordinance and ministers of God, and no more deserve that glorious character than common pirates and highwaymen. So that, whenever that argument for submission fails which is grounded upon the usefulness of magistracy to civil society—as it always does when magistrates do hurt to society instead of good—, the other argument, which is taken from their being the ordinance of God, must necessarily fail also; no person of a civil character being God's minister, in the sense of the apostle, any further than he performs God's will by exercising a just and reasonable authority, and ruling for the good of the subject.

If magistrates are unrighteous,—if they are respecters of persons,—if they are partial in their administration of justice,—then those who do well have as much reason to be afraid as those that do evil: there can be no safety for the good, nor any peculiar ground of terror to the unruly and injurious; so that, in this case, the main end of civil government will be frustrated. And what reason is there for submitting to that government which does by no means answer the design of government? "Wherefore ye must needs be subject not only for wrath, but also for conscience' sake." Here the apostle [Paul] argues the duty of a cheerful and conscientious submission to civil government from the nature and end of magistracy, as he had before laid it down; *i.e.*, as the design of it was to punish evil-doers, and to support and encourage such as do well; and as it must, if so exercised, be agreeable to the will of God. But how does what he here says prove the duty of a cheerful and conscientious subjection to those who forfeit the character of rulers?—to those who encourage the bad and discourage the good? The argument here used no more proves it to be a sin to resist such rulers than it does to resist the devil, that he may flee from us. For one is as truly the minister of God as the other. "For, for this cause pay you tribute also; for they are God's ministers, attending continually upon this very thing." Here the apostle argues the duty of paying taxes from this consideration, that those who perform the duty of rulers are continually attending upon the public welfare. But how does this argument conclude for paying taxes to such princes as are continually endeavoring to ruin the public; and especially when such payment would facilitate and promote this wicked design? . . .

I now add, further, that the apostle's argument is so far from proving it to be the duty of people to obey and submit to such rulers as act in contradiction to the public good, and so to the design of their office, that it proves the direct contrary. For, please to observe, that if the end of all civil government be the good of society; if this be the thing that is aimed at in constituting civil rulers; and if the motive and argument for submission to government be taken from the apparent usefulness of civil authority,—it follows, that when no such good end can be answered by submission, there remains no argument or motive to enforce it; and if, instead of this good end's being brought about by submission, a contrary end is brought about, and the ruin and misery of society effected by it, here is a plain and positive reason against submission in all such cases, should they ever happen. And therefore, in such cases, a regard to the public welfare ought to make us withhold from our rulers that obedience and submission which it would otherwise be our duty to render to them. If it be our duty, for example, to obey our king merely for this reason, that he rules for the public welfare (which is the only argument the apostle makes use of), it follows, by a parity of reason, that when he turns tyrant, and makes his subjects his prey to devour and destroy, instead of his charge to defend and cherish, we are bound to throw off our allegiance to him, and to resist; and that according to the tenor of the apostle's argument in this passage. Not to discontinue our allegiance in this case would be to join with the sovereign in promoting the slavery and misery of that society, the welfare of which we ourselves, as well as our sovereign, are indispensably obliged to secure and promote, as far as in us lies. It is true the apostle puts no case of such a tyrannical prince; but, by his grounding his argument for submission wholly upon the good of civil society, it is plain he implicitly authorizes, and even requires us to make resistance, whenever this shall be necessary to the public safety and happiness. . . .

But, then, if unlimited submission and passive obedience to the higher powers, in all possible cases, be not a duty, it will be asked, "How far are we obliged to submit? If we may innocently disobey and resist in some cases, why not in all? Where shall we stop? What is the measure of our duty? This doctrine tends to the total dissolution of civil government, and to introduce such scenes of wild anarchy and confusion as are more fatal to society than the worst of tyranny."

After this manner some men object; and, indeed, this is the most plausible thing that can be said in favor of such an absolute submission as they plead for. But the worst, or, rather, the best of it is, that there is very little strength or solidity in it; for similar difficulties may be raised with respect to almost every duty of natural and revealed religion. To instance only in two, both of which are near akin, and indeed exactly parallel to the case before us: It is unquestionably the duty of children to submit to their parents, and of servants to their masters; but no one asserts that it is their duty to obey and submit to them in all supposable cases, or universally a sin to resist them. Now, does this tend to subvert the just authority of parents and masters, or to introduce confusion and anarchy into private families? No. How, then, does the same principle tend to unhinge the government of that larger family the body politic? We know, in general, that children and servants are obliged to obey their parents and masters respectively; we know also, with equal certainty, that they are not obliged to submit to them in all things without exception, but may, in some cases, reasonably, and therefore innocently, resist them. These principles are acknowledged upon all hands, whatever difficulty there may be in fixing the exact limits of submission. Now, there is at least as much difficulty in stating the measure of duty in these two cases as in the case of rulers and subjects; so that this is really no objection—at least, no reasonable one—against resistance to the higher powers. Or, if it is one, it will hold equally against resistance in the other cases mentioned. It is indeed true, that turbulent, vicious-minded men may take occasion, from this principle that their rulers may in some cases be lawfully resisted, to raise factions and disturbances in the state, and to make resistance where resistance is needless, and therefore sinful. But is it not equally true that children and servants, of turbulent, vicious minds, may take occasion, from this principle that parents and masters may in some cases be lawfully resisted, to resist when resistance is unnecessary, and therefore criminal? Is the principle, in either case, false in itself merely because it may be abused, and applied to legitimate disobedience and resistance in those instances to which it ought not to be applied? According to this way of arguing, there will be no true principles in the world; for there are none but what may be wrested and perverted to serve bad purposes, either through the weakness or wickedness of men.

We may very safely assert these two things in general, without undermining government: One is, that no civil rulers are to be obeyed when they enjoin things that are inconsistent with the commands of God. All such disobedience is lawful and glorious; particularly if persons refuse to comply with any *legal establishment of religion*, because it is a gross perversion and corruption—as to doctrine, worship, and discipline—of a pure and divine religion, brought from heaven to earth by the Son of God,—the only King and Head of the Christian church,—and propagated through the world by his inspired apostles. All commands running counter to the declared will of the Supreme Legislator of heaven and earth are null and void, and therefore disobedience to them is a duty, not a crime. Another thing that may be asserted with equal truth and safety is, that no government is to be submitted to at the expense of that which is the sole end of all government—the common good and safety of society. Because, to submit in this case, if it should ever happen, would evidently be to set up the means as more valuable and above the end, than which there cannot be a greater solecism and contradiction. The only reason of the institution of civil government, and the only rational ground of submission to it, is the common safety and utility. If, therefore, in any case, the common safety and utility would not be promoted by submission to government, but the contrary, there is no ground or motive for obedience and submission, but for the contrary. . . .

Now, as all men are fallible, it cannot be supposed that the public affairs of any state should be always administered in the best manner possible, even by persons of the greatest wisdom and integrity. Nor is it sufficient to legitimate disobedience to the higher powers that they are not so administered, or that they are in some instances very ill-managed; for, upon this principle, it is scarcely supposable that any government at all could be supported, or subsist. Such a principle manifestly tends to the dissolution of government, and to throw all things into confusion and anarchy. But it is equally evident, upon the other hand, that those in authority may abuse their trust and power to such a degree, that neither the law of reason nor of religion requires that any obedience or submission should be paid to them; but, on the contrary, that they should be totally discarded, and the authority which they were before vested with transferred to others, who may exercise it more to those good purposes for which it is given. Nor is this principle, that resistance to the higher powers is in some extraordinary cases justifiable, so liable to abuse as many persons seem to apprehend it. . . . Mankind in general have a disposition to be as submissive and passive and tame under government as they ought to be. Witness a great, if not the greatest, part of the known world, who are now groaning, but not murmuring, under the heavy yoke of tyranny! While those who govern do it with any tolerable degree of moderation and justice, and in any good measure act up to their office and character by being public benefactors, the people will generally be easy and peaceable, and be rather inclined to flatter and adore than to insult and resist them. Nor was there ever any *general* complaint against any administration, which lasted long, but what there was good reason for. Till people find themselves greatly abused and oppressed by their governors, they are not apt to complain; and whenever they do, in fact, find themselves thus abused and oppressed, they must be stupid *not* to complain. To say that subjects in general are not proper judges when their governors oppress them and play the tyrant, and when they defend their rights, administer justice impartially, and promote the public welfare, is as great treason as ever man uttered. 'T is treason, not against one *single* man, but the state— against the whole body politic; 't is treason against mankind, 't is treason against common sense, 't is treason against God. And this impious principle lays the foundation for justifying all the tyranny and oppression that ever any prince was guilty of. The people know for what end they set up and maintain their governors, and they are the proper judges when they execute their trust as they ought to do it. . . .

3. *John Woolman's Journal* (c. 1760)

A man of profound humility and love, John Woolman was a tailor and tradesman who traveled among the colonial meetings of the Society of Friends, urging upon them the Christian necessity of absolute pacifism and the inescapably anti-Christian nature of slaveholding. His deepest motive, however, was not social or political but rather to act in harmony with "pure righteousness"; he tried to look "less at the effects of my labour, than at the pure motion and reality of the concern, as it arises from heavenly love." Still, the effects of his labor were considerable; he was remarkably successful in winning Quaker slaveholders to acts of emancipation.

Woolman was clear about his dependence on both divine grace and spiritual discipline; there was little in him of the saint who enjoys holiness as a matter of course or as an unwavering, exclusive principle of personality. He had an acute sense of the seductive ease with which one can become complicit in social evils; thus he declined employment as the draftsman of a will in which slaves were to be bequeathed to their owner's heirs rather than freed upon his death. The following passage from Woolman's famous *Journal* suggests his ability to sustain his peaceable but radical faith, even in the face of intense practical and social pressures, within an aroused and fearful community.

Reprinted from *John Woolman's Journal* (Philadelphia: Friends' Book Association, 1892), pp. 92–93, 94–98.

A few years past, money being made current in our province for carrying on wars, and to be called in again by taxes laid on the inhabitants, my mind was often affected with the thoughts of paying such taxes; and I believe it right for me to preserve a memorandum concerning it. I was told that Friends in England frequently paid taxes when the money was applied to such purposes. I had conversation with several noted Friends on the subject, who all favored the payment of such taxes, some of whom I preferred before myself; and this made me easier for a time; yet there was in the deeps of my mind a scruple which I never could get over, and at certain times I was greatly distressed on that account.

I all along believed that there were some upright-hearted men who paid such taxes, but could not see that their example was a sufficient reason for me to do so, while I believed that the spirit of Truth required of me, as an individual, to suffer patiently the distress of goods, rather than pay actively.

I have been informed that Thomas à Kempis lived and died in the profession of the Roman Catholic religion; and in reading his writings, I have believed him to be a man of a true Christian spirit; as fully so as many who died martyrs because they could not join with some superstitions in that church.

All true Christians are of the same spirit, but their gifts are diverse, Christ appointing to each one their peculiar office, agreeable to his infinite wisdom.

John Huss contended against the errors crept into the church, in opposition to the Council of Constance; which the historian reports to have consisted of many thousand persons. He modestly vindicated the cause which he believed was right; and though his language and conduct toward his judges appear to have been respectful, yet he never could be moved from the principles settled in his mind. To use his own words: "This I most humbly require and desire of you all, even for His sake who is the God of us all, that I be not compelled to the thing which my conscience doth repugn or strive against." And again, in his answer to the emperor: "I refuse nothing, most noble emperor, whatsoever the council shall decree or determine upon me, only this one thing I except, that I do not offend God and my conscience."—Fox's Acts and Monuments, page 233. At length, rather than act contrary to that which he believed the Lord required of him, he chose to suffer death by fire. Thomas à Kempis, without disputing against the articles then generally agreed to, appears to have laboured, by a pious example as well as by preaching and writing, to promote virtue and the inward spiritual religion; and I believe they were both sincere-hearted followers of Christ.

True charity is an excellent virtue; and sincerely to labour for their good, whose belief, in all points, doth not agree with ours, is a happy state. To refuse the active payment of a tax which our society generally paid, was exceedingly disagreeable; but to do [a thing] contrary to my conscience appeared yet more dreadful. When this exercise came upon me, I knew of none under the like difficulty, and in my distress I besought the Lord to enable me to give up all, that so I might follow him wheresoever he was pleased to lead me; and under this exercise I went to our Yearly meeting at Philadelphia, in the year 1755; at which a committee was appointed of some from each quarter, to correspond with the meeting for sufferings in London, and another to visit our Monthly and Quarterly Meetings; and after their appointment, before the last adjournment of the meeting, it was agreed in the meeting that these two committees should meet together in Friends' school-house in the city, at a time then concluded on, to consider some things in which the cause of Truth was concerned. And these committees meeting together, had a weighty conference in the fear of the Lord; at which time I perceived there were many Friends under a scruple like that before mentioned.

As scrupling to pay a tax on account of the application, hath seldom been heard of heretofore, even amongst men of integrity, who have steadily borne their testimony against outward wars in their time, I may here note some things which have opened on my mind, as I have been inwardly exercised on that account.

From the steady opposition which faithful Friends, in early times, made to wrong things then approved of, they were hated and persecuted by men living in the spirit of this world; and, suffering with firmness, they were made a blessing to the church, and the work prospered. It equally concerns men in every age to take heed to their own spirit; and in comparing their situation with ours, it looks to me there was less danger of their being infected with the spirit of this world, in paying their taxes, than there is of us now. They had little or no share in civil government, neither legislative nor executive; and many of them declared they were, through the power of God, separated from the spirit in which wars were; and being afflicted by the rulers on account of their testimony, there was less likelihood of uniting in spirit with them in things inconsistent with the purity of Truth. We, from the first settlement of this land, have known little or no troubles of that sort. Their profession, for a time, was accounted reproachful; but at length, the uprightness of our predecessors being understood by the rulers, and their innocent sufferings moving them, our way of worship was tolerated; and many of our members in these colonies became active in civil government. Being thus tried with favour and prosperity, this world hath appeared inviting; our minds have been turned to the improvement of our country, to merchandize and sciences; amongst which are many things useful, being followed in pure wisdom; but, in our present condition, that a carnal mind is gaining upon us, I believe will not be denied.

Some of our members who are officers in civil government, are, in one case or other, called upon in their respective stations to assist in things relative to the wars; such being in doubt whether to act, or crave to be excused from their office, seeing their brethren united in the payment of a tax to carry on the said wars, might think their case not much different, and so quench the tender movings of the Holy Spirit in their minds; and thus, by small degrees, there might be an approach toward that of fighting, till we came so near it, as that the distinction would be little else but the name of a peaceable people.

It requires great self-denial and resignation of ourselves to God, to attain that state wherein we can freely cease from fighting when wrongfully invaded; if, by our fighting, there were a probability of overcoming the invaders. Whoever rightly attains to it, does, in some degree, feel that spirit in which our Redeemer gave his life for us; and, through Divine goodness, many of our predecessors, and many now living, have learned this blessed lesson; but many others, having their religion chiefly by education, and not being enough acquainted with that cross which crucifies to the world, do manifest a temper distinguishable from that of an entire trust in God.

In calmly considering these things, it hath not appeared strange to me, that an exercise hath now fallen upon some, which, as to the outward means of it, is different from what was known to many of those who went before us.

Some time after the Yearly Meeting, a day being appointed, and letters wrote to distant members, the said committees met at Philadelphia; and by adjournments, continued several days. The calamities of war were now increasing; the frontier inhabitants of Pennsylvania were frequently surprised, some slain, and many taken captive by the Indians: and while these committees sat, the corpse of one so slain was brought in a wagon, and taken through the streets of the city, in his bloody garments, to alarm the people, and rouse them up to war.

Friends thus met were not all of one mind in relation to the tax; which to such who scrupled it, made the way more difficult. To refuse an active payment at such a time, might be construed an act of disloyalty, and appeared likely to displease the rulers, not only here but in England; still there was a scruple so fastened upon the minds of many Friends, that nothing moved it. It was a conference the most weighty that ever I was at; and the hearts of many were bowed in reverence before the Most High. Some Friends of the said committees who appeared easy to pay the tax, after several adjournments, withdrew; others of them continued till the last. At length, an epistle of tender love and caution to Friends in Pennsylvania, was drawn by some

Friends concerned on that account; which being read several times and corrected, was then signed by such of them as were free to sign it, and afterward sent to the monthly and Quarterly meetings. . . .

4. Isaac Backus: "An Appeal to the Public for Religious Liberty" (1773)

Throughout the second half of the eighteenth century Isaac Backus, a Baptist minister and preacher in Massachusetts and Rhode Island, was an important denominational spokesman and champion of the separation of church and state. As a leading member of the grievance committee of the Warren Baptist Association, he sought legislative and judicial remedies for the harassment and persecution of Baptists in New England, especially in Massachusetts. Though a good many of these efforts met with some success and the Massachusetts legislature exempted Baptist ministers from civil taxes after 1770, local practice often remained discriminatory. In any case, the system of exemption itself was in principle necessarily objectionable, since it embodied the power of the civil authorities to decline to impose (and therefore also to impose) taxes on dissenters for the benefit of the established Congregational churches of the Standing Order.[1]

By 1773 these considerations of theory and practice combined to lead many Massachusetts Baptists to adopt a more militant approach to the issue of religious liberty. Their program of civil disobedience is described and justified in Backus's "Appeal to the Public." It did not succeed in forcing the end of the system of certificates of exemption, but perhaps had an influence on the ecclesiastical provisions of the Massachusetts constitution adopted in 1780.[2]

Backus's own willingness to commit civil disobedience by refusing to pay religious taxes had deep personal as well as denominational roots: his mother and brother had been imprisoned for their separatism during his youth, and he had himself been arrested for tax refusal as early as 1748.[3]

❀   Reprinted from William G. McLoughlin, ed., *Isaac Backus on Church, State, and Calvinism: Pamphlets, 1754–1789* (Cambridge: Belknap Press of Harvard University Press, 1968), pp. 316–317, 324–325, 332–334, 338–340. Copyright © 1968 by the President and Fellows of Harvard College.

We are not insensible that an open appearance against any part of the conduct of men in power is commonly attended with difficulty and danger. And could we have found any way wherein with clearness we could have avoided the present attempt we would gladly have taken it. But our blessed Lord and only Redeemer has commanded us to *stand fast in the liberty wherewith he has made us free.* And things appear so to us at present that we cannot see how we can fully obey this command without refusing any active compliance with some laws about religious affairs that are laid upon us. And as those who are interested against us often accuse us of complaining unreasonably, we are brought under a necessity of laying open particular facts which otherwise we would gladly have concealed. And all must be sensible that there is a vast difference between exposing the faults, either of individuals or communities when the cause of truth and equity would suffer without it and the doing of it without any such occasion. We view it to be our incumbent duty to render unto Caesar the things that are his but also that it is of as much importance not to render unto him anything that belongs only to God, who is to be obeyed rather than any man. And as it is evident to us that God always claimed it as his sole prerogative to determine by his own laws what his worship shall be, who shall minister in it, and how they shall be supported, so it is evident that this prerogative has been, and still is, encroached upon in our land.

. . . In 1644 the court at Boston passed an act to punish men with banishment if they opposed infant baptism or departed from any of their congregations when it was going to be administered. And after they had acted upon this law one of their chief magistrates observed, that such methods tended to make hypocrites. To which a noted minister replied, that if it did so, yet such were better than profane persons because, said he, "Hypocrites give God part of his due, the outward man, but the profane person giveth God neither outward nor inward man." By which it seems that in that day they were zealous to have the outward man, if no more, *given to God.* But now that conduct is condemned as persecution by their children who profess to allow us full liberty of conscience because they do not hinder our giving our inward man to God, only claim a power to seize our outward man to get money for themselves. And though many of us have expended ten or twenty times as much in setting up and supporting that worship which we believe to be right as it would have cost us to have continued in the fashionable way, yet we are often accused of being covetous for dissenting from that way and refusing to pay more money out of our little incomes to uphold men from whom we receive no benefit but rather abuse. . . .

In civil states the power of the whole collective body is vested in a few hands that they may with better advantage defend themselves against injuries from abroad and correct abuses at home, for which end a few have a right to judge for the whole society. But in religion each one has an equal right to judge for himself, for we must all *appear* before the judgment seat of Christ, that *every one* may receive the things *done in his body* according to that *he hath done* (not what any earthly representative hath done for him), 2 *Cor.* v, 10. And we freely confess that we can find no more warrant from divine truth for any people on earth to constitute any men their representatives to make laws, to impose religious taxes than they have to appoint Peter or the Virgin Mary to represent them before the throne above. We are therefore brought to a stop about paying so much regard to such laws as to give in annual certificates to the other denomination [i.e. the Congregational or Standing Churches] as we have formerly done.

1. Because the very nature of such a practice implies an acknowledgement that the civil power has a right to set one religious sect up above another, else why need we give certificates to them any more than they to us? It is a tacit allowance that they have a right to make laws about such things which we believe in our consciences they have not. For,

2. By the foregoing address to our legislature and their committee's report thereon it is evident that they claim a right to tax us from *civil obligation* as being the representatives of the people. But how came a civil community by any ecclesiastical power? How came the kingdoms of *this world* to have a right to govern in Christ's kingdom which is *not of this world*!

3. That constitution not only emboldens people to *judge the liberty of other men's consciences* and has carried them so far as to

tell our General Assembly that they conceived it to be a *duty they owed to God* and their country not to be dispensed with, to lay before them the springs of their neighbors' actions, but it also requires something of the same nature from us. Their laws require us annually to certify to them what our belief is concerning the *conscience* of every person that assembles with us, as the condition of their being exempted from taxes to other's worship. And only because our brethren in Bellingham left that clause about the *conscience* out of their certificate last year a number of their society who live at Mendon were taxed, and lately suffered the spoiling of their goods to uphold pedobaptist worship.

4. The scheme we oppose evidently tends to destroy the purity and life of religion, for the inspired apostle assures us that the church is *espoused as a chaste virgin to Christ* and is obliged to be *subject to him in everything* as a true wife to her husband. Now the most chaste domestic obedience does not at all interfere with any lawful objection to civil authority. But for a woman to admit the highest ruler in a nation into her husband's place would be *adultery* or *whoredom*. And how often are *men's inventions* about worship so called in the sacred oracles? And does it not greatly concern us all earnestly to search out and put away such evils as we would desire to escape the awful judgments that such wickedness has brought on other nations! Especially if we consider that not only the purity but also the very life and being of religion among us is concerned therein, for 'tis evident that Christ has given as plain laws to determine what the duty of people is to his ministers as he has the duty of ministers to his people, and most certainly he is as able to enforce the one as the other. The common plea of our opponents is that people will not do their duty if rulers do not enforce it. But does not the whole book of God clearly show that ministers as often fail of doing their duty as the people do? And where is the care of rulers to punish ministers for their unfaithfulness? They often talk about *equality* in these affairs, but where does it appear! . . .

And now dear countrymen, we beseech you seriously to consider of these things. The great importance of a general union through this country in order to the preservation of our liberties has often been pleaded for with propriety, but how can such a union be expected so long as that dearest of all rights, equal liberty of conscience, is not allowed? Yea, how can any reasonably expect that HE who has the hearts of kings in his hand will turn the heart of our earthly sovereign to hear the pleas for liberty of those who will not hear the cries of their fellow subjects under their oppressions? Has it not been plainly proved that so far as any man gratifies his own inclinations without regard to the universal law of equity so far he is in bondage? So that it is impossible for anyone to tyrannize over others without thereby becoming a miserable slave himself, a slave to raging lusts and a slave to guilty fears of what will be the consequence. . . .

Suffer us a little to expostulate with our fathers and brethren who inhabit the land to which our ancestors fled for religious liberty. You have lately been accused with being disorderly and rebellious by men in power who profess a great regard for order and the public good. And why don't you believe them and rest easy under their administrations? You tell us you cannot because you are taxed where you are not represented. And is it not really so with us? You do not deny the right of the British Parliament to impose taxes within her own realm; only complain that she extends her taxing power beyond her proper limits. And have we not as good right to say you do the *same thing*? And so that wherein you judge others you condemn yourselves? Can three thousand miles possibly fix such limits to taxing power as the difference between civil and sacred matters has already done? One is only a difference of *space*, the other is so great a difference in the *nature* of things as there is between *sacrifices to God* and the *ordinances of man*. . . .

Many think it hard to be frowned upon only for pleading for their rights and laying open particular acts of encroachment thereon. But what frowns have we met with for no other crime? And as the present contest between Great Britain and America is not so much about the greatness of the taxes already laid, as about a submission to their taxing power, so (though what we have already suffered is far from being a trifle, yet) our greatest difficulty at present concerns the submitting to a taxing power in ecclesiastical affairs. It is supposed by many that we are exempted from such taxes, but they are greatly mistaken. For all know that paper is a money article and writing upon it is labor, and this tax we must pay every year as a token of submission to their power, or else they will lay a heavier tax upon us. And we have one difficulty in submitting to this power which our countrymen have not in the other case, that is, our case affects the conscience as theirs does not. And equal liberty of conscience is one essential article in our CHARTER which constitutes this government and describes the extent of our rulers' authority and what are the rights and liberties of the people. And in the confession of faith which our rulers and their ministers have published to the world they say, "God alone is Lord of the conscience and hath left it free from the doctrines and commandments of men which are in *anything* contrary to his word *or not contained in it*. So that to believe such doctrines or to obey such commands out of conscience is to *betray* true liberty of conscience, and the requiring of an implicit faith and an absolute blind obedience is to destroy liberty of conscience and reason also."

II CONSCIENCE VS. LAW IN THE MID-NINETEENTH CENTURY

In whatever country and whatever case a man may chance to be born, he is born a citizen of the world, and bound by the universal rule of right or law of God. God writes that law upon the man's perceptions, and we call it conscience, or God in him. Proper manhood is the fruit of obedience to that law. Countries and families are but nurseries and influences.
—George William Curtis, "Patriotism" (1857)

5. William Lloyd Garrison: "Review of Gerrit Smith's Letters" and "Trial of Rev. Mr. Cheever" (1835)

In dealing with the reformer and philanthropist Gerrit Smith, Garrison moderated somewhat the characteristically furious tone of his antislavery argument, for a good deal of mutual esteem survived between the two men despite their disagreements. But Garrison was severe enough in his criticism of what he saw as Smith's grossly inconsistent departures from their shared abolitionism. While Smith defended the American Colonization Society, Garrison attacked it; when Smith opposed all lawbreaking, Garrison fervently defended it in cases of conscience. Later Smith entered politics; Garrison continued to rely on "moral suasion." As the Civil War neared, Smith sent money to John Brown while Garrison tried to sustain the principles of nonresistance.

The first stage of their long debate was won by Garrison: by the end of 1835 Smith had broken with the colonizationists and joined the American Anti-Slavery Society.[1] And he got over his alarm at the Society's readiness for conscientious lawbreaking: in 1842 he urged slaves to break their masters' laws against learning to read and against escaping,[2] and later he himself articulated a more general theory of civil disobedience. (See his "True Office of Civil Government" in Part III.)

George B. Cheever, a Congregational minister in Salem, was a reformer and controversialist who castigated in print the proprietor of a Salem distillery and as a result was physically attacked, convicted of libel, fined, and briefly imprisoned. Garrison offers some criticisms of Cheever's tactics but is generally sympathetic toward him as an earnest advocate of temperance and as a representative of biblical rather than legal morality.[3] Together these two pieces, published in the *Liberator* early in Garrison's tumultuous career, represent his persistent antagonism toward any legal authority that seemed to be at odds with the will of God.

Reprinted from *Liberator* 5, no. 10 (March 7, 1835):39, and no. 27 (July 4, 1835):107.

Review of Gerrit Smith's Letters

The Declaration of the Anti-Slavery Convention maintains, "that all those laws which are now in force, admitting the *right* of slavery, are, before God, utterly null and void." Upon which position you make the following extraordinary comment: "This is the highest toned nullification we have met with. The doctrine involved in this Declaration, being once admitted, there is no longer any binding authority in human government and human laws." This comment is utterly perverse and fabulous, and it grants to tyrants and men-stealers all that they desire. It is thus that you "nullify" your own principles, and pour contempt upon your own doctrines. What, Sir! do you mean to affirm, "that all those laws which are now in force, admitting the *right of slavery*," i.e. the right of that which is "evil, and only evil continually"—the right of perpetuating "a soul-killing relation"— the right to "shut out the light of truth from the minds of the slaves, and to withhold from them all fitness for the responsibilities of freemen"—the right to seize, retain, buy, exchange and sell, to plunder, debase and lacerate, our fellow-creatures—I say, do you mean to affirm, that these heathenish and diabolical enactments are, "before *God*," (mark! not before *men*) just and equitable, and ought to be obeyed? Such a doctrine is the "highest toned" *blasphemy* against Almighty God. . . . It is evident that a strcng delusion fills your mind, which, in this particular instance, endangers your allegiance to the King of kings, and leads you to fall down and worship the bloody monster Slavery, because it has been formally set up by the American people! Sir, your attack upon Professor [Elizur] Wright, of New York,—one of the most devoted christians, one of the most consistent reformers, and one of the noblest philanthropists, of this or any other age,—is an outrage upon humanity, and a libel upon the christian religion. He has made no "seditious and incendiary appeals to the public mind"—his appeals have always been addressed to the *consciences* and *understandings* of men. As one who feels that the precepts of Jesus Christ ought to be obeyed, he has declared that he cannot assist in capturing the runaway slave, and sending him back again into bondage, but he will succor and hide him if practicable; and he calls upon every man, who professes to fear God and love his neighbors as himself, to give no aid to tyrants in this matter. This is "the head and front of his offending"—and for doing so, you accuse him of *sedition*!—thus plainly avowing that you are ready to seize, or assist in seizing, the captive who has fled from his oppressor, and to shackle his limbs anew with the galling fetters of slavery!— Now, Sir, for my own part,—talk as you will of the Constitution,—I would just as cheerfully steal a native of Africa, and carry him across the Atlantic to the shambles at New Orleans, as to abet the southern slaveholder in recovering his wandering slave. If "the laws and constituted authorities of the land" require me thus to aid the tyrant, then *I will not obey them*—then I will strenuously endeavor to bring them "into contempt"—then *I will resist them*, not by physical violence, but by christian boldness and by moral endurance. Every slave given up by Massachusetts to the slave States is *kidnapped by the State*; and every man who assists in returning the slave *is a kidnapper*. . . .

Trial of Rev. Mr. Cheever

The learned gentleman [James T. Austin, attorney general of Massachusetts] asks—"Can there be a safer mode of determining what is right or wrong than, is it *lawful?*" (i.e. does the law of the State or nation authorize or forbid it?) We answer in the affirmative. A resort to the Bible is the only sure method of coming to a just determination. Does Mr. Austin mean to make the statute-book of the Commonwealth paramount in obligation to the statute-book of Jehovah? Let us try the pertinency of his question by a few points of illustration. In India, they burn widows upon the funeral pile, and cast living infants into the Ganges, and bow down in worship to stocks and stones, and drag the car of Juggernaut over the bodies of prostrate men and women,—*lawfully*. If the Attorney General were in India, denouncing these horrid practices, might he not be asked by these idolators,—"Can there be a safer mode of determining what is right or wrong, than, is it lawful?" . . . We forbear multiplying examples, although it might be instructive to turn back to past ages, and recapitulate all the persecutions, heresies, indulgences and practices, which have obtained among mankind, *lawfully*—not forgetting to mention, that even in this renowned Commonwealth, Quakers, wizards, and witches have been *lawfully* hanged, as equally pernicious and damnable in their influence and profession. Now we regard the interrogation of the

Attorney General as savoring of practical atheism and treason against the government of God; and we maintain that the test of right or wrong which he proposes is a nose of wax that may be moulded into any shape—is full of uncertainty and danger, varying with every government and every nation—is the substitution of human fallibility for divine infallibility, the wisdom of man for the wisdom of God, and the policy of the world for the obedience of the gospel—and is now, and has ever been, the fruitful source of delusion, error and violence, the refuge of tyranny, the weapon of proscription, and the rack of martyrdom. We further maintain that it is because human enactments are consulted and obeyed, rather than the infallible code of laws given by the Almighty, so many hurtful customs and practices abound in [every] community. The doctrine, that what the law allows is right, and what it disallows is wrong, is a prevalent heresy which cannot be too soon repudiated. "Can there be a safer mode of determining what is right or wrong, than, is it lawful?" Can there be a more dangerous mode? . . . Now, I care not what the law allows me to do, or what it forbids my doing. If I violate it, I will submit to the penalty, unresistingly, in imitation of Christ, and his apostles, and the holy martyrs. But to learn my duty, I will not consult any other statute-book than THE BIBLE; and whatsoever requirement of man I believe is opposed to the spirit of the gospel, I will at all hazards disobey. Every man is bound to understand the laws of the country in which he lives, but he is not bound to obey any one of them, if it conflict with his allegiance to his Maker—and he alone is to judge in this matter, according to the monitions of his conscience and the dictates of his understanding. Who made the laws? Fallible men. Is a fallible standard the best by which to try human actions? The hues of the law are like those of the chameleon, ever shifting and evanescent. Human laws, as all history shows, waste like pillars of sand, or change their aspects with times and circumstances. Are they then to be trusted or obeyed in all cases? God forbid. It was not so under the Jewish dispensation—it is not so under the gospel. . . .

Now we ask, "can there be a safer mode of determining what is right or wrong, than, is it"—in accordance with the LAW OF GOD? All human enactments which run counter to this law, are necessarily null and void in his sight. . . .

From the beginning the law has been on the side of the distiller, the importer, and the vender, yet the Temperance reformation has swept over the land, and over the seas, and is traversing Europe, and will circumnavigate the globe. . . .

But it is the opinion of the Attorney General, "the best friends of temperance are those who would keep it within the strict line of law." "That's exactly my opinion," will be the response of every incorrigible distiller and rum seller in the land. . . . If we are not to travel beyond "the strict line of law" in the cause of moral reform, then the tongue is a useless machine, a gag is put into the mouth, personal freedom is lost, and human improvement is at an end. For whoever denounces a pursuit or practice which the law sanctions, necessarily impeaches the integrity of the law, and travels beyond it. And never, since the organization of human society, has a public reform been effected, without essentially altering the statute book. . . .

Moral right is ever paramount to legal right and may freely interrogate it. The controversy has never been with the legal right of the distiller or the rum seller (for that cannot be disputed), but with his moral right to poison and destroy his fellow creatures. A practice may be legal, and yet as atrocious as any that was permitted by Draco's code. At the South, it is a legal business to trade in human flesh and sinews; who disputes its legality? But will the Attorney General endorse its humanity and morality? Will he, as a man and a Christian, venture to maintain, that we have no more right to attack the domestic slave trader for carrying on his cruel business, than we have the tailor for making our clothes?

6. William Ellery Channing: "Lecture on War" (1838)

William Ellery Channing was for much of his adult life the preeminent spokesman for liberal Christianity in America. His arguments against Calvinism and his famous 1819 Baltimore sermon "Unitarian Christianity" helped to make him Unitarianism's most celebrated figure, a theologian and moralist with an international reputation and a national audience that reached far beyond the membership of his own denomination.

Though he was minister at Boston's prosperous and conservative Federal Street Church from 1803 until the end of his life, he found that his relationship with his congregation was strained in his later years by his increasing involvement in the antislavery movement. "His antislavery thinking was much more radical than that of the political Republicans of 1856–1860," John White Chadwick observed;[1] yet Channing illustrates perhaps more clearly than anyone else how much antislavery feeling could exist in one who was not actually an abolitionist, and his relationships with the Garrisonians were sometimes as strained as those with the staunch conservatives of his own church.

During the last fifteen years of his life he spoke and wrote more and more about poverty and slavery. This he conceived to be part of his ministry; Christianity, he wrote in 1838, is "at war with the present condition of society."[2] His emphases tended to remain both genteel and evangelical rather than politically programmatic, however. Though he took positions on such policy questions as the termination of slavery in the District of Columbia, his main interest was in the elevation of each person's individual character. He held, his son said, to an "uncompromising belief not only in the perfectibility of man, but in perfection as the practical aim of every human life."[3] Still he had an acute awareness of human vulnerability to selfishness and self-deception, to weakness and greed. His preaching, remote though it was from the Calvinist belief in an omnipotently threatening God and a predominantly sinful humanity, was still informed by an evangelical tension between exhortation and denunciation.

In so passionate a celebrant of the individual conscience it is not surprising to find support for civil disobedience. His death in 1842 spared him a confrontation with the most provocative law on the return of fugitive slaves; his clearest insistence on the supremacy of conscience over law came instead on the issue of military service. Never a complete pacifist, Channing was nonetheless horrified by the wars of his lifetime: he condemned the War of 1812, and in 1837 he wrote a famous open letter to Henry Clay that leaves no doubt about what his view of the Mexican War would have been. His "Lecture on War," in which he inexorably maintains the moral accountability of the individual citizen and soldier both before and after conscription, anticipates and transcends the principles adopted at Nuremberg more than a century later.

❀   Reprinted from William Ellery Channing, *Works* (Boston: American Unitarian Association, 1895), pp. 673–679.

The idea of "right" has always mixed itself with war, and this has kept out of view the real character of most of the conflicts of nations. The sovereign, regarding the right of war as an essential attribute of sovereignty, has on this ground ascribed a legitimacy to all national hostilities, and has never dreamed that in most of his wars he was a murderer. So the subject has thought himself bound to obey his sovereign, and, on this ground, has acquitted himself of crime, has perhaps imputed to himself merit, in fighting and slaughtering for the defense of the most iniquitous claims. Here lies the delusion, which we should be most anxious to remove. It is the legality ascribed to war, on account of its being waged by government, which produces insensibility to its horrors and crimes. . . .

I will allow that government has the right of war. But a right has bounds, and when these are transgressed by us, it ceases to exist; and we are as culpable as if it had never existed. The private citizen, it is generally acknowledged, has the right of taking life in self-defense; but if, under plea of this right, he should take life without cause, he would not stand absolved of murder. In like manner, though government be authorized to make war in self-defense, it still contracts the guilt of murder if it proclaim war from policy, ambition, or revenge. . . .

It is time that the right of war should not shield governments from the infamy due to hostilities to which selfish, wicked passions give birth. Let rulers learn that for this right they are held to a fearful responsibility. Let a war, not founded in plain justice and necessity, never be named but as murder. Let the Christian give articulate voice to the blood that cries from the earth against rulers by whom it has been criminally shed. Let no soft terms be used. On this subject, a new moral sense and a new language are needed throughout the whole civilized and Christian world, and just in proportion as the truth shall find a tongue, war will cease.

But the right of war, which is said to belong to sovereignty, not only keeps out of sight the enormous guilt of rulers in almost all national conflicts. It also hides or extenuates the frequent guilt of subjects in taking part in the hostilities which their rulers declare. In this way, much of the prevalent insensibility to the evils of war is induced, and perhaps on no point is light more needed. The ferocity and cruelty of armies impress us little, because we look on them as doing a work of duty. The subject or citizen, as we think, is bound to obey his rulers. In his worst deeds as a soldier he is discharging his obligations to the state; and thus murder and pillage, covered with a cloak of duty, excite no deep, unaffected reprobation and horror.

I know it will be asked, "And is not the citizen bound to fight at the call of his government? Does not his commission absolve him from the charge of murder or enormous crime? Is not obedience to the sovereign power the very foundation on which society rests?" I answer, "Has the duty of obeying government no bounds? Is the human sovereign a God? Is his sovereignty absolute? If he command you to slay a parent, must you obey? If he forbid you to worship God, must you obey? Have you no right to judge his acts? Have you no self-direction? Is there no unchangeable right which the ruler cannot touch? Is there no higher standard than human law?" These questions answer themselves. A declaration of war cannot sanction wrong, or turn murder into a virtuous deed. Undoubtedly, as a general rule, the citizen is bound to obey the authorities under which he lives. No difference of opinion as to the mere expediency of measures will warrant opposition. Even in cases of doubtful right he may submit his judgment to the law. But when called to do what his conscience clearly pronounces wrong, he must not waver. No outward law is so sacred as the voice of God in his own breast. He cannot devolve on rulers an act so solemn as the destruction of fellow-beings convicted of no offence. For no act will more solemn inquisition be made at the bar of God.

I maintain that the citizen, before fighting, is bound to inquire into the justice of the cause which he is called to maintain with blood, and bound to withhold his hand if his conscience condemn the cause. On this point he is able to judge. No political question, indeed, can be determined so easily as this of war. War can be justified only by plain, palpable necessity; by unquestionable wrongs, which, as patient trial has proved, can in no other way be redressed; by the obstinate, persevering invasion of solemn and unquestionable rights. The justice of war is not a mystery for cabinets to solve. It is not a state-secret which he must take on trust. It lies within our reach. We are bound to examine it.

We are especially bound to this examination, because there is always a presumption against the justice of war; always reason to fear that it is condemned by impartial conscience and God. This solemn truth has peculiar claims on attention. It takes away the plea that we may innocently fight, because our rulers have decreed war. It strips off the most specious disguise from the horrors and crimes of national hostilities. If hostilities were, as a general rule, necessary and just, if an unjust war were a solitary exception, then the citizen might extenuate his share in the atrocities of military life, by urging his obligation to the state. But if there is always reason to apprehend the existence of wrong on the part of rulers, then he is bound to pause and ponder well his path. Then he advances at his peril, and must answer for the crimes of the unjust, unnecessary wars in which he shares.

The presumption is always against the justice and necessity of war. This we learn from the spirit of all rulers and nations towards foreign states. It is partial, unjust. Individuals may be disinterested; but nations have no feeling of the tie of brotherhood to their race. A basic selfishness is the principle on which the affairs of nations are commonly conducted. A statesman is expected to take advantage of the weaknesses and wants of other countries. How loose a morality governs the intercourse of states! What falsehoods and intrigues are licensed diplomacy! What nation regards another with true friendship? What nation makes sacrifices to another's good? What nation is as anxious to perform its duties as to assert its rights? What nation chooses to suffer wrong, rather than to inflict it? What nation lays down the everlasting law of right, casts itself fearlessly on its principles, and chooses to be poor or to perish rather than to do wrong? Can communities so selfish, so unfriendly, so unprincipled, so unjust, be expected to wage righteous wars? Especially if with this selfishness are joined national prejudices, antipathies, and exasperated passions, what else can be expected in the public policy but inhumanity and crime? An individual, we know, cannot be trusted in his own cause, to measure his own claims, to avenge his own wrongs; and the civil magistrate, an impartial umpire, has been substituted as the only means of justice. But nations are even more unfit than individuals to judge in their own cause; more prone to push their rights to excess, and to trample on the rights of others; because nations are crowds, and crowds are unawed by opinion, and more easily inflamed by sympathy into madness. Is there not, then, always a presumption against the justice of war?

This presumption is increased, when we consider the false notions of patriotism and honor which prevail in nations. Men think it a virtuous patriotism to throw a mantle, as they call it, over their country's infirmities, to wink at her errors, to assert her most doubtful rights, to look jealously and angrily on the prosperity of rival states; and they place her honor not in unfaltering adherence to the right, but in a fiery spirit, in quick resentment, in martial courage, and especially in victory; and can a good man hold himself bound and stand prepared to engage in war at the dictate of such a state?

The citizen or subject, you say, may innocently fight at the call of his rulers; and I ask, who are his rulers? Perhaps an absolute sovereign, looking down on his people as another race, as created to toil for his pleasure, to fight for new provinces, to bleed for his renown. There are, indeed, republican governments. But were not the republics of antiquity as greedy of conquest, as prodigal of human life, as steeled against the cries of humanity, as any despots who ever lived? And if we come down to modern republics, are they to be trusted with our consciences? What does the Congress of these United States represent? Not so much the virtue of the country as a vicious principle, the spirit of party. It acts not so much for the people as for parties; and are parties upright? Are parties merciful? Are the wars, to which party commits a country, generally just?

Unhappily, public men under all governments are, of all moral guides, the most unsafe, the last for a Christian to follow. Public life is thought to absolve men from the strict obligations of truth and justice. To wrong an adverse party or another country, is not reprobated as are wrongs in private life. Thus duty is dethroned; thus the majesty of virtue insulted in the administration of nations. Public men are expected to think more of their own elevation than of their country. Is the city of Washington the most virtuous spot in this republic? Is it the school of incorruptible men? The hall of Congress, disgraced by so many brawls, swayed by local interest and party intrigues, in which the right of petition is trodden under foot, is this the oracle from which the responses of justice come forth? Public bodies want conscience. Men acting in masses shift off responsibility on one another. Multitudes never blush. If these things be true, then I maintain that the Christian has not a right to take part in war blindly, confidingly, at the call of his rulers. To shed the blood of fellow-creatures is too solemn a work to be engaged in lightly. Let him not put himself, a tool, into wicked hands. Let him not meet on the field his brother man, his brother Christian, in a cause on which heaven frowns. Let him bear witness against unholy wars, as his country's greatest crimes. If called to take part in them, let him deliberately refuse. If martial law seize on him, let him submit. If hurried to prison, let him submit. If brought thence to be shot, let him submit. There must be martyrs to peace as truly as to other principles of our religion. The first Christians chose to die rather than obey the laws of the state which commanded them to renounce their Lord. "Death rather than crime"; such is the good man's watchword, such the Christian's vow. Let him be faithful unto death.

Undoubtedly it will be objected, that if one law of the state may in any way be resisted, then all may be, and so government must fall. This is precisely the argument on which the doctrine of passive obedience to the worst tyrannies rests. The absolutist says, "If one government may be overturned, none can stand. Your right of revolution is nothing but the right of anarchy, of universal misrule." The reply is in both instances the same. Extreme cases speak for themselves. We must put confidence in the common-sense of men, and suppose them capable of distinguishing between reasonable laws and those which require them to commit manifest crimes. The objection which we are considering rests on the supposition that a declaration of war is a common act of legislation, bearing no strong marks of distinction from other laws, and consequently to be obeyed as implicitly as all. But it is broadly distinguished. A declaration of war sends us forth to destroy our fellow-creatures, to carry fire, sword, famine, bereavement, want, and woe into the fields and habitations of our brethren; whilst Christianity, conscience, and all the pure affections of our nature, call us to love our brethren, and to die, if need be, for their good. And from whence comes this declaration of war? From men who would rather die than engage in unjust or unnecessary conflict? Too probably from men to whom Christianity is a name, whose highest law is honor, who are used to avenge their private wrongs and defend their reputations by shedding blood, and who, in public as in private life, defy the laws of God. Whoever, at such men's dictation, engages in war without solemnly consulting conscience, and inquiring into the justice of the cause, contracts great guilt, nor can the "right of war," which such men claim as rulers, absolve him from the crimes and woes of the conflict in which he shares. . . .

I close with asking, "Must the sword devour for ever?" Must force, fear, pain, always rule the world? Is the kingdom of God, the reign of truth, duty, and love never to prevail? Must the sacred name of brethren be only a name among men? Must the divinity in man's nature never be recognized with veneration? Is the earth always to steam with human blood shed by man's hands, and to echo with groans wrung from hearts which violence has pierced? Can you and I, my friends, do nothing, nothing to impress a different character on the future history of our race? You say we are weak; and why weak? It is from inward defect, not from outward necessity. We are inefficient abroad, because faint within,—faint in love, and trust, and holy resolution. Inward power always comes forth, and works without. . . . We are dead, and therefore cannot act. Perhaps we speak against war; but if we speak from tradition, if we echo what we hear, if peace be a cant on our lips, our words are unmeaning air. Our own souls must bleed when our brethren are slaughtered. We must feel the infinite wrong done to man by the brute force which treads him in the dust. We must see in the authors of unjust, selfish, ambitious, revengeful wars, monsters in human form, incarnations of the dread enemy of the human race. Under the inspiration of such feelings, we shall speak, even the humblest of us, with something of prophetic force. This is the power which is to strike awe into the counsellors and perpetrators of now licensed murder; which is to wither the laurelled brow of now worshipped heroes. Deep moral convictions, unfeigned reverence and fervent love for man, and living faith in Christ, are mightier than armies: mighty through God to the pulling down of the strongholds of oppression and war. Go forth then, friends of mankind, peaceful soldiers of Christ! and in your various relations, at home and abroad, in private life, and, if it may be, in more public spheres, give faithful utterance to the principles of universal justice and love, give utterance to your deep, solemn, irreconcilable hatred of the spirit of war.

7. John Pierpont: *A Discourse on the Covenant with Judas* (1842)

Widely known as a poet and as a lecturer on reform subjects, John Pierpont served as minister of Boston's Unitarian Hollis Street Church from 1819 to 1845; he was a disciple of Channing and a friend of Theodore Parker in the latter's most embattled years. The last decade of Pierpont's ministry in Boston was marked by increasingly bitter divisions in his congregation over the nature of his spiritual leadership. Several prosperous distillers were among his parishioners, and they were antagonized by his temperance sermons.[1] When the dispute required adjudication, an ecclesiastical tribunal studied the case and vindicated Pierpont, though it spoke critically of some of his actions. He seems to have been a fierce moralist after the manner of Garrison and Parker; even his eulogists conceded that he was instinctively combative.[2]

In 1839 Pierpont preached his "Moral Rule of Political Action," a confident, theoretical exposition of the theme of Acts 5:29: "We ought to obey God rather than men." Three years later the case of the fugitive slave George Latimer (see the introductory note to Whittier's "Massachusetts to Virginia," below) gave him an occasion to apply the theory he had adopted earlier, and he did so with characteristic force. Liberty, Pierpont insists, is a right as precious and as inalienable as life; personal freedom is therefore a value that takes precedence over the interests of the majority, as enacted in constitutions and laws. This sermon anticipates by a decade the logic of much of the disobedience of the 1850s.

Reprinted from John Pierpont, *A Discourse on the Covenant with Judas* (Boston: Little & Brown, 1842), pp. 5–6, 16, 21–22, 26, 28, 32–34.

[I wish to consider] the general question of the binding force or obligation of all agreements, contracts, promises, vows or oaths, to do that which is a violation of natural right, and which, were there no such solemn engagement, would be acknowledged to be wrong.

This subject appears to me to be especially pertinent to the present occasion, when, at the Communion table, we are called to commemorate the death of one man, who was given up, or betrayed to those who were hunting after his life, by virtue of a covenant that he should be thus betrayed; and when, at the same time, our city is moved by the spectacle of another man, that is to be given up or betrayed to perpetual and hopeless bondage, if not to a cruel death, by virtue of a covenant that he shall be thus betrayed.

The essential morality of these two covenants is the same. The one was a covenant to give up an innocent man to death, in consideration of thirty pieces of silver. The other is a covenant to give up an innocent man to a bondage worse than death, in consideration of certain real or supposed political advantages, from which the covenanting parties expect to make *more* than thirty pieces of silver. Thus we see that, although there may be some difference in the *consideration* of the two covenants, by which, in one case the *life*, and, in the other the *liberty* of a man is to be sacrificed, the *essential morality* in both cases is precisely the same: both of them being to do an act which is a violation of a natural right; in the *one* case the natural right of a man to his *life*; and in the *other*, his natural right to his *liberty*. . . .

. . . All engagements, promises, covenants, vows or oaths to do a thing which is contrary to any one of the laws of God, or not to do a thing which any one of his laws requires, are utterly null, and void of binding force: . . . a man, so far from being justified or excused in doing wrong, by an oath which he has taken, that he will do wrong, is involved by that oath in still deeper guilt, since, by that very oath, he gives evidence of acting deliberately and with premeditation, and adds to the sin of violating God's law, the effrontery of swearing, in the presence of God, that he will violate it. He commits one sin in taking the oath, and another and still a greater sin in keeping it. And this I therefore venture to lay down as a general—nay, as a universal principle; that no vow or oath, to do that which is forbidden by any law of God, or not to do that which is required, is of any binding force, or imposes any obligation whatever; let the solemnities of the oath be as awful, and let the penalties imprecated with it, at the hand of either man or God, be as severe or as fearful as they may. . . .

This brings us directly upon the case that is now regarded with such intense interest in this community.

A man—a creature of God, made in his image,—a child of God, as much as any one of us is—who *was* a slave in Virginia, and, by the laws of that State, held to be a chattel—a *thing*—has been brought out of his house of bondage, and stands here, upon Massachusetts ground, and breathes Massachusetts air, in sight of the monument that stands on Bunker's Hill, to tell where Massachusetts men poured out their life-blood in the cause of Liberty. He is pursued by a man, who calls himself his *owner*. He is hunted down by slavery's minions in Boston; is seized and cast into a Boston jail; where, by direction of the Virginian, not even the ministers of Jesus Christ are allowed to come unto him; though, in the humane spirit—nay, by the letter —of Massachusetts law, they are allowed to visit a prisoner, whose hands are reeking with his brother's blood. His pursuer demands that he be given up. Will he be? I suppose, he will. On what ground? By virtue of a *covenant*, which, it is *said*, our fathers made with the Virginian's fathers, that, in such cases, the fugitive *should* be given up.

. . . Even if it *is* so—if it is clearly proved that this *was* the intention and understanding of the framers of the Constitution, then, I say that that provision, being against natural right, and, consequently, in derogation of a higher law, and requiring me to do what God forbids me to do, is of no binding force whatever, but is utterly void. This particular covenant,—for the Constitution of the United States is a covenant, or, rather, a number of covenants, entered into by the People of the United States, each with all the rest,—must come under the law of all human covenants, compacts or agreements, in this, that it is of no binding force, if it is contrary to the laws of God. The consideration that a Constitution is the act of a Convention, and an ordinary law, an act of a Congress; that the former is called the fundamental law, lying at the foundation of the government, or of the Union, does not alter its moral character. There is a government that hath still deeper foundations—foundations, that under-lie those of any human government, and on which, alone, the soul of man can build up for itself an 'everlasting habitation.'. . . .

Should [the Constitution] enjoin murder, which is, the taking away of a man's life, in violation of a natural or divine law, we are *bound* to transgress that Constitution. Now, the claimant, in this case, says, and for the sake of the argument, I admit, that the Constitution enjoins me to aid him in kidnapping, which is, the taking away of another man's liberty, in violation of a natural or divine law. Then I am *bound* to transgress that Constitution.—All writers on Natural Law admit our Declaration of Independence and many of our State Constitutions expressly declare, that a man's natural right to his liberty is as clear as his natural right to his life. Which is the greater blessing, I am not called upon, in this case, to decide. But I know, that thousands of the noblest of our revolutionary fathers and patriots judged, that life without liberty was not worth the holding: and especially do the words of one of the most eloquent of Virginia's own sons continually ring in my ear. 'Is life so dear, or peace so sweet, as to be purchased at the price of *chains and slavery*? Forbid it, Almighty God! I know not what course others may take, but as for me, give me liberty, or give me death!'

If, then, the clause of the Constitution that is appealed to, by the claimant in this case, *does* enjoin it upon me, as a judge, to deliver up the man before me to Virginia's 'chains and slavery,' I feel myself bound by a higher law,—by the authority of the Judge of all judges,—to declare that clause of the Constitution of no binding force before this tribunal, and the judgement of this court is, that the prisoner be discharged. . . .

However it may appear to the moral vision of other men, to mine, the morality that requires and compels me to deliver up a fellow man to chains and torture—to hopeless slavery, if not to death—because others have covenanted for me that I shall do so, and because of my own oath that I will keep that covenant, is, essentially, the morality of a Judas, who would deliver up the Son of Man to be scourged and crucified, because he had *covenanted to do so*—the morality of a Herod, who, *for his oath's sake*, would murder a prophet of God. . . .

I am aware that this is not popular doctrine. I know that the current of public sentiment, in the great thoroughfares of business, and along the channels of commerce, sets strongly against it. I know that in the eyes, of the many—yea, and of the mighty —the Constitution of these United States is supreme;—that it overrides God's laws, and that *it* must stand, though *they* be trodden under foot. But it is the object of this discourse to lift up God's law, to make it honorable in my hearers' eyes, and to make even the highest of human ordinances to do it homage. Though State may league with State, and millions covenant with millions more, to sustain a wrong, they cannot hold it up. Though hand join in hand, the wicked shall not go unpunished. Even yet, 'Righteousness exalteth a nation, but sin is a reproach to any people.'

. . . If, on my heavenward journey, I see even the Constitution of the United States standing in my path, like the visionary ladder of the patriarch, it shall not hinder—it shall help me on my way; for I will mount upward by treading it under my feet.

My brethren, much as we may venerate our fathers, we must venerate still more the rights of man, and his Maker's laws. Though we may reverently cherish their memory, and jealously guard their fame, we must not forget that there is One, whose authority is higher than theirs; and, if it be true that, in the laws which they made for us, they have required us to do any thing, so incompatible with the commands of the Most High, that we *cannot* obey them both, I most seriously ask you, Which *shall* we obey—our dead fathers? or, our LIVING GOD?

8. John Greenleaf Whittier: "Massachusetts to Virginia" (1843)

Several of Whittier's antislavery poems express or imply his support for civil disobedience, though their impassioned exhortations do not always make clear the depth of his feeling for nonviolence. (At an antislavery convention in 1838 Whittier introduced a resolution, which was narrowly defeated, urging antislavery workers not to employ physical violence even in self-defense.)[1]

"Massachusetts to Virginia" grew out of the arrest in Boston in 1842 of the fugitive slave George Latimer. Though Latimer's freedom was purchased, thus sparing Massachusetts abolitionists the full trauma of humiliation caused by the actual renditions of the 1850s, his case foreshadowed those later events in the intensity of feeling it aroused in some parts of the state; more than 60,000 signatures were affixed to a petition to the legislature asking for legal guarantees "against the future arrest of fugitive slaves within the borders of the state."[2] Whittier himself did not rely so heavily on legislation. In another poem, "The Rendition" (on the 1854 Anthony Burns case), Whittier describes Law as

> an unloosed maniac, strong,
> Blood-drunken . . . ,
> Hoarse-shouting in the ear of God
> The blasphemy of wrong.

At about the same time he wrote to Samuel E. Sewall (counsel for Anthony Burns): "I would die rather than aid in that wicked law; but I deplore all forcible resistance to it. I know the case is an aggravated one, but in the end forbearance will be best for all parties. . . . I beg thee to take especial pains with our colored friends to keep them from resort to force. May God in his mercy keep us from evil, in opposing evil."[3]

 Reprinted from Horace E. Scudder, ed., *The Complete Poetical Works of John Greenleaf Whittier* (Boston: Houghton Mifflin, 1894), pp. 286–288 (stanzas 3–11, 14, 21–24).

We hear thy threats, Virginia! thy stormy words and high
Swell harshly on the Southern winds which melt along our sky;
Yet, not one brown, hard hand foregoes its honest labor here,
No hewer of our mountain oaks suspends his axe in fear.

Wild are the waves which lash the reefs along St. George's bank;
Cold on the shores of Labrador the fog lies white and dank;
Through storm, and wave, and blinding mist, stout are the hearts
    which man
The fishing-smacks of Marblehead, the sea-boats of Cape Ann.

The cold north light and wintry sun glare on their icy forms,
Bent grimly o'er their straining lines or wrestling with the storms;
Free as the winds they drive before, rough as the waves they roam,
They laugh to scorn the slaver's threat against their rocky home.

What means the Old Dominion? Hath she forgot the day
When o'er her conquered valleys swept the Briton's steel array?
How side by side, with sons of hers, the Massachusetts men
Encountered Tarleton's charge of fire, and stout Cornwallis, then?

Forgets she how the Bay State, in answer to the call
Of her old House of Burgesses, spoke out from Faneuil Hall?

When, echoing back her Henry's cry, came pulsing on each breath
Of Northern winds the thrilling sounds of "Liberty or Death!"

What asks the Old Dominion? If now her sons have proved
False to their fathers' memory, false to the faith they loved;
If she can scoff at Freedom, and its great charter spurn,
Must we of Massachusetts from truth and duty turn?

We hunt your bondmen, flying from Slavery's hateful hell;
Our voices, at your bidding, take up the bloodhound's yell;
We gather, at your summons, above our father's graves,
From Freedom's holy altar-horns to tear your wretched slaves!

Thank God! not yet so vilely can Massachusetts bow;
The spirit of her early time is with her even now;
Dream not because her Pilgrim blood moves slow and calm and cool,
She thus can stoop her chainless neck, a sister's slave and tool!

All that a sister State should do, all that a free State may,
Heart, hand, and purse we proffer, as in our early day;
But that one dark loathsome burden ye must stagger with alone,
And reap the bitter harvest which ye yourselves have sown!

. . .

Lower than plummet soundeth, sink the Virginia name;
Plant, if ye will, your fathers' graves with rankest weeds of shame;
Be, if ye will, the scandal of God's fair universe;
We wash our hands forever of your sin and shame and curse.

. . .

The voice of Massachusetts! Of her free sons and daughters,
Deep calling unto deep aloud, the sound of many waters!
Against the burden of that voice what tyrant power shall stand?
No fetters in the Bay State! No slave upon her land!

Look to it well, Virginians! In calmness we have borne,
In answer to our faith and trust, your insult and your scorn;
You've spurned our kindest counsels; you've hunted for our lives;
And shaken round our hearths and homes your manacles and gyves!

We wage no war, we lift no arm, we fling no torch within
The fire-damps of the quaking mine beneath your soil of sin;
We leave ye with your bondmen, to wrestle, while ye can,
With the strong upward tendencies and godlike soul of man!

But for us and for our children, the vow which we have given
For freedom and humanity is registered in heaven;
No slave-hunt in our borders,—no pirate on our strand!
No fetters in the Bay State,—no slave upon our land!

9. James Russell Lowell: "On the Capture of Fugitive Slaves near Washington" (1845)

Though in the latter part of the 1840s Lowell was establishing himself as a poet and man of letters, the larger part of his income in this period was derived from antislavery poems and articles, most of which were published in the *National Anti-Slavery Standard*.[1] A staunch abolitionist and (beyond that) an articulate foe of racism, Lowell affirmed in prose and verse the doctrine of the higher law, placing "the Constitution of the Universe" above the federal constitution.[2] In an acerbic review of Daniel Webster's Seventh of March Speech, in which Webster supported passage of the Fugitive Slave Law as part of the Compromise of 1850, Lowell argued that "every contract to do an immoral act is void *ab initio*. The return of fugitives is clearly an immoral act. . . ."[3] Five years earlier, in response to a fugitive slave case, he had published in the *Boston Courier* a poem expressing the same attitude toward law. Like many of Whittier's and others of Lowell's own poems, this one became part of antislavery's established rhetoric for the next fifteen years.

✿   Reprinted from Horace E. Scudder, ed., *The Complete Poetical Works of James Russell Lowell* (Boston: Houghton Mifflin, 1896), pp. 82–83 (stanzas 1–7, 11).

Look on who will in apathy, and stifle they who can,
The sympathies, the hopes, the words, that make man truly man;
Let those whose hearts are dungeoned up with interest or with ease
Consent to hear with quiet pulse of loathsome deeds like these!

I first drew in New England's air, and from her hardy breast
Sucked in the tyrant-hating milk that will not let me rest;
And if my words seem treason to the dullard and the tame,
'T is but my Bay-State dialect,—our fathers spake the same!

Shame on the costly mockery of piling stone on stone
To those who won our liberty, the heroes dead and gone,
While we look coldly on and see law-shielded ruffians slay
The men who fain would win their own, the heroes of to-day!

Are we pledged to craven silence? Oh, fling it to the wind,
The parchment wall that bars us from the least of human kind,
That makes us cringe and temporize, and dumbly stand at rest,
While Pity's burning flood of words is red-hot in the breast!

Though we break our fathers' promise, we have nobler duties first;
The traitor to Humanity is the traitor most accursed;
Man is more than Constitutions; better rot beneath the sod,
Than be true to Church and State while we are doubly false to God!

We owe allegiance to the State; but deeper, truer, more,
To the sympathies that God hath set within our spirit's core;
Our country claims our fealty; we grant it so, but then
Before Man made us citizens, great Nature made us men.

He's true to God who's true to man; wherever wrong is done,
To the humblest and the weakest, 'neath the all-beholding sun,
That wrong is also done to us; and they are slaves most base,
Whose love of right is for themselves, and not for all their race.

.   .   .

'T is ours to save our brethren, with peace and love to win
Their darkened hearts from error, ere they harden it to sin;
But if before his duty man with listless spirit stands,
Erelong the Great Avenger takes the work from out his hands.

10. Francis Wayland: *The Duty of Obedience to the Civil Magistrate* (1847)

A Baptist minister like his father, Francis Wayland held a pastorate
in Boston and then, from 1827 to 1855, served as president of Brown
University. He was a successful administrator, a distinguished and effective teacher, and a preeminently innovative national leader—virtually, a prophet—in higher education.[1] Yet he probably had his greatest
influence as a moral philosopher. His *Elements of Moral Science* sold
hundreds of thousands of copies across the span of several decades.[2]
During that time his works were, in William McLoughlin's phrase, "the
most popular textbooks for the required course in moral philosophy in
colleges across the nation. . . . They were simply the best statements
of the common American consensus on religion, philosophy, ethics,
and political economy."[3]

In 1847, several months before Thoreau's first lecture on civil disobedience, Wayland developed some of his principles in a series of sermons preached in the Brown University chapel on the theme "The
Duty of Obedience to the Civil Magistrate." His concerns, which are a
good deal less conservative than his title, derived partly from the Mexican War, which he opposed though he did not offer an extended

discussion of it. He let the war serve as an unnamed but clearly understood illustration of his argument that no aggressive war could be justified.[4] Beyond that Wayland insists, first (like Channing), that the actions of a government are as properly subject to moral evaluation and judgment as are those of an individual; and second, that particularly in a democratic society the private citizen is flatly obliged to assess his government's actions in moral terms and to oppose those actions when he believes they have violated important moral values.

Wayland is as concerned with public results as with private integrity. Giving voice to a conception analogous to Thoreau's "wise minority," he exhorts his listeners to form what amounts to a pressure group dedicated to ensuring that Christian ethics will be respected by both political parties and by each segment of the government. One form the citizen's witness may take is civil disobedience, Wayland's conception of which closely resembles Thoreau's in one important respect: both regard the punishment that the disobedient is likely to incur as a penalty inflicted by the unjust magistracy, not as a moral obligation on the part of the conscientious lawbreaker. Further, though in characteristically evangelical fashion he urges each of his hearers to "begin not with his neighbor, but himself," still Wayland assumes the existence of "universal moral principle," which will give harmonious shape to the actions of men of conscience and goodwill. Wayland's disobedience, however, unlike Thoreau's, is necessarily nonviolent; and his thinking is far more social in its emphases than Thoreau's is. Even in his readiness to break the law Wayland is less concerned with preserving an extreme degree of individual freedom than with helping to bring about a peaceful and righteous society.

Reprinted from Francis Wayland, *The Duty of Obedience to the Civil Magistrate* (Boston: Little & Brown, 1847), pp. 16–21, 37–40.

. . . The Christian . . . is a party to every act of the society of which he is a member. He is an intelligent moral agent, responsible to God for his actions, whether they be personal or associated, and therefore he must think about civil government and act about it, according to the light which God has given him, all things else to the contrary notwithstanding.

I therefore, as a Christian citizen, look upon the civil government and the civil magistracy with as unblenching an eye as I look upon anything else. In simplicity and godly sincerity, not in the spirit of strife or partisanship, I may pronounce my opinion upon its enactments and measures, just as I would express my opinions in any other case. I see in Presidents, Cabinets, Senators, Representatives, and all the array of the civil magistracy, nothing but men, fallible men, of like passions with myself. Every page of the history of the past has shown that men placed in such situations have been exceedingly prone to err and to do wickedly. I cannot, therefore, worship men in power. In so far as they are virtuous men I love them. In so far as they are able men I respect them. In so far as, with an honest and true heart, they labor to discharge the solemn duties to which they have been appointed, I honor and I venerate them. I will pay all due deference to the offices which they hold, and will bow with seemly respect to the men who hold them. These men are to me the representatives on earth of eternal justice and unsullied truth; and may my arm fall palsied from my shoulder-blade when I refuse to raise it in token of respect to him who is called of God to minister under so solemn a responsibility.

But all this veneration is due, not to the man, but to the magistrate, and it is due to him therefore, only so long as he confines himself to the duties of his office, and discharges them with pure and patriotic intentions. I have a right to inquire whether his actions in his office conform to the principles of justice. He must claim for himself no immunity from scrutiny on account of the dignity of his station. If he use the power committed to him for any other purpose than that for which it was committed; if he prostitute his official influence to pander to the wishes of a political party; if he sacrifice the gravest interests of his country for the sake of securing to himself the emoluments of office; if he trample the national honor in the dust in order to minister to the grasping selfishness of a contemptible clique,—that moment every vestige of his sacredness is gone forever. He stands before me like Samson from the lap of Delilah. . . . I can look upon him henceforth with no other feelings than those of pity and disgust.

But this may become a yet more practical matter. The magistrate may not only do wrong himself, but he may command me to do wrong. How shall I regard this command? I will regard it as I do any other command to do wrong: I will not obey it. I will look the magistracy calmly and respectfully in the face, and declare to it that in this matter I owe it no allegiance. I will have nothing to do with its wrong-doing. I will separate myself as far as possible from the act and its consequences, whether they be prosperous or adverse. It is wickedness; it has the curse of God inwrought into it, and I will have nothing to do with it. From the beginning to the end I will eschew it and the rewards that it offers. The magistracy may punish me; I cannot help that. I will not resist, but I will not do wrong, nor will I be a party to wrong, let the magistracy or aught else command me.

In saying this I hope that I arrogate to myself nothing in the least peculiar. I am only in the plainest and simplest manner stating the rights and obligations of an intelligent moral being, accountable to God for his actions, and bound to reverence his Creator above all else in the universe. Created under such a responsibility, can I transfer the allegiance which I owe to God, to legislative assemblies, to political caucuses, to mass meetings, to packed or unpacked conventions representing or pretending to represent the assumed omnipotence of public opinion? My whole moral nature with loathing forbids it. I could not do it without feeling that I had become a despicable slave. I could not do it without knowing that I had exchanged the glorious and incorruptible God for an image made like to corruptible man, and to birds and four-footed beasts and creeping things, and worshipped the creature more than the Creator who is blessed forever. My fellow-citizens must not ask this of me; I will surrender for my country, my possessions, my labor, my life, but I will not sacrifice my integrity; and that is unworthy of being the country of a good man which shall ask it.

But here it seems proper that I illustrate more clearly the nature of that limit, beyond which the Christian obligation of obedience to the magistrate ceases. I proceed to offer a few suggestions on this part of our subject.

I have said that the great end for which civil society is established, and the magistracy appointed is, to secure to man the enjoyment of those rights with which he was endowed by his Creator. If society or the magistracy interfere with those rights, it is tyranny. If its acts transcend the limits of the authority committed to it, it is guilty of usurpation. In neither of these cases does the Gospel of Jesus Christ command us to render to it obedience.

The civil magistrate has frequently persecuted men even unto death for believing the Gospel of Jesus Christ. Here he not only does not secure the enjoyment of an inalienable right, he goes farther and actually prohibits it. . . . Here then is a plain case, in which the magistrate, by inhibiting instead of securing the rights conferred on man by his Creator, has forfeited his claim to obedience; I do not say to *all* obedience, but to obedience *in just so far* as his commands interfere with the rights of man or the commandments of God.

The magistrate may also forfeit his claim to obedience by usurpation, that is, by employing his official power for other purposes than those for which it was committed to him. One of the most common instances of this form of wrong is found in the case of war. To this case let us direct our attention.

. . . Suppose that a company of men should land upon our shores, for the purpose of destroying our property or pillaging our houses, or murdering our brethren. We and our fellow-citizens have mutually promised to protect each other in the enjoyment of our rights. We are therefore bound to protect them. We may rightfully unite together, and, if it be necessary, repel the wrong-doers by force of arms. But, in this case, our object recognizes no other persons than the wrong-doers themselves. Their wives, their children, their innocent fellow-citizens, have done us no harm, and we have no authority to inflict injury upon them. If it be said that in perpetrating wrong they only obey the commands of their government, I reply they are moral and accountable men and have no right to obey a wicked command. All that is necessary in order to protect our rights is to repel the invader; and hence our object allows us to employ force to no greater extent than is demanded for the accomplishment of this object.

Again, as soon as our object is accomplished, and our rights are no longer endangered, all reason for contention ceases. We wish the wrong-doer no harm. We have no desire of vengeance to gratify. Our object is not to harm him, but only to protect ourselves. He is still our brother, though he has intended evil against us. This danger being now averted, we will again treat him as a brother and overcome evil by good. We will turn his enmity to friendship, and thus all strife between us must by necessity forever cease.

Again, it is, I think, evident that our rights are of very different degrees of importance, and therefore justify very dissimilar efforts to enforce them. The right to life and liberty is very unlike our right to property. The invasion of the one would authorize us to use means of redress, which could not be authorized by the invasion of the other. I may have the right to repel a murderer at the risk of his life, but this by no means would justify me in slaying a man, because he owed me a dollar, or entering his house by force of arms and seizing upon his property at the risk of the destruction of his family. We are reasonable, accountable and sinful men. It becomes us, who owe a thousand talents, not to press too eagerly the payment of a hundred pence. There is, in our circumstances, much that persuades to forbearance and charity, both as individuals and as members of a community. It is surely better to suffer loss than to reclaim our property at the sacrifice of that which is of infinitely higher value. . . . These principles of action restrict the infliction of pain within the smallest possible limits, and thus they are in harmony with the attributes of a just and all-merciful God. . . .

Suppose that . . . a course of public wrong-doing has been actually commenced; what is then our duty?

I reply; the fact that our country has commenced a course of wrong-doing in no manner whatever alters the moral character of the action. The greater the number of persons combined to perpetrate injury, the greater is the wickedness and the more interminable the mischief. A nation seems a vast and magnificent conception to us the children of yesterday, but . . . [what] is the will of a nation in comparison with the command of Almighty God, and what can be the measure of that impiety which exclaims, "our country, whether right or wrong," that is, our country in defiance of the Eternal One himself.

Every virtuous man must shrink back with trembling from so glaring an impiety, and look with abhorrence upon a cause which requires such sentiments to sustain it. If his country has done or is doing wrong, he must boldly and fearlessly express his opinion of the transaction. He must, as I have before remarked, use all the constitutional power which he possesses, in order to bring the public wickedness to a close. Were the good men of this nation thus to unite, national wickedness among us would be of very limited duration.

But this is not all. While the wrong-doing is in progress we are bound to have no farther participation in it than our social condition renders indispensable. The punishment which God inflicts upon the nation for its crime, we must bear in common with our fellow-citizens. This we cannot avoid, and we must bear it manfully and uncomplainingly. But we can go no farther. We may have no share in the gains of iniquity. A good man can arm no privateers against his brethren of another nation because his government has styled them his enemies. He can loan no money to government, no matter how advantageous the terms of investment, in order to carry on an iniquitous war. He can undertake no contracts by which he may become rich out of the wages of unrighteousness. He may not say, if I do not reap these gains other men will reap them. They are the gains of wickedness, and let the wicked have them. If a good man believe that moral principle is better than gold, this is precisely the occasion on which he is called upon to show his faith by his works. The only question for a conscientious man to ask is this, Is the public act wrong in the sight of God? If it be wrong he must have nothing to do with it, and he can no more innocently aid it with his capital than with his personal service.

But it may be said, that a course of conduct like this would destroy all political organizations and render nugatory the designations in which we have for so very long prided ourselves. If this be all the mischief that is done, the republic, I think, may very patiently endure it. The voice of history has surely spoken in vain if it has not taught us that political parties have ever been combinations for the purposes of personal aggrandizement, advocating or denouncing whatever political principles would best subserve the selfish objects, which alone gave efficiency to their organization. And besides this, if a disciple of Christ has learned to value his political party more highly than he does truth and justice and mercy, it is surely time that his connection with it were broken off. . . . There is a power in truth and rectitude, which wise men would be wiser, did they duly appreciate. Let the moral principle of this country only find an utterance, and party organizations would quail before its rebuke. How often have we seen a combination, insignificant in point of numbers, breaking loose from the trammels of party, and uniting in the support of a *single* principle, hold the balance of power between contending parties, and wield the destinies of either at its will. Let virtuous men then unite on the ground of *universal moral principle*, and the tyranny of party will be crushed. Were the virtuous men of this country to carry their moral sentiments into practice, and act alone rather than participate in the doing of wrong, all parties would from necessity submit to their authority, and the acts of the nation would become a true exponent of the moral character of our people.

And unless we do this, it is both folly and injustice to complain of the magistracy which we have set over us. . . . If we expect moral independence in our representatives, we must show them that we possess it ourselves. If we ask them to peril their political influence for right, we must at least show them that the moral principle of their constituents will sustain them in well-doing.

We see then, that this whole discussion tends to one very simple practical conclusion. A virtuous man is bound to carry his principles into practice in all the relations of life. He can no more do wrong in company than alone, and be guiltless. If he be a true man, he must love right and justice and mercy, better than political party, or personal popularity. If he fear God, he must obey God rather than man, and this fear must govern his conduct universally. In this matter every man must begin not with his neighbor, but himself, and if he wish our country to be reformed, let him begin the work immediately. Let us all then lay these things solemnly to heart, and may God grant us grace to carry them into practice.

11. Henry David Thoreau: "Resistance to Civil Government" (1849)

Thoreau's first exercise in civil disobedience occurred in 1838, when as a citizen newly come of age he was subjected to a tax on behalf of the parish church to which his parents belonged. Since he had not been attending the church and did not consider himself a member of the congregation, he declined to pay the tax and would have been liable to arrest and imprisonment except that the tax was paid for him by someone else. In order to avoid repetitions of this challenge in the future, Thoreau agreed to submit to the town authorities a written declaration of nonmembership in the church. Had the issue been one of religious freedom, this "certificate bow" would have been regarded by many dissenters (Isaac Backus, for one) as a significant compromise of the principle that the state had no right to a role in the citizen's spiritual affairs.[1] But Thoreau's concern seems not to have been distinctly religious. Rather he was protecting his independent self: "Know all men by these presents, that I, Henry Thoreau, do not wish to be regarded as a member of any incorporated society which I have not joined."[2]

This was perhaps a crotchety beginning, but Thoreau took his memberships seriously, and in 1842 he began his refusal to pay his poll tax, on the grounds that to make the payment was to participate personally in the evil of slavery. This disobedient act was both symbolic and comprehensive. Thoreau's grievance was not against some single unjust statute; he was engaged in a summary rejection of the authority of the state, which through the federal compact and its own economic alliances was giving direct support to the slave system. By 1848 (when he first read this lecture publicly) the Mexican War had heightened the urgency of his concern.

Going to jail, insofar as it is a part of Thoreau's conception of civil disobedience, represents not submission, humility, good citizenship, or overall allegiance to the rule of law, but rather a personal declaration of political independence; it gives a concrete form to Thoreau's moral secession from a governmental system that has revealed itself to be corrupt. Imprisonment is the consequence and sign of refusing his citizenship, not the means of vindicating it. The excerpts that follow have been chosen mainly with an eye to clarifying Thoreau's insistence on this theme. For the same reason they are given under his original title, not the more famous one, which was first used after his death.

The essay as a whole is of course not limited to this single perspective. It is also, among other things, a criticism of our unexamined reverence for government, an examination of the relationship between poverty and true personal independence, an attempt at the political and moral education of his hearers and readers, and a meditation on the meaning of freedom.

Reprinted from Henry David Thoreau, *The Writings of Henry David Thoreau* (Cambridge, Mass.: Riverside Press, 1894), vol. 10, pp. 136–137, 138, 145–146, 147, 149–150, 152–153, 161–162.

How does it become a man to behave toward this American government to-day? I answer, that he cannot without disgrace be associated with it. I cannot for an instant recognize that political organization as *my* government which is the *slave's* government also.

All men recognize the right of revolution; that is, the right to refuse allegiance to, and to resist, the government, when its tyranny or its inefficiency are great and unendurable. But almost all say that such is not the case now. But such was the case, they think, in the Revolution of '75. If one were to tell me that this was a bad government because it taxed certain foreign commodities brought to its ports, it is most probable that I should not make an ado about it, for I can do without them. All machines have their friction; and possibly this does enough good to counterbalance the evil. At any rate, it is a great evil to make a stir about it. But when the friction comes to have its machine, and oppression and robbery are organized, I say, let us not have such a machine any longer. In other words, when a sixth of the population of a nation which has undertaken to be the refuge of liberty are slaves, and a whole country is unjustly overrun and conquered by a foreign army, and subjected to military law, I think that it is not too soon for honest men to rebel and revolutionize. What makes this duty the more urgent is the fact that the country so overrun is not our own, but ours is the invading army.

. . . This people must cease to hold slaves, and to make war on Mexico, though it cost them their existence as a people. . . .

One would think, that a deliberate and practical denial of its authority was the only offense never contemplated by government; else, why has it not assigned its definite, its suitable and proportionate penalty? If a man who has no property refuses but once to earn nine shillings for the state, he is put in prison for a period unlimited by any law that I know, and determined only by the discretion of those who placed him there; but if he should steal ninety times nine shillings from the state, he is soon permitted to go at large again.

If the injustice is part of the necessary friction of the machine of government, let it go, let it go: perchance it will wear smooth, —certainly the machine will wear out. If the injustice has a spring, or a pulley, or a rope, or a crank, exclusively for itself, then perhaps you may consider whether the remedy will not be worse than the evil; but if it is of such a nature that it requires you to be the agent of injustice to another, then, I say, break the law. Let your life be a counter friction to stop the machine. What I have to do is to see, at any rate, that I do not lend myself to the wrong which I condemn. . . .

I do not hesitate to say, that those who call themselves Abolitionists should at once effectually withdraw their support, both in person and property, from the government of Massachusetts, and not wait till they constitute a majority of one, before they suffer the right to prevail through them. I think that it is enough if they have God on their side, without waiting for that other one. Moreover, any man more right than his neighbors constitutes a majority of one already.

. . . I know this well, that if one thousand, if one hundred, if ten men whom I could name,—if ten *honest* men only,—ay, if *one* HONEST man, in this State of Massachusetts, *ceasing to hold slaves*, were actually to withdraw from this copartnership, and be locked up in the county jail therefor, it would be the abolition of slavery in America. For it matters not how small the beginning may seem to be: what is once well done is done forever. . . .

Under a government which imprisons any unjustly, the true place for a just man is also a prison. The proper place to-day, the only place which Massachusetts has provided for her freer and less desponding spirits, is in her prisons, to be put out and locked out of the State by her own act, as they have already put themselves out by their principles. It is there that the fugitive slave, and the Mexican prisoner on parole, and the Indian come to plead the wrongs of his race should find them; on that separate, but more free and honorable ground, where the State places those who are not *with* her, but *against* her,—the only house in a slave State in which a free man can abide with honor. If any think that their influence would be lost there, and their voices no longer afflict the ear of the State, that they would not be as an enemy within its walls, they do not know by how much truth is stronger than error, nor how much more eloquently and effectively he can combat injustice who has experienced a little in his own person. Cast your whole vote, not a strip of paper merely, but your whole influence. A minority is powerless while it conforms to the majority; it is not even a minority then; but it is irresistible when it clogs by its whole weight. If the alternative is to keep all just men in prison, or give up war and slavery, the State will not hesitate which to choose. If a thousand men were not to pay their tax-bills this year, that would not be a violent and bloody measure, as it would be to pay them, and enable the State to commit violence and shed innocent blood. This is, in fact, the definition of a peaceable revolution, if any such is possible. If the tax-gatherer, or any other public officer, asks me, as one has done, "But what shall I do?" my answer is, "If you really wish to do anything, resign your office." When the subject has refused allegiance, and the officer has resigned his office, then the revolution is accomplished. But even suppose blood should flow. Is there not a sort of blood shed when the conscience is wounded? Through this wound a man's real manhood and immortality flow out, and he bleeds to an everlasting death. I see this blood flowing now. . . .

When I converse with the freest of my neighbors, I perceive that, whatever they may say about the magnitude and seriousness of the question, and their regard for the public tranquillity, the long and the short of the matter is, that they cannot spare the protection of the existing government, and they dread the consequences to their property and families of disobedience to it. For my own part, I should not like to think that I ever rely on the protection of the State. But, if I deny the authority of the State when it presents its tax-bill, it will soon take and waste all my property, and so harass me and my children without end. This is hard. This makes it impossible for a man to live honestly, and at the same time comfortably, in outward respects. . . . [Nevertheless] I can afford to refuse allegiance to Massachusetts, and her right to my property and life. It costs me less in every sense to incur the penalty of disobedience to the State than it would to obey. I should feel as if I were worth less in that case. . . .

I have never declined paying the highway tax, because I am as desirous of being a good neighbor as I am of being a bad subject; and as for supporting schools, I am doing my part to educate my fellow-countrymen now. It is for no particular item in the tax-bill that I refuse to pay it. I simply wish to refuse allegiance to the State, to withdraw and stand aloof from it effectually. I do not care to trace the course of my dollar, if I could, till it buys a man or a musket to shoot one with,—the dollar is innocent,—but I am concerned to trace the effects of my allegiance. In fact, I quietly declare war with the State, after my fashion, though I will still make what use and get what advantage of her I can, as is usual in such cases.

If others pay the tax which is demanded of me, from a sympathy with the State, they do but what they have already done in their own case, or rather they abet injustice to a greater extent than the State requires. If they pay the tax from a mistaken interest in the individual taxed, to save his property, or prevent his going to jail, it is because they have not considered wisely how far they let their private feelings interfere with the public good.

This, then, is my position at present. But one cannot be too much on his guard in such a case, lest his action be biased by obstinacy or an undue regard for the opinions of men. Let him see that he does only what belongs to himself and to the hour. . . .

III DISOBEDIENCE TO THE FUGITIVE SLAVE LAW OF 1850

There is no power but of God: the powers that be are ordained of God. Whosoever therefore resisteth the power, resisteth the ordinance of God.

—Romans 13:1–2

Then Peter and the other apostles answered and said, We ought to obey God rather than men.

—Acts 5:29

Introduction

During the 1840s, even as northern antislavery feeling gathered momentum, most northerners continued to reject radical measures. One of their guiding assumptions was that slavery was at odds with "the spirit of the age" and with God's providential design for human history, so that with time and patience slavery was certain to disappear and there was no obligation or necessity to risk sectional hostility through aggressive actions aimed at speeding abolition. A letter from Daniel Webster to William Henry Furness shows how, through this assumption, antislavery feeling and a theoretical approval of emancipation could be accommodated to political quietism. "The mild influence of Christianity," Webster argues, will itself eventually abolish slavery:

> If we see that the course is onward and forward, as it certainly is, in regard to the final abolition of human slavery, while we give to it our fervent prayers, and aid it by all the justifiable influences which we can exercise, it seems to me we must leave both the progress and the result in His hands, who sees the end from the beginning, and in whose sight a thousand years are but as a single day.[1]

With the annexation of Texas and the Mexican War, however, the view that history would move ever "onward and forward" without human assistance received a great jolt. These events were seen by many as shameless means of extending the power and influence of slavery; and Webster's sort of patience was hard to sustain if the direction of events could be so drastically reversed. William Lloyd Garrison and his nonresistant followers were by no means the only ones to be outraged; the Massachusetts legislature adopted "a comprehensive and strong antiwar report."[2] Nonetheless, very few Americans were brought at this time into direct conflict with the law, especially because Congress did not enact a military draft bill.

Two years after the war's victorious conclusion, however, Congress passed the Compromise of 1850, one element of which was an aggressive new fugitive slave law.[3] This law invaded the North's moral as well as geographical territory in an unprecedented way. Until the Fugitive Slave Law was passed, Emerson said, he had lived "without suffering any known inconvenience from American slavery. I never saw it; I never heard the whip."[4] Now his distance from it had been suddenly and inescapably bridged. Among the law's provisions were the exclusion from fugitive slave cases of jury trials and writs of habeas corpus; a modest but symbolically weighty financial incentive for federal commissioners to decide cases in favor of the southern claimants; and, above all, a specific requirement that any northern citizen was liable to be deputized by federal marshals and obliged to participate personally in the capture and return of fugitives who had reached what had long been regarded as free soil.

"Outcries of contempt and defiance came from every free State," Samuel May said.[5] Protest meetings were held in many communities. At one of them, in New York City, a large group "of Negroes, mostly women, passed resolutions condemning the Fugitive Slave Law and counselled armed resistance to it."[6] Another, at Canfield, Ohio, was addressed by Benjamin Wade, later a U.S. senator; Matthew Birchard, Milton Sutliff, and Rufus Ranney, later judges of the Ohio Supreme Court; and John Hutchins, later a member of Congress. The meeting voted among others the following resolution, "unanimously passed with a hurricane of shouts":

> *Resolved*, That, come life or come imprisonment,—come fine or come death—we will neither aid nor assist in the return of any fugitive slave, but, on the contrary, we will harbor and secrete, and by all just means protect and defend him, and thus give him a practical God speed to liberty.[7]

Despite all this, sentiment in the North was far from united. If Canfield had its eminent advocates of disobedience, many prominent northerners were arrayed on the other side. Daniel Webster, who had been instrumental in securing passage of the law (believing the compromise necessary to preserve the Union), was reviled by the radicals as a new Benedict Arnold; but he had the fervent support of many citizens, especially businessmen. In Massachusetts three thousand people ("accomplices in crime," Garrison called them) signed a public letter endorsing Webster's climactic Seventh of March speech and thanking him for "recalling us to our duties under the Constitution. . . . In a time . . . when multitudes have been unable to find solid ground on which to rest with security and peace, you have pointed out to a whole people the path of duty, have convinced the understanding and touched the conscience of a nation."[8] A similar division prevailed in the churches; a number of eminent ministers of several denominations preached and published sermons on the duty of citizens to obey the law. Clergymen who preached disobedience could usually expect to antagonize many parishioners in doing so; some were dismissed from their pulpits.[9]

Throughout the early 1850s, then, the idea of civil disobedience received its first broad national debate. It was a debate in which the stakes were felt on all sides to be very high. In the eyes of the advocates of disobedience, the passage of the Fugitive Slave Law had uniquely jeopardized the preservation of justice in the United States; in the view of their opponents, the disobedients themselves posed a terrifying threat to the preservation of the Union and the rule of law. Neither side minced words. All of the objections to civil disobedience that had been posed from the very beginning were raised again now, urgently and sometimes belligerently; in order to maintain their position the disobedients had to find persuasive answers to them. Webster spoke at dinners in his honor in several northern cities, making mocking references to an illusory higher law of conscience and emphatically equating disobedience to the Fugitive Slave Law with treason.[10] Rufus Choate spoke at Harvard Law School before the Story Association to urge his hearers "to cherish the Religion of the Law. . . . To exercise this conservative influence, to beget a distrust of individual and unenlightened judgment, on matters of such vast import and extent, and to foster a religious reverence for the laws, is the *new duty* which the times demand of the legal profession."[11] At a mass meeting in Faneuil Hall, held in response to a call signed by "about five thousand citizens of Massachusetts," resolutions were voted including the following:

> Resolved, That every species and form of resistance to the execution of a regularly enacted law, except by peaceable appeal to the regular action of the judicial tribunals upon the question of its constitutionality—an appeal which ought never to be opposed or impeded—is mischievous, and subversive of the first principles of social order, and tends to anarchy and bloodshed.[12]

One of the speakers deplored a previous Faneuil Hall meeting that had voted a resolve that "Constitution or no Constitution, law or no law, we will not allow a fugitive slave to be taken from Massachusetts." Another speaker, B. F. Hallett, warned of "a new form of moral treason, which assumes, by the mysterious power of an unknown 'higher law' to trample down all law." To treat the Fugitive Slave Law like the Stamp Act, he said, "is revolution or it is treason." His argument was based on a political theory that most Americans had historically taken for granted:

> It is rightful revolution if in the exercise of the reserved sovereignty of the people, it puts down one government, and by organic laws forms another. That is the only American theory of the higher law that is not rebellion, but a sacred right of the

people. But if it only resists law, and obstructs its officers, while it seeks no new organic form of government through the collected will of the people, it is treason, rebellion, mobism, and anarchy, and he who risks it must risk hanging for it.

"May not a law be too high?" asked another speaker ironically. "It is *above* justice, for it refuses to return the property of our brethren of the South when found within our precincts." This conception of fugitive slaves as property, however, besides being anathema to the Parkers and the Thoreaus, was a position with which many of the conservatives were uncomfortable. Most of them preferred to pose the issue in terms of fealty to law and to Constitutional obligations. Hallett used a more effective idiom when he said to the crowd: "If there be any wild enough hereafter to resort to a fancied higher law to put down law, they will find in your determined will a stronger law to sustain all the laws of the land." His rhetorical prediction turned out, however, to be wide of the mark: hundreds of fugitive slaves passed safely through Boston in the next several years, and the two who were captured and returned were the victims not of the population's "determined will" but of federal power exercised through legal channels and particularly through the armed strength of the militia.[13] Nonetheless, especially in the first years of the Fugitive Slave Law's operation, opposition to disobedience was a formidable force in northern public opinion.

In highly charged public meetings, on both sides converts preached to others already, or nearly, converted. When genuine efforts at persuasion were made, the advocates of civil disobedience were obliged to adopt more conciliatory rhetorical approaches. Often the speaker used a tone that was painstakingly restrained, so that skeptical listeners would be able to hear; sometimes the logical structure of the argument was defensive even if its tone was not. The disobedients' styles ranged from Nathaniel Hall's perfect rationality and sweetness to the headlong vituperation of Daniel Foster. There was a good deal of disagreement among the disobedients about what kind of disobedience was justified. "I would die rather than aid in that wicked law," Whittier said; "but I deplore all forcible resistance to it."[14] This approach was not likely to help free embattled fugitives, so others adopted a more militant ethic. Theodore Parker, for example, said he would use "all means moral," by which he meant that "it is the natural duty of citizens to rescue every fugitive slave from the hands of the marshal who essays to return him to bondage, to do it peaceably if they can, forcibly if they must, but by all means to do it."[15]

Whatever the disobedient's precise position, he generally acknowledged the obligation to define the nature of the authority that he elevated above the Constitution and the law. ("The higher law" was a fairly broad rubric covering a number of ethics, theologies, and epistemologies. To cite the extreme case, it embraced Andrews Norton as well as Emerson.) The transcendentalists (especially Thoreau, Parker, and Thomas Stone), unlike most others, emphasized the unaided voice of an intuitive conscience; but they denied that their position was tantamount to anarchy or subjectivism. They too vindicated their disobedience by an appeal to law, a law that in being "higher" was all the more inexorably binding. Though their solution to the epistemological problem of authority was more radical and more divisive than the solutions of other higher-law advocates, still in an important sense they shared the restraint and self-subordination of Whittier. To read the dictates of the conscience they looked inward much more than to the Bible, to the collective judgment of the community, to persons in positions of moral leadership, or even to an inherited tradition of English law based on natural rights. Nonetheless, they too assumed that they were the bearers of a moral nature whose essence was shared with other men and which had been ordained for all time by a power beyond themselves. To those who worried about social safeguards, they might have replied simply that their own disobedience was as well rooted in piety as Whittier's.

For a larger number of disobedients, however, this testimony of the individual conscience was to be shaped, restrained, guided, and corrected by other resources, especially the Bible. Perhaps the period's most extraordinary testimony to the centrality of biblical interpretation and biblical authority in people's thinking on these issues was given in 1851, when the slaveholder Edward Gorsuch entered Pennsylvania in pursuit of several escaped slaves. He found them under the armed protection of a number of (mostly black) Pennsylvanians, whereupon he and the protectors' leader, a black named William Parker, cited contradictory biblical passages at each other. The exchange of texts was, of course, a standoff; in the ensuing fight Gorsuch was killed.[16]

In the years that followed 1850 northern sentiment was increasingly on the side of disobedience, and by 1854 its advocates found themselves in a far more supportive social environment than the one they had encountered at first. There were several reasons for this shift in feeling. One was the continued proslavery thrust of congressional action, culminating in the Kansas-Nebraska Act of 1854, which repealed the Missouri Compromise and opened to the possibility of slavery territory previously guaranteed to be free; this was widely felt in the North to be a flagrant breach of contract and good faith. A second influence was the return, under the 1850 Fugitive Slave Law, of fugitives who had reached northern communities, especially Boston, in which anti-slavery feeling was already strong. These dramatic events, combined with the support for the law proclaimed by the platforms of both major parties in the campaign of 1852, tended to "radicalize" (at least in this one respect) a considerable portion of the general public. A third stimulus was *Uncle Tom's Cabin*, which was published serially in 1851–52 and sold 300,000 copies in the first year after its release in book form in March 1852.[17] Richard Henry Dana, who was quick to offer his legal services to captured fugitive slaves, noted in his journal in the midst of the furor over the Anthony Burns case: "The most remarkable exhibition is from the Whigs, the Hunker Whigs, the Compromise men of 1850. Men who wd. not speak to me in 1850&51, & who were enrolling themselves as special policemen in the Sims affair, stop me in the street & talk treason."[18] In the years between the passage of the Compromise and midsummer 1854, Protestant clergymen alone preached dozens of sermons espousing the Christian duty of disobedience to the Fugitive Slave Law. They were joined, as the following selections show, by lecturers, poets, essayists, congressmen, and private citizens. In short, by mid-decade there existed in several parts of the North the nearest thing in our history to a popular consensus in support of civil disobedience.

12. Lewis Hayden, William C. Nell, and others: "Declaration of Sentiments of the Colored Citizens of Boston, on the Fugitive Slave Bill" (1850)

In the weeks following the enactment of the Fugitive Slave Law, protest meetings were held all over the North, many of them by groups of blacks. These meetings generally adopted a series of resolutions that advocated a comprehensive program of opposition and resistance to the new law and pointed toward court tests of the law's constitutionality, political organizing aimed at securing repeal, individual and collective acts of disobedience, and, in Boston as elsewhere, forcible resistance undertaken in self-defense and as a last resort.[1] Blacks had necessarily to view these measures in comparison with their obvious and stark alternatives: the chance of capture by a slaveholder or his agents, and flight from the United States. (For whites the alternative was of course direct personal complicity in the act of enslavement.)

The chief participants in the Boston meeting whose resolutions and minutes are excerpted here were leading figures among the city's abolitionists. Lewis Hayden, an escaped slave and by 1850 a Boston clothier, was active in the underground railroad and later in the Vigilance Committee.[2] William Nell was a black journalist, historian, and anti-slavery organizer who led a long, ultimately successful campaign of boycotts and petitions aimed at the abolition of segregation in Massachusetts schools. (Boston became, in 1855, the only major city in the United States to desegregate its schools before the Civil War.)[3] John T. Hilton, a black barber, was prominent in the Massachusetts Anti-Slavery Society and with Nell a durable leader of the school integration campaign.[4] Robert Johnson, also black, was another associate in that work. Robert Morris was a well-known black lawyer and activist. Joshua B. Smith was a black caterer who in a sort of private boycott "refused to serve a banquet to honor Daniel Webster,"[5] one of the Fugitive Slave Law's major sponsors. Father Josiah Henson, an escaped slave and Methodist Episcopal preacher, was the leader of a settlement for black fugitives in Ontario; his militant contribution to the Boston meeting casts a rather ironic light on his long-standing popular identification with Harriet Beecher Stowe's Uncle Tom.[6] Charles L. Remond, a black from Salem, was well known as a traveling agent and effective speaker for the American Anti-Slavery Society.[7] Originally a Garrisonian nonresistant, he had come by the late 1840s to support "any means that will abolish slavery."[8] Another dominant participant in the meeting was Garrison himself, who reaffirmed his own absolute non-resistance and his belief in the superiority of moral to physical force but at the same time invoked (somewhat equivocally) the names of Washington and William Tell as examples worthy to be followed by all those present who were not conscientiously committed to nonviolence.

Robert Morris, Esq., called for the Report of the Committee, which was submitted by William C. Nell, as follows:

The Fugitive Slave Bill, exhibited in its hideous deformity at our previous meeting, has already in hot haste commenced its bloody crusade o'er the land, and the liability of ourselves and families becoming its victims at the caprice of Southern men-stealers, imperatively demands an expression, whether we will tamely submit to chains and slavery, or whether we will, at all and every hazard, Live and Die freemen.

The system of American slavery, the vilest that ever saw the sun, is a violation of every sentiment of Christianity and the antipodes of every dictate of humanity. The slaveholder's pretensions to a claim on human property are of no more weight than those of the midnight assassin or the pirate on the high seas. "God made all men Free,—free as the birds that cleave the air or sing on the branches,—free as the sunshine that gladdens the earth,—free as the winds that sweep over sea and land,—free at his birth,—free during his whole life,—free today,—this hour,—this moment."

The Massachusetts Bill of Rights declares that ALL MEN are born free and equal, and have certain natural, essential and in-alienable rights, among which may be reckoned the right of enjoying and defending their liberties.

The example of the Revolutionary Fathers in resisting British oppression, throwing the tea overboard in Boston Harbor, rather than submit to a three-penny tax, is a most significant one to us, when Man is likely to be deprived of his God-given liberty.

Among the incidents of that seven years' struggle for liberty, and to which the page of impartial history bears record, is the fact that the first Martyr in the attack on residents was a colored man, Crispus Attucks by name, who fell in State Street on the 5th of March, 1770. In that conflict, as also in the War of 1812, colored Americans were devoted and gallant worshippers at Freedom's shrine; and pre-eminently at New Orleans they were warranted in believing that when the victory was achieved, they, as all who fought shoulder to shoulder, would be invited to the banquet. But lo! the white man's banquet has been held, and loud peals to liberty have reached the sky above; but the colored American's share has been to stand outside and wait for the crumbs that fell from Liberty's festive board. And to cap the climax at this advanced hour of the nation's prosperity, and the spread over all Christendom of a sentiment of liberty, fraternity and equality, the colored man, woman and child, bond and nominally free, are hunted like partridges on the mountain, if their hearts aspire for freedom.

The American people glory in the struggle of 1776, and laud the names of those who made the bloody resistance to tyranny. The battle cry of Patrick Henry of Virginia—"GIVE ME LIBERTY, OR GIVE ME DEATH,"—and that of General Warren, "MY SONS SCORN TO BE SLAVES," are immortalized, and we are proud in not being an exception to that inspiration. It warms our hearts, and will nerve our right arms, to do all, and suffer all for Liberty.

The laudation and assistance volunteered by the United States to the Poles and Greeks and South Americans in their struggles for freedom,—the recent manifestations of sympathy with the Blouses of Paris, the oppressed of Italy, and with Kossuth and his band of noble Hungarians, are so many incentives to the victims of Republican American despotism, to manfully assert their independence, and martyr-like, die freemen, rather than live slaves; confirming also, our pre-determined resolution to abide the issue made with us by the slave power—counting our lives not worth preserving at the expense of our liberties.

In connection with what has been previously adopted, the committee would submit the following preamble and resolutions:

Whereas, the Fugitive Slave Bill is unconstitutional, and in direct conflict with the higher law enjoined by our Saviour, "whatsoever ye would that men should do unto you, do you even so to them."

Whereas, from time immemorial, unrighteous enactments have been nullified by all who feared God rather than man; by Moses the deliverer of Israel, against wicked Pharoah, and Daniel who welcomed incarceration in a den of lions, rather than perjure his own soul in obedience to the tyrant's mandate.

Whereas, St. Paul expressly declares that he who will not provide for his own household, is an infidel, having denied the faith.

Whereas, the history of nations attests numerous instances where the gallows, stake, and gibbet have been welcomed when security of life and limb might have been purchased by obedience to inhuman statutes.

Whereas, Thousands in the land from every class and profession in life, without exception, are eagerly registering their vows to oppose this infamous enactment, at whatever cost of money, reputation or life.

Whereas, Sustained as we are, by examples of Mosaic and Christian practice, and from the history of civil society from the earliest ages; encouraged by the voices of our brethren from the East and the West, from the North, and even the tyrant's domain, the bloody South (where many true hearts beat for freedom). But above all, and independent of any suggestions, counsels or examples, guided by our own promptings for the freedom of ourselves and families (by which we mean, of course, all those in any way exposed to danger from the slave power), and believing that Resistance to tyrants is obedience to God, we are now

Resolved, To organize a League of Freedom, composed of all those who are ready to resist this law, rescue, and protect the slave, at every hazard, and who remember that

> "Whether on the scaffold high,
> Or in the battle's van,
> The fittest place where Man can die,
> Is where he dies for Man."*

Resolved, That in view of the imminent danger, present and looked for, we caution every colored man, woman and child, to

*Michael J. Barry, "The Place Where Man Should Die."—Ed.

be careful in their walks through the highways and byways of the city by day, and doubly so, if out at night, as to where they go—how they go—and who they go with; to be guarded on side, off side and all sides; as watchful as Argus with his hundred eyes, and as executive as was Brierius, with as many hands; if seized by any one, to make the air resound with the signal-word, and as they would rid themselves of any wild beast, be prompt in their hour of peril.

Resolved, That any Commissioner who would deliver up a fugitive slave to a Southern highwayman, under this infamous and unconstitutional law, would have delivered up Jesus Christ to his persecutors for one-third of the price that Judas Iscariot did.

Resolved, That in the event of any Commissioner of Massachusetts being applied to for remanding a fugitive, we trust he will emulate the example of Judge Harrington, of Vermont, and "be satisfied with nothing short of a bill of sale from the Almighty."

Resolved, That though we learn that bribes have already been offered to our Judiciary to forestall their influence against the panting fugitive, we would not attempt any other offset, than to remind said officers that

> "Man is more than Constitutions—
> He'd better rot beneath the sod,
> Than be true to Church and State
> And doubly false to God";*

that should he in the emergency obey God rather than the devil, by letting the oppressed go free, he will have done his part in wiping out from the escutcheon of Massachusetts the foul stain inflicted by Daniel Webster in promoting, and Samuel A. Eliot in voting for this Heaven-defying law.

Resolved, That though we gratefully acknowledge that the mane of the British Lion affords a nestling place for our brethren in danger from the claws of the American Eagle, we would, nevertheless, counsel against their leaving the soil of their birth, consecrated by their tears, toils and perils, but yet to be rendered truly, the "land of the free and the home of the brave."

*James Russell Lowell, "On the Capture of Fugitive Slaves Near Washington." See Chapter 9.—Ed.

The ties of consanguinity, bid *all* remain who would lend a helping hand to the millions now in bonds. But at all events, if the soil of Bunker Hill, Concord and Lexington is the last bulwark of liberty, we can nowhere fill more honorable graves.

Resolved, That we do earnestly express the hope that the citizens of Boston will rally in Faneuil Hall, and send forth in the ear of all christendom their opinion of the infamous Fugitive Slave Bill, and their intention to *disobey* its decrees; their voice, uttered in the Cradle of Liberty, will assure us as nothing else can, whether they are to be reckoned on the side of liberty or slavery—whether they will vouchsafe to us their aid, or will assist the manthief in hurling us and our little ones into interminable bondage.

Resolved, That this meeting would invite the clergymen in this city and vicinity to dedicate a day or part thereof, in presenting to their people by prayer and sermon, their Christian duty to the flying fugitive, and also in acceding [*sic*] to requisitions of this atrocious Bill.

Resolved, That as in union is strength, and in this crisis a combination of power is all-important, this meeting recommend the calling of a New England Convention of the friends of Liberty to operate against the Fugitive Law, and to devise ways and means for consolidating their resources here on the soil.

Resolved, That the doings of this and preceding meeting be published for wide circulation.

The report was accepted and the resolutions adopted by a unanimous vote.

John T. Hilton in an eloquent and earnest speech advocated the resolutions—remarking that twenty-five years ago he eulogized, as the greatest talent in the country, Daniel Webster for his efforts on Plymouth Rock on the slavery question, and he regretted exceedingly that that talent should have been used in favor of the odious bill. He was no longer to be trusted by the friends of liberty, for he had done more evil, and committed more sin than a thousand such men as the late Professor Webster ever did.* This speaker concluded his remarks, which were listened to with marked attention, by saying that when his

*John White Webster, a chemistry professor at Harvard, was convicted of murder in a sensational trial in 1850.—Ed.

services should be wanted in defense of their rights, he would desire no greater office than to lead them on to battle and to victory.

Joshua B. Smith hoped no one in that meeting would preach *Peace*, for as Patrick Henry said, *"There is no Peace."* . . . He advised every fugitive to arm himself with a revolver—if he could not buy one otherwise to sell his coat for that purpose. As for himself, and he thus exhorted others, he should be kind and courteous to all, even the slave dealer, until the moment of an attack upon his liberty. He should not be taken alive, but upon the slave catcher's head be the consequences. When he could not live here in Boston a *freeman*, in the language of Socrates, *"He had lived long enough."* Mr. Smith in conclusion made a demonstration of one mode of defense, which those who best know him say would be exemplified to the *hilt*.

Robert Johnson proclaimed that the meeting was largely composed of actors, and not speakers merely; they were men of over-alls—men of the wharf—those who could do heavy work in the hour of difficulty. He administered a timely caution to the women who, in pursuit of washing and other work, visited the hotels and boarding houses, that they should be on the constant look-out for the Southern slave catcher or the *Northern accessory*, and as they valued their liberty be prepared for any emergency. (This word to the *wise* women and others, was greeted with lively demonstrations; some remarking that the spirit exhibited by the women some years since, in a slave rescue from the Supreme Court, was yet alive and ready for action.) He would have it a well understood point in our creed of vigilance, in no case to be ourselves the aggressors; in this it was all-important to be cautious; we will not go to the depots or elsewhere after the slave hunter, but when he rushes upon our buckler—*kill him*. . . .

Father Henson—would tell our oppressors that in condemning resistance on the part of the colored people, they were denouncing the examples of Washington and Jefferson and all Martyrs of Liberty. He concurred with Mr. Garrison and others in a reliance upon moral power, but the meeting well understood that in a crisis for *Liberty or Death*, the speaker would not be quietly led like a lamb to the slaughter. . . .

Charles Lenox Remond— . . . The idea of leaving our homes

and firesides was in every sense a mistaken one; the Old Bay State should be our Canada. Boston is the Thermopylae of the anti-slavery cause. Let us be ready in the trial hour to insure its analogy with that classic spot rendered so illustrious by Leonidas and his Spartan Band, or like the more modern but not less significant—Bunker Hill. The history of our country's struggles for Liberty had never been disgraced by a *colored* Arnold; if then we have not proved traitors to the white man, in God's name shall we not prove true to ourselves? He believed that the Fugitive Slave Law had been enacted in great part at the instance of the hand maid of slavery, the Colonization Society, in the wicked hope that the fear of being recaptured into bondage would move the colored man to emigrate to Liberia. But this feature only made the whole more damnable, and was to be opposed at all and every point. After rebuking the colored people for lack of anti-slavery character, he declared that he would not yield to any institution or individual that would abridge his liberties or his efforts for the fugitive, and was happy in believing that the colored citizens of Boston would do their whole duty and defend themselves. . . .

LEWIS HAYDEN, *President*. WILLIAM C. NELL, *Secretary*.

13. Theodore Parker: *The Function and Place of Conscience, in Relation to the Laws of Men* (1850)

A great preacher who has been called the conscience of his generation,[1] Theodore Parker focused the ideal vision of his transcendentalism directly on the workaday world. Not for him the withdrawals and privacies of Emerson and Thoreau; "transcendental politics," Parker said, ". . . aims to organize the ideals of man's moral and social nature into political institutions."[2]

Parker derived his politics in large measure from the Declaration of Independence, whose natural-rights ideas he explicitly identified as transcendental—by which he meant that they were in harmony with the eternal moral laws that were inherent in the universe and sanctioned by God. He felt no such enthusiasm for the Constitution, however. On the contrary, his belief that the most reliable determinations of truth were made intuitively by the individual conscience gave him a considerable detachment both from civil law and from decisions arrived at through majority vote.

Parker preached "The Function and Place of Conscience in Relation to the Laws of Men" on September 22, 1850. It was both a part of his continuing rebuttal of Webster's Seventh of March Speech and, as it turned out, a prophecy of Parker's own role over the next several years in resisting enforcement of the Fugitive Slave Law. One aspect of the prophecy is perhaps misleading, however: when Parker speaks of obtaining "the freedom of every fugitive slave in Boston, without breaking a limb or rending a garment," he is expressing a naive hope, not a principle. He is closer to the disobedience that actually took place when he insists that the citizens are obliged to free all fugitive slaves "peaceably if they can, forcibly if they must, but by all means to do it." By the end of the decade he had extended this principle and become one of the "Secret Six" who provided John Brown with funds not long before the attack on Harpers Ferry.

Reprinted from Theodore Parker, *The Function and Place of Conscience, in Relation to the Laws of Men* (Boston: Crosby & Nichols, 1850), pp. 7–8, 11–16, 21, 24–26, 32.

There are some things which are true, independent of all human opinions. Such things we call facts. Thus it is true that one and one are equal to two, that the earth moves round the sun, that all men have certain natural and unalienable rights, rights which a man can alienate only for himself, and not for another. No man made these things true; no man can make them false. If all the men in Jerusalem and ever so many more, if all the men in the world, were to pass a unanimous vote that one and one were not equal to two, that the earth did not move round the sun, that all men had not natural and unalienable rights, the opinion would not alter the fact, nor make truth false and falsehood true.

So there are likewise some things which are right, independent of all human opinions. Thus it is right to love a man and not to hate him, to do him justice and not injustice, to allow him the natural rights which he has not alienated. No man made these things right; no man can make them wrong. If all the men in Jerusalem and ever so many more, if all the men in the world, were to pass a unanimous vote that it was right to hate a man and not love him, right to do him injustice and not justice, right to deprive him of his natural rights not alienated by himself, the opinion would not alter the fact, nor make right wrong and wrong right. . . .

Before men attain a knowledge of the absolute right, they often make theories which do not rest upon the facts of man's moral nature, and enact human rules for the conduct of men, which do not agree with the moral nature of man. These are rules which men make and do not find made. They are not a part of man's moral nature, writ therein, and so obligatory thereon, no more than the false rules for the conduct of matter are writ therein, and so obligatory thereon. You and I are no more morally bound to keep such rules of conduct, because king Pharoah or king People say we shall, than the sun is materially bound to go round the earth every day, because Hipparchus and Ptolemy say it does. The opinion or command of a king, or a people, can no more change a fact and alter a law of man's nature, than the opinion of a philosopher can do this in material nature.

. . . As the mind has for its object absolute Truth, so Conscience has for its object absolute Justice. Conscience enables us not merely to learn the right by experiment and induction, but intuitively and in advance of experiment; so in addition to the experimental way, whereby we learn Justice from the facts of human history, we have a transcendental way, and learn it from the facts of human nature, from immediate consciousness.

It is the function of Conscience to discover to men the moral law of God. It will not do this with infallible certainty, for, at its best estate, neither Conscience nor any other faculty of man is absolutely perfect, so as never to mistake. Absolute perfection belongs only to the faculties of God. But Conscience, like each other faculty, is relatively perfect,—is adequate to the purpose God meant it for. . . .

. . . Though the Conscience of a man lacks the absolute perfection of that of God, in all that relates to my dealing with men, it is still the last standard of appeal. I will hear what my friends have to say, what public opinion has to offer, what the best men can advise me to, then I am to ask my own Conscience, and follow its decision—not that of my next friend, the public, or the best of men. . . . If I do the best thing I can know to-day, and to-morrow find a better one and do that, I am not to be blamed, nor to be called a sinner against God because not so just to-day, as I shall be to-morrow. I am to do God's will soon as I know it, not before, and to take all possible pains to find it out; but am not to blame for acting childish when a child, nor to be ashamed of it when grown up to be a man. . . .

Having determined what is absolutely right by the Conscience of God, or at least relatively right according to my Conscience to-day, then it becomes my duty to keep it. I owe it to God to obey His law, or what I deem His law; that is my Duty. It may be uncomfortable to keep it, unpopular, contrary to my present desires, to my passions, to my immediate interests; it may conflict with my plans in life: that makes no difference. I owe entire allegiance to my God. It is a duty to keep His law, a personal duty, my duty as a man. I owe it to myself, for I am to keep the integrity of my own consciousness; I owe it to my brother and to my God. Nothing can absolve me from this duty, neither the fact that it is uncomfortable or unpopular, nor that it conflicts with my desires, my passions, my immediate interests and my plans in life. . . .

I believe all this is perfectly plain, but now see what it leads to. In the complicated relations of human life, various rules for the moral conduct of men have been devised, some of them in the form of statute-laws, some in the form of customs, and, in virtue of these rules, certain artificial demands are made of men, which have no foundation in the moral nature of man; these demands are thought to represent duties. We have the same word to describe what I ought to do as subject to the law of God, and what is demanded of me by custom, or the statute. We call each a duty. Hence comes no small confusion; the conventional and official obligation is thought to rest on the same foundation as the natural and personal duty. As the natural duty is at first sight a little vague, and not written out in the law-book, or defined by custom, while the conventional obligation is well understood, men think that in case of any collision between the two, the natural duty must give way to the official obligation.

For clearness' sake, the natural and personal obligation to

keep the law of God as my Conscience declares it, I will call
Duty; the conventional and official obligation to comply with
some custom, keep some statute, or serve some special interest,
I will call Business. Here then are two things—my natural and
personal duty, my conventional and official business. Which of
the two shall give way to the other,—personal duty or official
business? Let it be remembered that I am a MAN first of all, and
all else that I am is but a modification of my manhood, which
makes me a clergyman, a fisherman, or a statesman; but the
clergy, the fish, and the state are not to strip me of my manhood. They are valuable in so far as they serve my manhood,
not as it serves them. My official business as clergyman, fisherman, or statesman is always beneath my personal duty as man.
In case of any conflict between the two, the natural duty ought
to prevail and carry the day before the official business; for the
natural duty represents the permanent law of God, the absolute
right, Justice the balance-point of all interests, while the official
business represents only the transient conventions of men,
some partial interest; and besides the man who owes the personal duty is immortal, while the officer who performs the official business is but for a time. At death the man is to be tried
by the Justice of God, for the deeds done, and character at-
tained, for his natural duty, but he does not enter the next life
as a clergyman with his surplice and prayer-book, or a fisherman with his angles and net, nor yet as a statesman with his
franking privilege and title of Honorable and Member of Congress. The officer dies, of a vote or a fever. The man lives forever. From the relation between a man and his occupation it is
plain, in general, that all conventional and official business is to
be overruled by natural, personal duty. This is the great circle,
drawn by God and discovered by Conscience, which girdles my
sphere, including all the smaller circles, and itself included by
none of them. The law of God has eminent domain everywhere,
over the private passions of Oliver and Charles, the special interests of Carthage and of Rome, over all customs, all official
business, all precedents, all human statutes, all treaties between
Judas and Pilate, or England and France, over all the conventional affairs of one man or mankind. My own Conscience is to

declare that law for me, yours for you, and is before all private
passions, or public interests, the decision of majorities, and a
world full of precedents. You may resign your office and escape
its obligations, forsake your country and owe it no allegiance,
but you cannot move out of the dominions of God, nor escape
where Conscience has not eminent domain. . . .

Of old time the Roman law commanded the Christians to sacrifice to Jupiter; they deemed it the highest sin to do so, but it
was their official business as Roman citizens. Some of them
were true to their natural duty as men, and took the same cross
Jesus had borne before them; Peter and John had said at their
outset to the authorities—"whether it be right in the sight of
God to hearken unto you more than unto God, judge ye." The
Emperor once made it the official business of every citizen to
deliver up the Christians. But God made it no man's duty. Nay,
it was each man's duty to help them. . . . As I have stood among
their graves, have handled the instruments with which they
tasted of bitter death, and crumbled their bones in my hands, I
have thought there was a little difference between their religion,
and the pale decency that haunts the churches of our time and
is afraid lest it lose its dividends, or its respectability, or hurt its
usefulness, which is in no danger. . . .

The natural duty to keep the law of God overrides the obligation to observe any human statute, and continually commands
us to love a man and not hate him, to do him Justice, and not
injustice, to allow him his natural rights not alienated by himself, yes to defend him in them, not only by all means legal but
by all means moral. . . .

If a troop of wolves or tigers were about to seize a man, and
devour him, and you and I could help him, it would be our duty
to do so, even to peril our own limbs and life for that purpose.
If a man undertakes to murder or steal a man, it is the duty of
the bystanders to help their brother, who is in peril, against
wrong from the two-legged man, as much as against the four-
legged beast. But suppose the invader who seizes the man is an
officer of the United States, has a commission in his pocket, a
warrant for his deed in his hand, and seizes as a slave a man
who has done nothing to alienate his natural rights, does that

give him any more natural right to enslave a man than he had before? Can any piece of parchment make Right wrong, and Wrong right? . . . It is plain to me that it is the natural duty of citizens to rescue every fugitive slave from the hands of the marshal who essays to return him to bondage, to do it peaceably if they can, forcibly if they must, but by all means to do it. Will you stand by and see your countrymen, your fellow citizens of Boston, sent off to slavery by some commissioner? . . .

I am not a man who loves violence. I respect the sacredness of human life. But this I say, solemnly, that I will do all in my power to rescue any fugitive slave from the hands of any officer who attempts to return him to bondage. I will resist him as gently as I know how, but with such strength as I can command; I will ring the bells, and alarm the town; I will serve as head, as foot, or as hand to any body of serious and earnest men, who will go with me, with no weapons but their hands, in this work. I will do it as readily as I would lift a man out of the water, or pluck him from the teeth of a wolf, or snatch him from the hands of a murderer. What is a fine of a thousand dollars, and jailing for six months, to the liberty of a man? My money perish with me, if it stand between me and the eternal law of God. I trust there are manly men enough in this house to secure the freedom of every fugitive slave in Boston, without breaking a limb or rending a garment.

One thing more I think is very plain, that the fugitive has the same natural right to defend himself against the slave catcher, or his constitutional tool, that he has against a murderer or a wolf. The man who attacks me to reduce me to slavery, in that moment of attack alienates his right to life, and if I were the fugitive, and could escape in no other way, I would kill him with as little compunction as I would drive a mosquito from my face. It is high time this was said. What grasshoppers we are before the law of men; what Goliaths against the law of God! . . . When a man's liberty is concerned—we must keep the law, must we? betray the wanderer, and expose the outcast? . . . Justice, the law paramount of the universe, extends over armies and nations.

14. Samuel Willard:
The Grand Issue (1851)

Samuel Willard was minister of the First Congregational Church in Deerfield, Massachusetts, from 1807 to 1829. Since he was a liberal theologian whose views were more nearly attuned to those of his colleagues in Boston than to those of ministers closer to his own parish, his was for a long time virtually an isolated voice in western Massachusetts. But of the numerous Protestant clergymen who debated the issue of civil disobedience in the wake of the enactment of the Fugitive Slave Law, he was one of the most peaceable. Deeply committed to the maintenance of the rule of law, he tried to develop a rationale and a form for civil disobedience that would minimize the risk of its lending itself to anarchy. Having satisfied himself on this point, however, he was unafraid of urging his position on others, and he was instrumental in getting the American Unitarian Association, a group always skittish in the extreme about mixing religion and politics, to go on record as opposed to the Fugitive Slave Law.[1]

The Unitarian cast of Willard's mind is reflected in his introductory promise to examine the question "first in the perspective of reason, and then in the light of the Holy Scripture." This is not to trivialize his scriptural argument, which is earnest and deliberate. (Willard recalls among other things the example of Jesus' disobedience to the priests and elders.) Another long section of his tract attempts to demonstrate the Fugitive Slave Law's unconstitutionality.

When Willard published this pamphlet, he was (as many of his readers knew) seventy-five years old and had been blind for more than twenty years.[2]

Reprinted from Samuel Willard, *The Grand Issue: An Ethico-Political Tract* (Boston: John P. Jewett, 1851), pp. 11, 36–37.

. . . What real Christian can pay any other regard to the recent law for the restoration of fugitive slaves, than that of quietly submitting to its penalties? If we have the slightest faith in Christ as the present Governor and final Judge of the world, we cannot without infinite presumption shut our doors against him, when he comes pleading for shelter, as he may do in the person of a fugitive slave. For myself, I will not boast of an invincible resolution. The example of Peter should teach us not to presume on our own strength. But, if sustained by Almighty grace, I will perform toward the fugitive slave all the acts of kindness that I should do if there were no prohibition against it; and I will quietly endure the consequences, though enormous fines or exactions should deprive me of my last cent, and though I be thrown into prison for six months, or six years, or all the residue of life; and I will not put the Government of my country to the expense of a single lock and key for my safe keeping. Though the doors be open day and night, I will not come out, till the magistrates come themselves and bring me out. I do not say that all this submissiveness to human authority is clearly required by any Divine principle. I am not now deciding a question of casuistry for others, nor even for myself; but so important in my view is the maintenance of civil order, that I am willing, so far as I alone am involved in the consequences, to make all the concessions expressed above. . . .

What is to be the end of these things, or how the existing evils are to be removed, is known to that Being alone, with whom there is no distinction between the present and the future. One thing, however, is certain. Government is too strong to be forcibly resisted, even if Christian principle would allow such resistance; and if the Fugitive Slave law should be continued, and be strenuously enforced, another thing is equally certain; viz.: That those who believe in the unchangeable supremacy of the Divine law, and the consequent injustice of every aid that is given to slavery, must be prepared to endure persecution. . . . It was persecution that spread and established Christianity in the primitive ages, and this mighty agent may be required to give life to those religious professions, which often seem to be nothing more than professions and empty forms; to call forth the regenerating power of the Gospel, and abolish everything in our Constitution and Laws which is opposed to its philanthropic spirit. Let the law in question be rigorously enforced, and the sufferers have everything to hope for, and persecutors everything to fear. Suffering innocence, bleeding under oppression and cruelty, acts on the heart of man, so long as he has any heart, with a power surpassing everything else upon earth; and where the heart is gained, the understanding is apt to follow, and all the noblest energies of the soul. Let, then, the advocates of that law exert all their power and influence to crush opposition to it. They will only hasten the downfall of their political system. They will sooner or later produce a moral earthquake, which will cause our whole country, from ocean to ocean, to rock like a cradle, or rather, like a ship on a tempestuous sea. Such moral earthquakes, and their kindred storms, are, I think, means appointed by the Almighty and Allwise for demolishing the strongholds of inveterate abuses. . . .

15. Nathaniel Hall: *The Limits of Civil Obedience* (1851)

Nathaniel Hall, for forty years the pastor of the First Church of Dorchester (Unitarian), is reminiscent of John Woolman in his ability to integrate the traits of "the lion and the lamb" into a single, mature, effective personality.[1] This combination of tenacious courage with infallible gentleness and generosity is a theme insisted on by all of his eulogists and biographers. Andrew Peabody, referring to Hall's early and enduring opposition to slavery, says that "he held his post and fulfilled his mission when the general conscience around him was torpid; when the iniquity that he denounced coursed through the life-blood of the whole community; when to show people their transgression, was stigmatized as treason"; in the next paragraph he attributes to this warrior "a meekness and gentleness which betokened his close kindred with the Saviour."[2]

These qualities inform the tone and style of Hall's sermon on the Fugitive Slave Law, in which a determined advocacy of civil disobedience is securely fastened to conservative anchors. He affirms the need of deliberation, meditation, and self-criticism; stresses the general agreement among the dictates of the consciences of "the great majority of men . . . if not allowed to be blinded and turned aside"; and even invokes a divine sanction for the government that is to be disobeyed: "Civil government exists by Divine appointment, and is therefore to be respected and obeyed." But he frees himself from the most conservative implications of this principle by maintaining that God's sanction of human government and laws is limited and conditional. Our first obligation, he insists, is always to "those moral relations which we sustain to Him by whose appointment [government] exists." Though his

discussion is unusual in its subtlety, Hall's rhetoric and logic are similar
to those of other ante bellum Unitarian advocates of civil disobedience.

Reprinted from Nathaniel Hall, *The Limits of Civil Obedience* (Boston:
Crosby & Nichols, 1851), pp. 6–12, 18–19, 23–26.

. . . Government is of Divine appointment, inasmuch as society cannot fulfill its ends, cannot exist to any good purpose,
without it. The very idea of civil society supposes the surrender,
in certain directions, and to a certain extent, of individual rights,
and the suppression of individual impulses and desires, in submission to a general, constituted authority, and for the sake of
benefits not otherwise to be secured. And if civil government be
of Divine appointment, it follows, that obedience to its authority
and laws is a sacred obligation. . . . [But] no one would say, that
obedience to civil government was a sacred obligation in *all cases*
—*whatever* it might command. Were it to command, for instance, that parents should cruelly maim or torture their children, or teach them any gross immorality, or that people generally should practise theft, or utter profanity, or the like,—who
would say that it was a sacred obligation to obey it, as regards
these things? Where, then, if limit there be, does that limit lie?
By what principle is it defined? We want a *principle*,—something
which shall keep us from being driven hither and thither,
now towards this conclusion and now towards that, as others
may urge us by their reasoning, or their rhetoric, or their sophistries. . . .

Does not the answer lie in this consideration? that the relations we sustain to civil government, do not, and cannot, over-
lay and interrupt those moral relations which we sustain to Him
by whose appointment it exists. Whatever society, through its
government, may do, it may not disturb those relations—it may
not come between the soul and God—it may not come between
the soul's sense of duty to Him and the performance of that
duty. Whatever authority God may have delegated to human
governments, it cannot be an authority—every sentiment and
principle within us forbid the thought—to abrogate or suspend
any one of those moral requirements which spring out of the
essential attributes of His nature, and are eternal as himself. *It*

cannot be that the laws upon the statute books of States, are, in any conceivable or possible circumstances, to limit or lessen our obligation to the law, traced by the very hand of the Almighty, ineffaceably, upon the tables of the heart. . . . In setting at naught, by its enactments, an eternal moral law, [civil government] is criminally false to the purposes of its existence. In commanding others to set it at naught in their practice, it has, so far, forfeited its claim to their obedience. . . .

Civil government has its constituted limits; its God-appointed sphere. In its requisitions within those limits and that sphere, to its laws which violate no sense of obligation to a moral law, we are to be obedient. We may deem its enactments unwise and inexpedient, but may not, for that reason, disobey them. We have confided the judgment of these points to the government, and must abide by that judgment. We may feel its enactments to be oppressive and injurious,—they may abridge our comforts, they may waste our fortunes, they may restrain us in the exercise of natural rights and civil privileges; but we may not, for this reason, disobey and resist them. The authority of government is a rightful one, even in its abuse, while it keeps itself within its constituted limits. We are to bear with the personal evils which the State inflicts, or take ourselves from its jurisdiction, until, through legitimate and constitutional methods, we may obtain relief—excepting always those instances of general and extreme oppression, constitutionally irremediable, which justify revolution. We have no right, in view of our personal grievances, so far as they relate to physical and secular interests, to put in jeopardy, by a resistance to government, and by our example of disobedience to its authority, the good which, on the whole, it may be the medium of conferring. So much we may concede. But when government, by its enactments, demands of us the doing of an *unrighteous* and *inhuman* act, known and felt as such by the enlightened judgment of mankind; demands what seems to us a palpable violation of the law of God; when it thus invades the region of the moral sentiments; when it breaks into the sacred court of Conscience; the case is widely different. It has, in so doing, transcended its constituted limits. It has gone out from its appointed sphere. It has assumed a right which was never given it—which it was never designed it should possess. It has dared the attempt to extend its sway where God has reserved to Himself the sole prerogative of reigning; and *disobedience* is the sacred obligation. Government may sin against me, if it will, and answer for it to its great Ordainer; but it may not compel *me* to sin. It may inflict injury upon me, if so, in its perversity or its ignorance, it choose to do;—I will endure it;—but it may not compel me to inflict injury upon another, whom God is telling me to befriend. It may not compel me to violate the immortal sentiments of justice and mercy which God's own spirit breathed within me when he gave me being. It has no right to do this; and I have no right, as a moral and accountable being, to obey it, if it should. I have no *right*. It is not left to my choice. The line of duty is proclaimed to me by the voice of the Infinite within my soul. The question of consequences, *then*, is an impertinence. As I have a soul to save and an account to give, I must, at all hazards, obey God.

. . . [This principle] is not strained after for an emergency, ingeniously evoked from the mists of sophistry, or elaborately wrought of metaphysical subtleties. It is simple as Nature. It is clearly to be discerned as the lights of heaven. It is one of the fundamental truths of religion, and the strangeness is, that, at this late day, there should be a necessity for restating it. . . . [Some argue that] men would plead conscientious convictions, as an excuse for disobedience to an offensive law, when there was no conscience about it, but only an imagined self-interest, or a stubborn self-will. Allow that, to some extent, it might be so,—is not every principle, and every prescribed rule of action, however sound and true, liable to be abused? Is not evil incident to the practical workings of civil government, always and every where? And what do we, when we say that the individual is not to judge for himself, what is morally right and obligatory in the requirements of the State? Is it not to dishonor and disown the very principle which lies at the foundation of our Protestantism? Does the right of private judgment have reference only to matters of belief, and not to those of conduct? Yea, and it is a right which we may not surrender. It involves a priceless privilege not only, but a solemn duty. God has bound it upon us in the trust of a moral nature. If, as moral beings, we are individually accountable; if, at the great day, each must answer for himself as to his fidelity to the law of Right; by each for himself must be the decision as to what that law requires of him. In giving to each the capacity of moral judgment, God requires of each its exercise, in relation to civil as to all other matters; and each,—let this be felt,—each is responsible for the *manner* of its exercise. Not rashly or lightly or irreverently, not in prejudice or passion or excitement, not in a self-sufficient inconsiderateness of others' views and arguments; but deliberately, soberly, humbly, seeking all helps around us and above, in the love of truth and in the fear of God, are we severally to form our judgment as to what is right and obligatory. And thus judging and thus acting, I cannot conceive that any great harm would come to society in the application of our principle.

"But," again it is said, "your principle strikes at the authority of all government; and government, as you allow, there must be. You counsel resistance, and resistance is rebellion." The reply is, that the resistance counselled is not the forcible resistance which is rebellion, but that which consists in disobedience, with a passive submission to whatever penalty may be thereto attached. The authority is acknowledged which enacts the law, and enforces the penalty. We would resist that authority, not in its legitimate exercise; not in its unlawful exercise, unless it go to the length of commanding us to do iniquity; and not *then* as an authority to punish for our disobedience to its command. The moral *right* to do it we deny, in relation to God; but not the *authority*, in relation to man. I will submit to government so far as to *endure* wrong, but never to *do* it. . . .

And let us not imagine that the evils consequent upon our action, as a people, in relation to this law, are all on the side of disobedience to it. Let views like those which have come forth from the high places of the land, and been echoed back from many a pulpit of the Church, be practically adopted, become a part of the public morality; let the pleading sentiments of humanity be put down, and the Law of God dethroned from its supremacy, in obedience to this most inhuman and unrighteous law— and is there no evil worthy to be deprecated in that demoralization, public and private, which cannot but ensue? Looking at it merely in its civil bearings, is there nothing to fear from it? What constitutes the stability of a State, and gives security beneath its laws, but a reverence for moral principles,—for the great Fountain of Law,—in the hearts of the people? Who are the real disorganizers? they who teach the absolute morality, or they who advocate the morality of expediency? they who announce and heed a Higher Law, or they who scout the idea of it? What is it that really endangers the permanency of our Republic? What but that monster Wrong,—fostered beneath its shade, coeval with its birth and strengthening with its strength, which is denying to three millions of human beings the sacred rights of humanity? What but that terrible Iniquity, whose retribution is already upon us, in a blunted national conscience, a lessening love of freedom, a depressed humanity, a fettered gospel; and which, if much longer upheld and fostered, must bring down upon us, as God is just, his more fearful judgments? And yet, we are told that our safety lies in conciliating and strengthening it, by committing ourselves more fully to its support, and sharing more directly in its deeds. Do we realize what a blighting censure is passed upon our nation and ourselves, when it is thus assumed that our civil safety is dependent upon our holding, with tightened grasp, the chains of the enslaved, and in aiding with our own hands to rebind them upon those who, in the might of an intrepid manhood, have sundered them and fled? . . . What will all our prosperity be worth, if, underneath its dazzling glare, the work of moral deterioration and decline, —by that very prosperity fed and fostered,—shall be going forward? . . .

. . . The path of duty and of safety—they are ever identical— is in an uncompromising fidelity to whatever GOD shall show us, through the sentiments of our hearts and the teachings of Christianity, to be right. Let no human authority ever restrain us from this path. Let no leanings of sordid desire tempt us from it. Let no view of consequences allure or affright us from it. And let nothing—no fear of men, no alienation of friends, no edict from whatever source—prevent us from advocating the cause of the oppressed,—from obeying the dictates of humanity in their behalf, whenever Providence shall grant us the opportunity.

16. Daniel Foster: *Our Nation's Sins and the Christian's Duty* (1851)

Daniel Foster, a Massachusetts schoolteacher and abolitionist minister who was highly regarded by Thoreau,[1] held successive pastorates in Salem, Danvers, Chester, and Concord between 1847 and 1851. The length of his service was restricted again and again by the inability of small congregations to support him economically and by the hostile resistance of some parishioners to his aggressive antislavery preaching.[2]

Renouncing sectarianism as unchristian, Foster asked to be known as a "Union Minister"—"not as a Methodist, nor as a Congregational Minister, but as a Christian Reformer."[3] But his sympathies, however broadly interdenominational, were scarcely catholic, and his sermons are full of severe personal attacks that seem of dubious consistency with his credo that duty lies "not in the belief or rejection of any abstract doctrine, [but] in the daily application of the example and precepts of Christ to every situation and act of life."[4] Adopting a style that is the rhetorical antithesis of Nathaniel Hall's, Foster calls Daniel Webster "the arch-traitor who secured this disastrous result"; ministers who preach obedience to the Fugitive Slave Law are Judases; Orville Dewey, a highly distinguished Unitarian minister whose sermon espousing obedience to the Fugitive Slave Law had become notorious among abolitionists, has committed "treason against Christ"; President Fillmore is a "renegade," a "traitor before God and a hypocrite before the world."[5]

These men were in Foster's eyes representative of the worst and dominant side of a society that had been morally all but destroyed by its connection with slavery. One of his main themes is that of national corruption and decline, made visible in the gloomy contrast between the patriarchal judges, ministers, and politicians of the Republic's first days and their contemptible successors of Foster's own time. Another target of his wrath is the racism that he believes pervades the white community and that is a great, unconfessed resource for those who advocate obedience to the Fugitive Slave Law.

Reprinted from Daniel Foster, *Our Nation's Sins and the Christian's Duty* (Boston: White & Potter, 1851), pp. 13–15, 26–27.

The ministers who preach that we ought to obey, or ought not to disobey this infernal fugitive slave bill, because it has passed both houses of Congress, and received the sanction of the Presi-

dent, and thus become the constitutionally recognized law of
the land, in so doing, cast off their allegiance to God, and for
some paltry present consideration, sell to his cruel foe, the Redeemer of this lost world. This is strong language, I am aware,
but the truth is stronger. Daniel disobeyed the Persian law, was
cast into the midst of the ravenous lions for his disobedience,
and God delivered him. That law only required of him to refrain
for thirty days from public prayer. This law requires you to
seize, and render back to the hell of American slavery, the
brother who seeks shelter and safety in your home. *If the prophet
Daniel now lived would he obey this infamous statute?* The three
Hebrew children refused to obey a law less atrocious than this,
and God sustained them in doing it. The Apostles were lawbreakers, and when called to account for their treason, this was
their excuse—"Whether it be right in the sight of God to heark-
en unto you more than unto God, judge ye." Peter and the
other Apostles answered and said—"We ought to obey God
rather than man." "And when they had called the Apostles and
beaten them, they *commanded that they should not speak in the
name of Jesus,* and let them go. And they departed from the
presence of the council, rejoicing that they were counted worthy
to suffer shame for his name. And daily in the temple and in
every house, *they ceased not to teach and preach Jesus Christ.*"
Plainer cases could not be found of open disobedience to wicked
law. And the history of the early Christians abounds with such
cases. Now remember these ministers know these things. They
have the Bible in their hands, and *they* cannot plead *ignorance* to
justify their course. . . . *I distinctly impeach these men of treason
against Christ.* And mark you this prediction, the revelation of
Eternity will sustain this fearful charge. *Those ministers who take the
Bible in their hands and preach the duty of obedience to this bill of
abominations are traitors before God and hypocrites before men.*

The capitalists who call so loudly upon us to obey this law,
and the politicians, who join with them in the cry, are themselves the violators of our Temperance and Usury laws. For the
sake of Southern trade they go in for this wicked law, and for
the sake of profit or appetite, they go in for a systematic violation of the just and necessary laws on Temperance and Usury.
They seem to act on this principle, viz: if a law is just and its

execution is necessary to secure the public good, then we will disobey it and set its enactment at defiance. But if our Government enacts injustice into law and requires us to disobey God, then we will obey *this* law ourselves, and denounce and brand and persecute to the last extremity, the man who takes his stand on the old apostolic platform, and disobeys a wicked law that he may obey God.

. . . The military power of the United States is pledged to insure the successful execution of this tyrannical law in Boston. Does any one imagine this comes of a reverence for the Constitution and an honest purpose to execute the requirements thereof? It is hardly possible to be so deceived. Just look at the well known facts. The President is bound by his oath to observe in all his official conduct the provisions of the Constitution, and to enforce the same through the land. Does any one suppose that Mr. Fillmore was ignorant of the fact that this fugitive slave bill is utterly repugnant to the spirit and the letter of the Constitution? He owns that he feared it struck down one of the old bulwarks of personal freedom, viz: the writ of habeas corpus and so he addressed Mr. Attorney General Crittenden to show that this was not done. And in answer Mr. C. states that this great right is not touched by the provisions of the bill. Well now I undertake to say that every person in the country, of common intelligence, on reading that bill, could but see the base falsehood of Mr. Crittenden's *professional* opinion. *The President knew that this right was destroyed by that bill and we all knew it.* And so now we see Judge Shaw refusing this writ of personal replevin in the case of a brother in Boston, seized as an alleged fugitive, but claiming to be free by the law of Georgia as well as by the law of Massachusetts. *Oh, it is infinite baseness for the renegade Fillmore to profess to reverence the Constitution while signing this bill, which he knew to be as unconstitutional as it is infernal.* . . .

I have never been disposed to stop to ask the question whether this pretended law be constitutional or unconstitutional, as a question to be settled before I should decide whether duty bade me to obey or disobey the infamous statute. It is clearly proved, however, by argument and logic which cannot be answered, and which no man will ever attempt to answer, that this law is entirely unconstitutional. It subverts the Constitution, and severs the bond of Union, just as much as it contravenes the eternal constitution of Right which God has enacted. *But I am prepared to say, that I will disobey that law, by aiding the fugitive slave, and by active obstructions in the way of the abominable kidnapper, although the Constitution of my country should sanction the law in all the length and breadth of its immeasurable infamy.* I am devoutly thankful that this law is as unconstitutional as it is bad, but we must remember this rule, which is binding upon men always and everywhere, a rule higher in authority and more ancient than any human law or Constitution, *obey God rather than man,—disobedience to a wicked law is loyalty to God,—deliberate obedience to a wicked statute like this bill of utter abominations is blank Atheism, and those who counsel it are sheer Atheists.* And in this matter the old doctrine of the Protestants is true, each one must examine and decide according to the convictions of *his own* conscience. As each one will go to the judgment alone, and answer for *himself* and for *no other*, according to that which *he* hath done, so must each one, by *his own* private individual conscience, decide for *his own soul*, and thus forever bear the result of that decision, what duty demands of *him*. . . .

17. Charles Beecher: *The Duty of Disobedience to Wicked Laws* (1851)

A son of Lyman Beecher and a brother of Henry Ward Beecher and Harriet Beecher Stowe, Charles Beecher struggled through a crisis of faith and then became a Presbyterian minister in Indiana in 1844. Because his views were sometimes outside the usual boundaries of orthodoxy, his career was marked by uncomfortable relations with denominational establishments. In 1851 he moved to Newark, New Jersey, to become minister of the First Congregational Church there; in the same year he was expelled from his ministerial association for having preached the sermon that is excerpted here. In 1863 in Georgetown, Massachusetts, he was tried for heresy for preaching his doctrine on the preexistence of souls; he was convicted but was ultimately vindicated.[1]

In *The Duty of Disobedience to Wicked Laws* Beecher develops a radical conception of law which, like Parker's, owes much to eighteenth-century natural rights philosophy. Since human statutes are subordinate to eternal principles of natural right, Beecher argues, the binding authority of any human law is contingent upon its being in harmony with those principles, which correspond to the revealed will of God. But while Parker would have the higher law interpreted by the intuitions of the individual conscience, Beecher seeks to avoid such radical individualism through his emphasis on the clarity and authority of the Bible. He simply assumes that disobedience that is seriously based on biblical interpretation will be almost universally shared (and thus, apparently, legitimized): "The deep instinct of every heart pronounces sentence here. . . . [The Bible] is a common-sense book, to be interpreted by common-sense minds in a common-sense way."

Reprinted from Charles Beecher, *The Duty of Disobedience to Wicked Laws* (Newark, N.J.: J. McIlvaine, 1851), pp. 5, 6, 13, 16, 21–22.

There is to be a day of judgment—a day when God will reveal his righteous judgment concerning all deeds done in the body. In that review no part of human conduct will be exempt from scrutiny. The public as well as the private acts of every man will undergo impartial examination. Nor will the acts of individuals, only, be considered. The acts of organic bodies of men constitute a very large part of all history, and must be judged. The acts of nations, governments, and all authorities will be diligently examined; and especially the *laws* which were by different nations passed, accepted, obeyed.

. . . My object tonight will be to take such a view of the late Fugitive Slave Law, passed by the Congress of these United States, and approved by the President. I wish to inquire how that law will look when examined before the bar of God. I wish to ask how the men that made it, the men that execute, the citizens that obey, and the nation that tolerates that law, will look when they stand before the judgment seat. And,

1. I observe that laws are to be judged of by certain principles of natural right, and by those same principles as more clearly evolved in the gospel—that gospel, I mean, which was preached before Moses, as well as after. (Gal. iii. 8.)

These principles of right are eternal, not made. They are the foundation of law, not its product. The law of God is his declaration of what is from eternity, and must be *right*—not his arbitrary decision of what shall be right. Neither is it in the power of God himself (with reverence be it spoken) to repeal those principles, nor by a law to make anything right which was wrong intrinsically before, or wrong which was right before. To say that things are right only because God's will has so decided, is to nullify right; it is to say that might makes right, and that if the devil were omnipotent, malice would be right and benevolence wrong. God's will is always right, and the measure of right in fact; but it is because he perceives omnisciently what is eternally and immutably right, and conforms to his own perceptions, and legislates accordingly.

But if divine legislation does not *make* things right or wrong, still less can human legislation. God's legislation is declaratory of what is absolutely right. Man's legislation is declaratory of what he conceives to be right. Hence human law is nothing but a declaration of the public idea of right; or, at least, it can rise no higher than the public idea. Of course, then, as the public idea of right is obscure and progressive, law must be progressive. Ancient laws are now seen to have been barbarous, not because they had not some elements of right, but because they had some elements of wrong admixed. Hence modern laws continually amend, supersede, or annul laws that are older. And just in proportion as the national intellect and conscience are developed, just in proportion as *man* returns toward the image and likeness of God, will this process of improved legislation be apparent.

Hence the mind of man is destined to be always testing its own legislation by those principles on which God tests it and will render verdict in the judgment. For, in the language of Sir William Blackstone, "The law of nature, being coeval with mankind and dictated by God himself, is of course superior in obligation to any other. It is binding all over the globe, in all countries, at all times; NO HUMAN LAWS ARE OF ANY VALIDITY IF CONTRARY TO THIS; and such of them as are valid derive all their force, and all their validity, mediately or immediately, from this original." . . .

This law then is wrong in the sight of God and man—it is an

unexampled climax of sin. It is the monster iniquity of the present age, and it will stand for ever on the page of history, as the vilest monument of infamy of the nineteenth century. Russia knows nothing like it. . . .

[But] there is yet one thing more guilty than the act of passing this law. There is yet one step wanting to render complete and awful in the sight of God our mighty guilt; and that step is obedience to the law. That is a sin even more exquisitely sinful than the making of the law itself, for two reasons: first, because it has the whole atrociousness of the law itself; and secondly, because it has the whole atrociousness of a stab at the freedom of conscience, and of private judgment. . . .

Why does any man imagine he ought to obey the law? What is the Jesuitical plea which is industriously inculcated by the high priests of Moloch and Mammon? It is because he wants to keep on the safe side, by obeying law. Because he is told that the proper way is to obey, until the law can be altered. Because he is told it is wrong to do right, unless the Government gives him leave—right to do wrong, whenever an aristocracy of politicians, and a hierarchy of office-holders, command. Because he pins his faith on the sleeve of Government, and makes Congress his pope, cardinals, and holy college of Jesuits, to act the part of infallible interpreter for him, of the Bible and of duty. This is the reason, and the only reason why he obeys. The law says so, and the law must be obeyed, right or wrong, till it is altered. Argument always used by Jesuits and despots, on weak consciences, and weaker brains. Argument first begotten of Satan, Father of Lies. . . .

The men that refuse obedience to such laws are the sure, the only defenders of law. If they will shed their own blood rather than sin by keeping a wicked law, they will by the same principle shed their blood rather than break a law which is righteous. In short, such men are the only true law-abiding men. For they never break a law, except when they see that to keep it would be to violate *all* law in its very foundation, and overturn the very government of God; while those men who clamor for blind obedience to all law—right or wrong—are striking at the throne of God. . . .

In conclusion, therefore, my application of the subject is—
DISOBEY THIS LAW. If you have ever dreamed of obeying it, re-
pent before God, and ask his forgiveness. I counsel no violence.
I suggest no warlike measures of resistance. I incite no man to
deeds of blood. I speak as the minister of the Prince of Peace. As
much as lieth in you, live peaceably with all men. To the
fugitive, touching the question of self-defense, I offer no advice,
as none can be necessary. The right of self-defense is unquestionable here, if ever. Of the expediency of its exercise, every
man must judge for himself. I leave the question of self-defense
undiscussed, to the settlement of every man's own judgment,
according to circumstances.

But if a fugitive claim your help on his journey, break the law
and give it him. The law is broken as thoroughly by INDIRECTLY
aiding his escape as DIRECTLY, for both are penal. Therefore
break the law, and help him on his way, *directly* if you can, *indirectly* if you must. Feed him, clothe him, harbor him, by day
and by night, and conceal him from his pursuers and from the
officers of the law. If you are summoned to aid in his capture,
refuse to obey. If you are commanded by the officer to lay hands
on the fugitive, decline to comply; rather, if possible, detain the
officer, if you conveniently can, without injury to his person,
until the victim is clean gone. If for these things you are accused
and brought to trial, appear and defend yourself. If asked how
you dared disobey the laws of this realm, answer with Bunyan's
Pilgrim in Vanity Fair: tell the court that you obey Christ, not
Belial. If they fine you, and imprison you, take joyfully the
spoiling of your goods, wear gladly your chain, and in the last
day you shall be rewarded for your fidelity to God. Do not think
any true disgrace can attach to such penalties. It is the devil, and
the devil's people only, who enact, enforce, or respect such penalties. If you are disgraced, it is the disgrace that Washington
bore when he was called a rebel, and it is inflicted on you for the
support of a cause and of principles as holy as his.

You will suffer with Wickliffe and Huss, with the Albigenses
and Huguenots, with the early Christian martyrs, with the
Apostles, and Jesus their head; and with that mighty army of
still more ancient worthies, who were stoned, sawn asunder,

and of whom the world was not worthy. With them to suffer is honor; with them to be defamed, reviled, and spit upon, is glory. With them to rise and reign eternally, will be ample reward.

18. Gerrit Smith: *The True Office of Civil Government* (1851)

Gerrit Smith was an immensely wealthy New York landowner, reformer, and philanthropist who (like many of his contemporaries) revised his political principles and strategies under the pressure of the frustrations, the anxieties, and the changing antislavery perspectives of the decades before the Civil War. In the early 1830s he supported the American Colonization Society and opposed the American Anti-Slavery Society's declaration of support for conscientious lawbreaking; two decades later he had been arrested for his role in the escape of a fugitive slave, he had publicly advocated civil disobedience, and (like Emerson, Parker, and Wendell Phillips) he was raising money for rifles that would arm the free-soil settlers in Kansas.[1] One has to view even his ultimate abolitionism as either wildly inconsistent or extraordinarily comprehensive, since at the end of the 1850s he simultaneously supported a program for compensated emancipation and the armed enterprises of John Brown.[2]

For much of the ante bellum period Smith was engaged in the effort to develop an effective antislavery political organization. In 1847 he was nominated for the presidency by the Liberty League; and the year after he gave the speech that is partially reprinted here, he was elected to Congress.

Reprinted from Gerrit Smith, *The True Office of Civil Government: A Speech in the City of Troy* (New York: S. W. Benedict, 1851), pp. 5–6, 11, 29–30.

The legitimate action of Civil Government is very simple. Its legitimate range is very narrow. Government owes nothing to its subjects but protection. And this is a protection, not from competitions, but from crimes. It owes them no protection from the foreign farmer, or foreign manufacturer, or foreign navigator. As it owes them no other protection from each other than from the crimes of each other, so it owes them no other protection from foreigners, than from the crimes of foreigners. . . .

No protection does Government owe to the morals of its subjects. Still less is it bound to study to promote their morals. To call on Government to increase the wealth of its subjects, or to help the progress of religion among them, or, in short, to promote any of their interests, is to call on it to do that, which it has no right to do, and which, it is probably safe to add, it has no power to do. Were Government to aim to secure to its subjects the free and inviolable control of their persons and property—of life and of the means of sustaining life—it would be aiming at all, that it should aim at. And its subjects, if they get this security, should feel that they need nothing more at the hands of Government to enable them to work their way well through the world. Government, in a word, is to say to its subjects: "You must do for yourselves. My only part is to defend your right to do for yourselves. You must do your own work. I will but protect you in that work."

That, the world over, Government is depended on to instruct, improve, guide, and enrich its subjects, proves, that, the world over, there is little confidence in the democratic doctrine of the people's ability to take care of themselves: and that the opposite doctrine, that the many must be taken care of by the aristocratic and select few, is well nigh universally entertained. The people's lack of confidence in themselves is not only proved, but it is accounted for, by this dependence on Government. This dependence of the people on the policy, providence, and guidance of Government, as well in peace as in war, has necessarily begotten in them a distrust of their ability to take care of themselves.

One of the consequences of this self-distrust on the part of the people is, that Government is employed, for the most part, in doing what it belongs to the people to do. And one of the consequences of this illegitimate work of Government is, that Government has become too great, and the people too little—that Government has risen into undue prominence, and the people sunk into undue obscurity. . . .

There are several points, on which an explanation may, perhaps, be desired of me.

1st. *Do I mean, that Government shall invariably and absolutely forbid slavery?* Yes—as invariably and absolutely, as it forbids murder. God no more creates men to be enslaved than to be murdered. And that does not deserve the name of Civil Government, which permits its subjects to be enslaved. And he is a pirate, instead of a Civil Ruler, who lays his hand on men to enslave them. And that is not law, but anti-law, which is enacted to reduce men to slavery, or to hold them in slavery. Hence, they are pirates, mobocrats, and anarchists, who are for the "Fugitive Slave law"; and they are law-abiding, who trample it under foot.

Law is for the protection of rights. And they, who believe, that enactments for the destruction of rights are law, know not what are the elements of true law. The American people in their folly, and madness, and devilishness, are busied, under their Fugitive Slave Law, in trying the questions, whether this man and that man are slaves—whether this being and that being, "made in the image of God," are chattels and commodities. As well, (and not one whit more blasphemously,) might they try the question, whether God is entitled to His throne, or whether God shall be permitted to live. The American people proudly imagine, that theirs is the highest style of Christian civilization. And, yet, where shall we look for ranker atheism, or more revolting features of barbarism? . . .

Perhaps, it will be asked, whether Government, under my definition of its province, would be at liberty to carry the mail; build asylums; improve harbors; and build light-houses? I answer, that nothing of all this is, necessarily, the work of Government. The mail can be carried, as well without, as with, the help of Government. Some of the best and most extensive asylums in our country are those with which Government has nothing to do. And the interest and humanity of individuals and communities might be relied on to improve harbors and build light-houses, as well as to keep bridges and roads in repair. . . .

. . . The work of Civil Government is not so much to take care of its subjects, as to leave them in circumstances, in which they may take care of themselves:—and not so much to govern its subjects, as to leave them free to govern themselves. Civil Government is to hold a shield over the heads of its subjects, beneath which they may, in safety from one another, and from all others, pursue their respective callings and discharge their respective duties. Whilst confining itself to this employment, it is a blessing above all praise—above all price. But, when it forsakes its own work to usurp that of the people; and, especially, when, as it has been recently known to do, it arrays itself against the great and holy God, who ordained Civil Government, and blasphemously enacts laws, which are opposed to His laws, then is it a curse and a monster, which deserves to be hated with all our hatred, and resisted at every hazard.

19. Thomas Treadwell Stone:
An Address before the Salem Female Anti-Slavery Society (1852)

Thomas Treadwell Stone (1801–1895) was born and educated in Maine and began his career there as a schoolmaster and then a Congregational minister. His views became increasingly liberal and then unreservedly transcendental. In 1846 he accepted a call to the First Church in Salem (Massachusetts), but his fervently antislavery preaching caused division in his congregation, and in 1852 he was dismissed by a majority of a single vote. Subsequently he was minister of other congregations in Massachusetts, Pennsylvania, and Connecticut.[1]

His address to the Salem Female Anti-Slavery Society fuses transcendental theology with antislavery politics. God is, Stone declares, immanent both in nature ("There is One, in all, through all, around all") and in man: "The Word of God . . . is indeed contained, as we have been taught, in the Scriptures; but it is not confined to them; it existed before they were written; it exists where they remain unknown. . . . By it, the soul in every man is quickened and enlightened." Since enlightenment can occur directly, independently of the Bible, Stone views that book much as Daniel Foster does the Constitution. He doesn't think that the Bible justifies either slavery or the Fugitive Slave Law; but if it should, so much the worse for the Bible: "The sole grounds on which the sacredness of the Bible or any book can possibly stand, fall from under it the instant it is shown to contradict the eternal laws, the secret oracle, the everlasting God within." These principles, Stone asserts in an idiom similar to that of Emerson and Parker, "need no proofs. They stand above the realm of question and argument. They transcend logic; they seek not discussion, but hearty acceptance." Viewed in this bright light, the Fugitive Slave Law "contains in itself the principle which annuls and makes it void. . . . Tell me what you will of Laws making men property; I reverence Law,— therefore do I pronounce these [proslavery] statutes lawless and anarchic, impieties to God and tyrannies to men." The issue as he sees it is whether men will recognize as supreme the law God has inscribed on every human soul, or whether they will bow instead to "human passions and interests, expressed by majorities and enacted in statutes."

❦ Reprinted from Thomas Treadwell Stone, *An Address before the Salem Female Anti-Slavery Society* (Salem, Mass.: William Ives, 1852), pp. 15–17.

Sin is no better, because it has been enacted by King or Congress. . . . I reverence Law; just for this reason do I hate lawless tyranny. . . . Tell me what you will of Laws making men property; I reverence Law,—therefore do I pronounce these statutes lawless and anarchic, impieties to God and tyrannies to men. I will try to prove my fidelity to true government by my treason to demoniac usurpation. I reverence Law; therefore I will obey it, though states, republics, congresses, the world itself, blaspheme its name by connecting herewith their own enormities. Not who made the statute determines whether it be true law; but what it is. Never can a majority impose obligation; the question is forever open, Have the majority done right? Very often they have done wrong. . . .

[Even] the Bible cannot make wrong, right; falsehood, truth; darkness, light; and the sole grounds on which the sacredness of the Bible or any Book can possibly stand, fall from under it the instant it is shown to contradict the eternal laws, the secret oracle, the everlasting God within. . . . The true man may put away from himself the smooth speeches, the plausible arguments, the cunning sophistries, by which American tyranny, just like all other despotisms of ancient or modern times, strives to reconcile itself with the religious faith, the moral sense, the conscience, the reason, and the humanities of the living soul. . . .

20. Joshua Giddings: *Speeches in Congress* (1850–1852)

Joshua Giddings was for two decades (1839–1859) the representative in Congress of the Western Reserve district of Ohio. For the first several years of his tenure, he tried to reconcile his antislavery positions, based on principle, with Whig loyalties rooted in political expediency. To some extent he was able, through shrewdness, to enlist his pragmatism in the service of his ideals. "By defending his own constituents from taxation to support slavery," Jane and William Pease observe, "he popularized his antislavery position at home and retained his seat."[1] Often, however, this tenuous equilibrium was threatened by pressure from both sides: while his antislavery fervor made him all but a pariah in the House, he was criticized by abolitionists for his moral compromises, as when, in the 1840 contest for Speaker, he supported a proslavery Whig over an antislavery Democrat.[2]

The frustrations of his experience in the House, which reached a peak when Congress supported the Mexican War, led him increasingly to place his antislavery commitments above his party interests. In any case, having established himself with his constituency, he was able to shift his affiliation from the Whigs to the Free Soilers to the Republicans without losing his seat.

Much of his energy as a congressman was directed at the achievement of limited (though remote) political objectives, such as the abolition of the slave trade in the District of Columbia; but some of his views rejected the constitutional framework altogether. Believing that slavery was inherently "a state of war" that placed its victims outside the realm of law, he accepted their right to use extralegal force;[3] and by 1859 he was publicly avowing his personal willingness to resist the Fugitive Slave Law "by violence if necessary."[4] Though his speeches on the floor of Congress did not generally go so far, the final passage given here moves beyond an advocacy of civil disobedience to a call, only slightly oblique, for slave insurrection.

Reprinted from Joshua R. Giddings, *Speeches in Congress* (Boston: John P. Jewett, 1853), pp. 424–427, 462, 481–485.

December 9, 1850

Mr. Chairman, our opposition to the fugitive law is based upon the soundest principles of ethics and of law, as well as the dictates of the common sense of mankind. While the southern men are thus seizing northern freemen, enslaving and brutalizing them, they turn round and call on us to leave our employments, give chase, arrest, and return their fugitive slaves. While violating our national compact in its most vital features, they ask us not merely to observe and keep our stipulations, but to go far beyond our covenants to uphold their slavery.

Now, Sir, these southern men have no claim whatever on us to observe the compact, while they disregard and trample upon it. Such are the dictates of law, and of justice, and the teachings of common sense. A compliance with such demand would constitute us the mere subsidiaries, the appendages of southern slavery. This feeling has thus far been suppressed by our intelligent people, hoping that Congress would relieve them from the position in which they have long been placed. If this fugitive law be kept in force, and Congress shall exert its power and influence to degrade our people, I, Sir, will not predict the consequences. They may be read in our past history. One thing may be regarded as admitted truth,—while northern freemen are held in southern chains, the people of the free States will not arrest, nor return fugitive slaves. I speak for no other portion of the country. But the South and the North, the East and the West, may understand, that, while the inhabitants of our State shall be held in slavery, (and there are many there,) few, *very few*, slaves will return to bondage from that section of country where I reside.

Sir, suppose a man born among us, educated in our schools, baptized in our churches, professing our religion, but who has been seized and held in southern slavery, should make his escape, and revisit the scenes of his birth and childhood; but, while quietly and peaceably among us, the baying of human bloodhounds should be heard upon his track, and the whole army of slave-catchers, including certain high dignitaries who procured the passage of the fugitive law, should be seen coming in hot pursuit, with handcuffs and chains and fetters prepared and clanking in their hands; do you, Sir, think they would take him, and fetter him, in the presence of our people, and drag him back to a land of sighs and tears? Sir, if the President, or members of this body, or that class of clergymen who are preaching that obedience to this law is a religious duty, believe this can be done, they had better study the character of our population more thoroughly.

Under that law, such cases may frequently occur; and whether there be a neighborhood north of Mason and Dixon's line, where such a freeman can be taken back to a land of whips and chains, I leave for others to judge; I will not argue the point.

But the President is not satisfied with quoting the words of the Constitution; he closes the paragraph with the following sentence: "You, gentlemen, and the country, may be assured, that to the utmost of my ability, and to the extent of the power vested in me, I shall at all times, and in all places, take care that the laws be faithfully executed."

This language is understood by the House and by the country. No one can mistake its import. It is the language of menace,—of *intimidation*. He distinctly avows that, *"to the extent of the power vested in him, he will see"* this infamous law executed. The power of the army and the navy is vested in the President. This power, he assures us, will be used to shoot down northern freemen, if necessary to enforce this law. This attempt at menace is unworthy of the President. It is unbecoming his station. I feel pained while contemplating the position in which the President has thus placed himself. No language could have been more destructive to his influence. This taunting menace should never have been addressed to freemen; to men who understand the Constitution, and know their rights. I have shown some reasons why our people of northern Ohio will *not obey that law*. The President may speak to them of the *"power vested in him"*; of the army and navy; and he may tell them that he will use the whole military power of the nation at all *times*, and in all *places*, to enforce this detestable law; but, Sir, they will hurl back defiance both at him and his army. He may send his troops,—his Swiss guards of slavery; he may put all the machines of human butchery in operation; he may drench our free land with blood; he may entitle himself to the appellation of a second *"Haynau"*;* but he will *never compel them to obey that law*. They will govern themselves; they will obey every constitutional enactment; but they will discard and repudiate this fugitive bill. I speak what I feel before God and man. I speak what every enlightened statesman

*An Austrian general notorious for brutality, especially during the revolutions of 1848–49.—Ed.

must feel and admit, when I say that no free, enlightened, and independent people ever was, or ever will be, governed by the bayonet and the sword. No, Sir. I will say to the President with all kindness, but with unhesitating confidence, our people will never be compelled by the bayonet or the cannon, or in any other manner, to lend any aid or assistance in executing that infamous law; *nor will they obey it.*

The President should have learned ere this, that public sentiment, with an enlightened and patriotic people, is stronger than armies or navies; that he himself is but the creature of the people's will,—their servant,—elected to execute their purposes. In the enactment of this law, their feelings were not consulted, their honor was disregarded, and their wishes were treated with scorn. Sir, a large portion of the northern people were not represented in this body at the passage of that law. Their servants fled from this hall, and left the interests, the rights, and the honor of their constituents to be disposed of by slave-holders and their obsequious allies. This law "was conceived in sin," and literally "brought forth in iniquity." It is due to our southern friends that we should inform them distinctly that the law *cannot* and *will not* be enforced. Our people, Sir, know what constitutes law. This enactment I call a law merely for convenience, because our language furnishes no proper term in which to characterize it. It has the *form*, but is entirely destitute of the spirit,—the essence of law. It *commands* the perpetration of crimes, which no human enactment can justify. In passing it, Congress overstepped the limits of civil government, and attempted to usurp powers which belong only to God. In this attempt to involve our people in crimes forbidden by inspiration, by every impulse of humanity, and to command one portion of the people to wage a war upon another, Congress was guilty of tyranny unexampled.

This enactment is beyond the power, outside the duties of human government; it imposes no obligation to commit the crimes it commands, it can justify no one for committing them. For this reason, the people *will not obey it.* . . .

February 26, 1851

No cry of "danger to the Union" can alarm the people, or frighten them into obedience to this law. This *"ignis fatuus"* of *dissolution* has for more than a year constituted the entire capital on which certain political leaders have traded. A greater *humbug* was never conceived or brought forth. The gigantic intellect of the Secretary of State [Webster], aided by the political experience of certain distinguished senators and politicians, could alone have given birth to this *"splendid failure,"* which, if put forth by men in the more humble walks of life, would have entitled them to lodgings in some lunatic asylum. . . . The history of the times will show these things in their true light, and place these disunion panics among the most extraordinary *inventions* of any age. The authors should at once obtain patents both here and in Europe. . . .

March 16, 1852

We know, historically, that it was the intention of the framers of [the Constitution] to do no more than to secure to the master the same right to pursue and capture his slave in a free State, that he possessed to pursue and capture his horse or mule. We are not to obstruct the master in reclaiming him. . . . [But] to the full extent to which the law of 1850 involves this government, its officers, and the people of the free States in the burden, the expense, and disgrace of recapturing and returning fugitive slaves, it is *unconstitutional.* . . . This law, which takes from the laboring men of the North a portion of their earnings, to pay for catching and returning fugitive slaves, is a thousand times more repugnant to their feelings than was the stamp act, or the tax on tea. Under this law, they are involved in supporting an institution which they detest; compelled to contribute to the commission of crimes abhorrent to humanity. This oppression, this violation of conscience and of their constitutional rights, this tyranny they feel and deprecate. It is impossible that an intelligent, a patriotic people, can long be subjected to such violations of their rights and the rights of humanity.

The conscience of the nation cannot be long separated from its government. It will be in vain for navy-yard chaplains to deliver lectures, and write essays, to convince our people that it is their duty to uphold the slave-trade and the fugitive law. It will be in vain for "ministers of the lower law," to preach up the duty of Christians to commit crimes against God and humanity, at the contemplation of which our very natures revolt. The voice of reason and of conscience will find utterance. The escape of Shadrach at Boston, the just and holy manifestation of the popular mind at Syracuse, the merited death of Gorsuch at Christiana, should teach the advocates of the fugitive law, and of the compromise, that the "higher law" of our natures, dictated by God, and imprinted upon the hearts of a Christian people, will eventually set these barbarous enactments at defiance.* The shooting [of] slaves in the mountains of Pennsylvania, the inhuman murder of a fugitive in Indiana, as stated in the public papers, could not fail to be followed by the resistance to which I have referred. . . .

By an inscrutable law which pervades the moral world, our very efforts to sustain slavery are converted into the means of its overthrow. The slave-trade in this district is upheld for the purpose of sustaining slavery in our southern States. But where is the reflecting man, who does not see that every slave sold from this city carries with him intelligence of his rights, and becomes a missionary of freedom when transferred South? Why, Sir, in that mournful procession of fifty-two victims of this infamous commerce, taken from this city in 1848, was an individual of unusual intellect. His name was Edmondson. He called on me at different times to aid him in raising money to redeem his sisters. They were, however, sold, and subsequently repurchased by some benevolent people at the East, and are now free. I am told that his whole family were endowed with intellects of the highest order. He was himself, so far as propriety of language, gentlemanly deportment, and intelligence are concerned, not the inferior of gentlemen here, or of the President of the United States. But he was a victim to this slave-trade; and unless he now sleeps in a servile grave, he is preparing the minds of southern slaves for that work which lies before them; a work which, if not accomplished by the voice of truth and justice, will be perfected in blood. That, too, is the case with every

---

*The reference is to three famous cases in which fugitive slaves were rescued from their former owners and from the processes of the Fugitive Slave Law. Edward Gorsuch, a Maryland slaveholder, was killed in Christiana, Pennsylvania, in September 1851 as he tried to recapture several of his escaped slaves. —Ed.

fugitive slave who is returned to bondage. The whole northern slave population are becoming intelligent. They read, or hear read, the discussions of our northern press. They learn what is said in this hall. The remarks I am now making will reąch the ears of many thousands who are borne down by oppression. To them I say, "All men are created equal"; "you are endowed by your Creator with an inalienable right to liberty"; and I add the words of one of Virginia's noblest sons, *"give me liberty, or give me death."*

21. Wendell Phillips: Speech at the Melodeon on the First Anniversary of the Rendition of Thomas Sims (1852)

Wendell Phillips—lawyer, reformer, and radical orator—became a major figure in American abolitionism within a few years of his graduation from Harvard College and Harvard Law School in the early 1830s. Throughout the ante bellum period he stood with William Lloyd Garrison on most issues of principle, but Phillips was not a thoroughgoing nonresistant. Before the end of the 1850s he would, like Theodore Parker, be arrested and indicted in the aftermath of the abortive effort to rescue Anthony Burns by force of arms; he would raise funds to buy rifles for the Kansas free-soilers; he would express approval of John Brown's raid on Harpers Ferry. Yet he accepted the necessity for violence always with extreme reluctance. A year after Thomas Sims was returned to slavery from the streets of Boston, Phillips observed the grim anniversary with a speech that takes the obligation of civil disobedience practically for granted, and is less an exhortation than a complex meditation on the issue of means.[1]

Reprinted from Wendell Phillips, *Speeches, Lectures, and Letters* (Boston: James Redpath, 1863), pp. 76–82.

. . . The best use that we can now make of this occasion, it seems to me, is to look about us, take our bearings, and tell the fugitives, over whom yet hangs this terrible statute, what course, in our opinion, they should pursue.

And, in the first place, it is neither frank nor honest to keep

up the delusive idea that a fugitive slave can be protected in
Massachusetts. I hope I am mistaken; I shall be glad to be
proved incorrect; but I do not believe there is any such antislavery sentiment here as is able to protect a fugitive on whom the
government has once laid its hand. We were told this afternoon,
from this platform, that there were one hundred and fifty men
in one town ready to come with their muskets to Boston,—all
they waited for was an invitation. I heard, three weeks before
the Sims case, that there were a hundred in one town in Plymouth County pledged to shoulder their muskets in such a cause.
We saw nothing of them. I heard, three weeks after the Sims
rendition, that there were two hundred more in the city of
Worcester ready to have come, had they been invited. We saw
nothing of them. On such an occasion, from the nature of the
case, there cannot be much previous concert; the people must
take their own cause into their own hands. Intense earnestness
of purpose, pervading large classes, must instinctively perceive
the crisis, and gather all spontaneously for the first act which is
to organize revolution. When the Court was in pursuit of John
Hampden, we are not told that the two thousand men who rode
up to London the next morning, to stand between their representative and a king's frown, waited for an invitation. They assembled of their own voluntary and individual purpose, and
found themselves in London. Whenever there is a like determination throughout Massachusetts, it will need no invitation.
When, in 1775, the British turned their eyes toward Lexington,
the same *invitation* went out from the Vigilance Committee of
Mechanics in Boston, as in our case of April, 1851. Two lanterns
on the North Church steeple telegraphed the fact to the country;
Revere and Prescott, as they rode from house to house in the
gray light of that April morning, could tell little what others
would do,—they flung into each house the startling announcement, "The red-coats are coming!" and rode on. None that day
issued orders, none obeyed aught but his own soul. Though
Massachusetts rocked from Barnstable to Berkshire, when the
wire flashed over the land the announcement that a slave lay
chained in the Boston court-house, there was no answer from
the antislavery feeling of the State. It is sad, therefore, but it
seems to me honest, to say to the fugitive in Boston, or on his

way, that, if the government once seize him, he cannot be protected here. I think we are bound, in common kindness and honesty, to tell them that there are but two ways that promise any refuge from the horrors of a return to bondage: one is to fly [to Canada]—to place themselves under the protection of that government, which, with all her faults, has won the proud distinction that slaves cannot breathe her air,—the fast-anchored isle of empire, where tyrants and slaves may alike find refuge from vengeance and oppression. AND THIS IS THE COURSE I WOULD ADVISE EVERY MAN TO ADOPT. THIS, UNLESS THERE ARE, IN HIS PARTICULAR CASE, IMPERATIVE REASONS TO THE CONTRARY, IS HIS DUTY. If this course be impossible, then the other way is to arm himself, and by resistance secure in the Free States a trial for homicide,—trusting that no jury will be able so far to crush the instincts of humanity as not to hold him justified.

But some one may ask, Why countenance, even by a mention of it, this public resistance,—you, whose whole enterprise repudiates force? Because this is a very different question from that great issue, the abolition of slavery. On that point, I am willing to wait. I can be patient, no matter how often that is defeated by treacherous statesmen. The cause of three millions of slaves, the destruction of a great national institution, must proceed slowly; and, like every other change in public sentiment, we must wait patiently for it, and there the best policy is, beyond all question, the policy of submission; for that gains, in time, on public sympathy. But this is a different case. Who can ask the trembling, anxious fugitive to stop and submit patiently to the overwhelming chances of going back, that his fate may, in some indirect manner, and far-off hour, influence for good the destiny of his fellow-millions? Such virtue must be self-moved. Who could stand and ask it of another? True, Thomas Sims returned is a great public event, calculated to make Abolitionists; but the game sickens me when the counters are living men. We have no right to use up fugitives for the manufacture of antislavery sentiment. There are those who hang one man to benefit another, and to create a wholesome dread of crime. I shrink from using human life as raw material for the production of any state of public opinion, however valuable. I do not think we have a right to use up fugitive slaves in this pitiless way, in order to extend or deepen an antislavery sentiment. At least, I have no right to use them so, without their full consent. It seems to me, therefore, we are bound to tell those who have taken refuge under the laws of Massachusetts, what they must expect here. The time was when we honestly believed they might expect protection. That time, in my opinion, has passed by. . . .

. . . I do say, in private, to every one that comes to me, "But one course is left for you. There is no safety for you here; there is no law for you here. The hearts of the judges are stone, the hearts of the people are stone. It is in vain that you appeal to the Abolitionists. They may be ready, may be able, ten years hence." But the "brace of Adamses," to which our friend [Theodore Parker] alluded this morning, if they had mistaken 1765 for 1775, would have ended at the scaffold instead of the Declaration of Independence and the treaty of 1783. We must bide our time, and we must read, with anointed eyes, the signs of our time. If public opinion is wrong, we want to know it; know it, that we may remodel it. We will ourselves trample this accursed Fugitive Slave Law under foot. But we are a minority at present, and cannot do this to any great practical effect; we are bound to suggest to these unfortunates who look to us for advice, some feasible plan. This, in my view, should be our counsel: "Depart if you can,—if you have time and means. As no one has a right to ask that you stay, and, if arrested, submit, in order that your case may convert men to antislavery principles; so you have no right, capriciously, to stay and resist, merely that your resistance may rouse attention, and awaken antislavery sympathy. It is a grave thing to break into the bloody house of life. The mere expectation of good consequences will not justify you in taking a man's life. You have a perfect right to live where you choose. No one can rightfully force you away. There may be important and sufficient reasons, in many cases, why you should stay and vindicate your right at all hazards. But in common cases, where no such reasons exist, it is better that you surrender your extreme right to live where you choose, than assert it in blood, and thus *risk* injuring the movement which seeks to aid your fellows. Put yourselves under the protection of the British flag; appeal to the humanity of the world. Do not linger here." . . .

. . . Still, circumstances may prevent flight, imperative reasons may exist why he should remain here: he may be seized before he succeeds in escaping. I say to him, then, There is a course left, if you have the courage to face it. There is one appeal left, which has not yet been tried; it may avail you; I cannot insure you even that. It has now reached that pass when even the chance of a Boston gibbet may be no protection from a Georgia plantation; but if I were in your place, I would try! The sympathies of the people will gather round you, if put on trial for such an act. . . . There may be something in an appeal to a Massachusetts jury impanelled to try a man's INALIENABLE right to liberty, the pursuit of happiness, and to protect himself; and I hope—I dare not hope much, but I do hope—that there is still humanity enough to bring you in "not guilty." . . . I think, therefore, that it is possible an appeal to the criminal jurisdiction of the State might save a man. Perhaps it might be just that final blow which would stun this drunken nation into sobriety, and make it heed, at last, the claims of the slave.

Mark me! I do not *advise* any one to take the life of his fellow, —to brave the vengeance of the law, and run the somewhat, after all, unequal risk of the hard technical heart of a Massachusetts jury. Such an act must be, after all, one's own impulse. To burst away from all civil relations, to throw one's self back on this great primal right of self-protection, at all hazards, must be the growth of one's own thought and purpose. I can only tell the sufferer the possibilities that lie before him,—tell him what I would do in his case,—tell him that what I would do myself I would countenance another in doing, and aid him to the extent of my power. . . .

22. Harriet Beecher Stowe:
Uncle Tom's Cabin (1852)

In the months following the passage of the Fugitive Slave Law, while three of her brothers denounced the new law from their pulpits, Harriet Beecher Stowe began *Uncle Tom's Cabin.* The principal aims of her literary evangelicalism seem to have been large and broad—if not the conversion of her readers, especially southern women, to antislavery, then at least the alteration of their conception of slaves as property.[1] Yet one of her important themes was her specific sense of the law as "the machinery of the devil"[2] in its violation of fundamental Christian precepts, precepts that take (or ought to take) precedence over all political considerations. In the novel, at least, women are more likely than men to put this perspective into practice. Mrs. Bird the senator's wife, Barbara Cross has observed, is only one of a number of women in *Uncle Tom's Cabin* who, secure within the "enclosed havens" of their benign domestic authority, "quietly and persistently subvert the laws of the land."[3]

Beyond the awesome numbers of copies sold (abroad as well as in the United States), the impact of *Uncle Tom's Cabin* is of course difficult to assess. Sometimes the effects were grossly hostile: Mrs. Stowe was abusively portrayed by some southern readers "as a sexually driven 'nigger lover.'"[4] Sometimes, on the other hand, the response was powerfully sympathetic—though Wendell Phillips observed ironically that "there is many a man that weeps over *Uncle Tom* who votes the Whig or the Democratic ticket."[5] Even so, the novel's dramatic pathos must have affected many northern and southern readers in more lastingly powerful nonrational ways. The conclusion of Chapter 9 (given here) illustrates both Mrs. Stowe's explicit appeal to the South and the suspicion, current among abolitionists in the early 1850s, that at least some of the legislators who had voted for the Fugitive Slave Law would shrink from any personal role in enforcing it.

Reprinted from Harriet Beecher Stowe, *Uncle Tom's Cabin; or, Life among the Lowly* (Boston: Houghton Mifflin, 1896), chap. 9, pp. 94–105, 107.

The light of the cheerful fire shone on the rug and carpet of a cosey parlor, and glittered on the sides of the teacups and well-brightened teapot, as Senator Bird was drawing off his boots, preparatory to inserting his feet in a pair of new handsome slippers, which his wife had been working for him while away on his senatorial tour. Mrs. Bird, looking the very picture of delight, was superintending the arrangements of the table, ever and anon mingling admonitory remarks to a number of frolicsome juveniles, who were effervescing in all those modes of untold gambol and mischief that have astonished mothers ever since the flood.

"Tom, let the door-knob alone,—there's a man! Mary! Mary!

don't pull the cat's tail,—poor pussy! Jim, you must n't climb on that table,—no, no!—You don't know, my dear, what a surprise it is to us all, to see you here to-night!" said she, at last, when she found a space to say something to her husband.

"Yes, yes, I thought I'd just make a run down, spend the night, and have a little comfort at home. I'm tired to death, and my head aches!"

Mrs. Bird cast a glance at a camphor-bottle, which stood in the half-open closet, and appeared to meditate an approach to it, but her husband interposed.

"No, no, Mary, no doctoring! a cup of your good hot tea, and some of our good home living, is what I want. It's a tiresome business, this legislating!"

And the senator smiled, as if he rather liked the idea of considering himself a sacrifice to his country.

"Well," said his wife, after the business of the tea-table was getting rather slack, "and what have they been doing in the Senate?"

Now, it was a very unusual thing for gentle little Mrs. Bird ever to trouble her head with what was going on in the house of the state, very wisely considering that she had enough to do to mind her own. Mr. Bird, therefore, opened his eyes in surprise, and said,—

"Not very much of importance."

"Well; but is it true that they have been passing a law forbidding people to give meat and drink to those poor colored folks that come along? I heard they were talking of some such law, but I did n't think any Christian legislature would pass it!"

"Why, Mary, you are getting to be a politician, all at once."

"No, nonsense! I wouldn't give a fig for all your politics, generally, but I think this is something downright cruel and unchristian. I hope, my dear, no such law has been passed."

"There has been a law passed forbidding people to help off the slaves that come over from Kentucky, my dear; so much of that thing has been done by these reckless Abolitionists, that our brethren in Kentucky are very strongly excited, and it seems necessary, and no more than Christian and kind, that something should be done by our state to quiet the excitement."

"And what is the law? It don't forbid us to shelter these poor creatures a night, does it, and to give 'em something comfortable to eat, and a few old clothes, and send them quietly about their business?"

"Why, yes, my dear; that would be aiding and abetting, you know."

Mrs. Bird was a timid, blushing little woman, of about four feet in height, and with mild blue eyes, and a peach-blow complexion, and the gentlest, sweetest voice in the world;—as for courage, a moderate-sized cock-turkey had been known to put her to rout at the very first gobble, and a stout house-dog, of moderate capacity, would bring her into subjection merely by a show of his teeth. Her husband and children were her entire world, and in these she ruled more by entreaty and persuasion than by command or argument. There was only one thing that was capable of arousing her, and that provocation came in on the side of her unusually gentle and sympathetic nature;—anything in the shape of cruelty would throw her into a passion, which was the more alarming and inexplicable in proportion to the general softness of her nature. Generally the most indulgent and easy to be entreated of all mothers, still her boys had a very reverent remembrance of a most vehement chastisement she once bestowed on them, because she found them leagued with several graceless boys of the neighborhood, stoning a defenceless kitten.

"I'll tell you what," Master Bill used to say, "I was scared that time. Mother came at me so that I thought she was crazy, and I was whipped and tumbled off to bed, without any supper, before I could get over wondering what had come about; and, after that, I heard mother crying outside the door, which made me feel worse than all the rest. I'll tell you what," he'd say, "we boys never stoned another kitten!"

On the present occasion, Mrs. Bird rose quickly, with very red cheeks, which quite improved her general appearance, and walked up to her husband, with quite a resolute air, and said, in a determined tone,—

"Now, John, I want to know if you think such a law as that is right and Christian?"

"You won't shoot me, now, Mary, if I say I do!"

"I never could have thought it of you, John; you did n't vote for it?"

"Even so, my fair politician."

"You ought to be ashamed, John! Poor, homeless, houseless creatures! It's a shameful, wicked, abominable law, and I'll break it, for one, the first time I get a chance; and I hope I *shall* have a chance, I do! Things have got to a pretty pass, if a woman can't give a warm supper and a bed to poor, starving creatures, just because they are slaves, and have been abused and oppressed all their lives, poor things!"

"But, Mary, just listen to me. Your feelings are all quite right, dear, and interesting, and I love you for them; but, then, dear, we must n't suffer our feelings to run away with our judgment; you must consider it's not a matter of private feeling,—there are great public interests involved,—there is such a state of public agitation rising, that we must put aside our private feelings."

"Now, John, I don't know anything about politics, but I can read my Bible; and there I see that I must feed the hungry, clothe the naked, and comfort the desolate; and that Bible I mean to follow."

"But in cases where your doing so would involve a great public evil—"

"Obeying God never brings on public evils. I know it can't. It's always safest, all round, to *do as he* bids us."

"Now, listen to me, Mary, and I can state to you a very clear argument, to show—"

"O, nonsense, John! you can talk all night, but you would n't do it. I put it to you, John,—would *you*, now, turn away a poor, shivering, hungry creature from your door, because he was a runaway? *Would* you, now?

Now, if the truth must be told, our senator had the misfortune to be a man who had a particularly humane and accessible nature, and turning away anybody that was in trouble never had been his forte; and what was worse for him in this particular pinch of the argument was, that his wife knew it, and, of course, was making an assault on rather an indefensible point. So he had recourse to the usual means of gaining time for such cases made and provided; he said "ahem," and coughed several times, took out his pocket-handkerchief, and began to wipe his glasses. Mrs. Bird, seeing the defenceless condition of the enemy's territory, had no more conscience than to push her advantage.

"I should like to see you doing that, John,—I really should! Turning a woman out of doors in a snow-storm, for instance; or, may be you'd take her up and put her in jail, would n't you? You would make a great hand at that!"

"Of course, it would be a very painful duty," began Mr. Bird, in a moderate tone.

"Duty, John! don't use that word! You know it is n't a duty,— it can't be a duty! If folks want to keep their slaves from running away, let 'em treat 'em well,—that's my doctrine. If I had slaves (as I hope I never shall have), I'd risk their wanting to run away from me, or you either, John. I tell you folks don't run away when they are happy; and when they do run, poor creatures! they suffer enough with cold and hunger and fear, without everybody's turning against them; and, law or no law, I never will, so help me God!"

"Mary! Mary! My dear, let me reason with you."

"I hate reasoning, John,—especially reasoning on such subjects. There's a way you political folks have of coming round and round a plain right thing; and you don't believe in it yourselves, when it comes to practice. I know *you* well enough, John. You don't believe it's right any more than I do; and you would n't do it any sooner than I."

At this critical juncture, old Cudjoe, the black man-of-all-work, put his head in at the door, and wished "Missis would come into the kitchen"; and our senator, tolerably relieved, looked after his little wife with a whimsical mixture of amusement and vexation, and, seating himself in the arm-chair, began to read the papers.

After a moment, his wife's voice was heard at the door, in a quick, earnest tone,—"John! John! I do wish you'd come here, a moment."

He laid down his paper, and went into the kitchen, and started, quite amazed at the sight that presented itself:—A young and slender woman, with garments torn and frozen, with one shoe gone, and the stocking torn away from the cut and bleeding foot, was laid back in a deadly swoon upon two chairs. There was the impress of the despised race on her face, yet none could help feeling its mournful and pathetic beauty, while its stony sharpness, its cold, fixed, deathly aspect, struck a solemn chill over him. He drew his breath short, and stood in silence. His wife, and their only colored domestic, old Aunt Dinah, were busily engaged in restorative measures; while old Cudjoe had got the boy on his knee, and was busy pulling off his shoes and stockings, and chafing his little cold feet.

"Sure, now, if she an't a sight to behold!" said old Dinah, compassionately; "'pears like 't was the heat that made her faint. She was tol'able peart when she cum in, and asked if she could n't warm herself here a spell; and I was just a askin' her where she cum from, and she fainted right down. Never done much hard work, guess, by the looks of her hands."

"Poor creature!" said Mrs. Bird, compassionately, as the woman slowly unclosed her large, dark eyes, and looked vacantly at her. Suddenly an expression of agony crossed her face, and she sprang up, saying, "O, my Harry! Have they got him?"

The boy, at this, jumped from Cudjoe's knee, and, running to her side, put up his arms. "O, he's here! he's here!" she exclaimed.

"O, ma'am!" said she wildly, to Mrs. Bird, "do protect us! don't let them get him!"

"Nobody shall hurt you here, poor woman," said Mrs. Bird, encouragingly. "You are safe; don't be afraid."

"God bless you!" said the woman, covering her face and sobbing; while the little boy, seeing her crying, tried to get into her lap.

With many gentle and womanly offices, which none knew better how to render than Mrs. Bird, the poor woman was, in time, rendered more calm. A temporary bed was provided for her on the settle, near the fire; and, after a short time, she fell into a heavy slumber, with the child, who seemed no less weary, soundly sleeping on her arm; for the mother resisted, with nervous anxiety, the kindest attempts to take him from her; and, even in sleep, her arm encircled him with an unrelaxing clasp, as if she could not even then be beguiled of her vigilant hold.

Mr. and Mrs. Bird had gone back to the parlor, where, strange as it may appear, no reference was made, on either side, to the preceding conversation; but Mrs. Bird busied herself with her knitting-work, and Mr. Bird pretended to be reading the paper.

"I wonder who and what she is!" said Mr. Bird, at last, as he laid it down.

"When she wakes up and feels a little rested, we will see," said Mrs. Bird.

"I say, wife!" said Mr. Bird, after musing in silence over his newspaper.

"Well, dear!"

"She could n't wear one of your gowns, could she, by any letting down, or such matter? She seems to be rather larger than you are."

A quite perceptible smile glimmered on Mrs. Bird's face, as she answered, "We'll see."

Another pause, and Mr. Bird again broke out,—

"I say, wife!"

"Well! what now?"

"Why, there's that old bombazine cloak, that you keep on purpose to put over me when I take my afternoon's nap; you might as well give her that,—she needs clothes."

At this instant, Dinah looked in to say that the woman was awake, and wanted to see Missis.

Mr. and Mrs. Bird went into the kitchen, followed by the two eldest boys, the smaller fry having, by this time, been safely disposed of in bed.

The woman was now sitting up on the settle, by the fire. She was looking steadily into the blaze, with a calm, heartbroken expression, very different from her former agitated wildness.

"Did you want me?" said Mrs. Bird, in gentle tones. "I hope you feel better now, poor woman!"

A long-drawn, shivering sigh was the only answer; but she lifted her dark eyes, and fixed them on her with such a forlorn and imploring expression, that the tears came into the little woman's eyes.

"You need n't be afraid of anything; we are friends here, poor woman! Tell me where you came from, and what you want," said she.

"I came from Kentucky," said the woman.

"When?" said Mr. Bird, taking up the interrogatory.

"To-night."

"How did you come?"

"I crossed on the ice."

"Crossed on the ice!" said every one present.

"Yes," said the woman, slowly, "I did. God helping me. I crossed on the ice; for they were behind me,—right behind,— and there was no other way!"

"Law, Missis," said Cudjoe, "the ice is all in broken-up blocks, a swinging and a teetering up and down in the water."

"I know it was,—I know it!" said she, wildly; "but I did it! I would n't have thought I could,—I did n't think I should get over, but I did n't care! I could but die, if I did n't. The Lord helped me; nobody knows how much the Lord can help 'em, till they try," said the woman, with a flashing eye.

"Were you a slave?" said Mr. Bird.

"Yes, sir; I belonged to a man in Kentucky."

"Was he unkind to you?"

"No, sir; he was a good master."

"And was your mistress unkind to you?"

"No, sir,—no! my mistress was always good to me."

"What could induce you to leave a good home, then, and run away, and go through such dangers?"

The woman looked up at Mrs. Bird with a keen, scrutinizing glance, and it did not escape her that she was dressed in deep mourning.

"Ma'am," she said, suddenly, "Have you ever lost a child?"

The question was unexpected, and it was a thrust on a new wound; for it was only a month since a darling child of the family had been laid in the grave.

Mr. Bird turned around and walked to the window, and Mrs. Bird burst into tears; but, recovering her voice, she said,—

"Why do you ask that? I have lost a little one."

"Then you will feel for me. I have lost two, one after another, —left 'em buried there when I came away; and I had only this one left. I never slept a night without him; he was all I had. He was my comfort and pride, day and night; and, ma'am, they were going to take him away from me,—to *sell* him,—sell him down south, ma'am, to go all alone,—a baby that had never been away from his mother in his life! I could n't stand it, ma'am. I knew I never should be good for anything, if they did; and when I knew the papers were signed, and he was sold, I took him and came off in the night; and they chased me,—the man that bought him, and some of Mas'r's folks,—and they were coming down right behind me, and I heard 'em. I jumped right on to the ice; and how I got across, I don't know,—but, first I knew, a man was helping me up the bank."

The woman did not sob nor weep. She had gone to a place where tears are dry; but every one around her was, in some way characteristic of themselves, showing signs of hearty sympathy.

The two little boys, after a desperate rummaging in their pockets, in search of those pocket-handkerchiefs which mothers know are never to be found there, had thrown themselves disconsolately into the skirts of their mother's gown, where they were sobbing, and wiping their eyes and noses, to their hearts' content;—Mrs. Bird had her face fairly hidden in her pocket-handkerchief; and old Dinah, with tears streaming down her black, honest face, was ejaculating, "Lord have mercy on us!" with all the fervor of a camp-meeting;—while old Cudjoe, rubbing his eyes very hard with his cuffs, and making a most uncommon variety of wry faces, occasionally responded in the same key, with great fervor. Our senator was a statesman, and of course could not be expected to cry, like other mortals; and so he turned his back to the company, and looked out of the window, and seemed particularly busy in clearing his throat and wiping his spectacle-glasses, occasionally blowing his nose in a manner that was calculated to excite suspicion, had any one been in a state to observe critically.

"How came you to tell me you had a kind master?" he suddenly exclaimed, gulping down very resolutely some kind of rising in his throat, and turning suddenly round upon the woman.

"Because he *was* a kind master; I'll say that of him, any way;— and my mistress was kind; but they could n't help themselves. They were owing money; and there was some way, I can't tell how, that a man had a hold on them, and they were obliged to give him his will. I listened, and heard him telling mistress that, and she begging and pleading for me,—and he told her he could n't help himself, and that the papers were all drawn;—and then it was I took him and left my home, and came away. I knew 't was no use of my trying to live, if they did it; for 't 'pears like this child is all I have."

"Have you no husband?"

"Yes, but he belongs to another man. His master is real hard to him, and won't let him come to see me, hardly ever; and he's grown harder and harder upon us, and he threatens to sell him down south;—it's like I'll never see *him* again!"

The quiet tone in which the woman pronounced these words might have led a superficial observer to think that she was entirely apathetic; but there was a calm, settled depth of anguish in her large, dark eye, that spoke of something far otherwise.

"And where do you mean to go, my poor woman?" said Mrs. Bird.

"To Canada, if I only knew where that was. Is it very far off, is Canada?" said she, looking up, with a simple, confiding air, to Mrs. Bird's face.

"Poor thing!" said Mrs. Bird, involuntarily.

"Is 't a very great way off, think?" said the woman, earnestly.

"Much further than you think, poor child!" said Mrs. Bird; "but we will try to think what can be done for you. Here, Dinah, make her up a bed in your own room, close by the kitchen, and I'll think what to do for her in the morning. Meanwhile, never fear, poor woman; put your trust in God; he will protect you."

Mrs. Bird and her husband re-entered the parlor. She sat down in her little rocking-chair before the fire, swaying thoughtfully to and fro. Mr. Bird strode up and down the room, grumbling to himself. "Pish! pshaw! confounded awkward business!" At length, striding up to his wife, he said,—

"I say, wife, she'll have to get away from here, this very night. That fellow will be down on the scent bright and early to-morrow morning; if 't was only the woman, she could lie quiet till it was over; but that little chap can't be kept still by a troop of horse and foot, I'll warrant me; he'll bring it all out, popping his head out of some window or door. A pretty kettle of fish it would be for me, too, to be caught with them both here, just now! No; they'll have to be got off to-night."

"To-night! How is it possible?—where to?"

"Well, I know pretty well where to," said the senator, beginning to put on his boots, with a reflective air; and, stopping when his leg was half in, he embraced his knee with both hands, and seemed to go off in deep meditation.

"It's a confounded awkward, ugly business," said he, at last, beginning to tug at his boot-straps again, "and that's a fact!" After one boot was fairly on, the senator sat with the other in his hand, profoundly studying the figure of the carpet. "It will have to be done, though, for aught I see,—hang it all!" and he drew the other boot anxiously on, and looked out of the window.

Now, little Mrs. Bird was a discreet woman,—a woman who never in her life said, "I told you so!" and, on the present occasion, though pretty well aware of the shape her husband's meditations were taking, she very prudently forbore to meddle with them, only sat very quietly in her chair, and looked quite ready to hear her liege lord's intentions, when he should think proper to utter them.

"You see," he said, "there's my old client, Van Trompe, has come over from Kentucky, and set all his slaves free; and he has bought a place seven miles up the creek, here, back in the woods, where nobody goes, unless they go on purpose; and it's a place that is n't found in a hurry. There she'd be safe enough; but the plague of the thing is, nobody could drive a carriage there to-night, but *me*."

"Why not? Cudjoe is an excellent driver."

"Ay, ay, but here it is. The creek has to be crossed twice; and the second crossing is quite dangerous, unless one knows it as I do. I have crossed it a hundred times on horseback, and know exactly the turns to take. And so, you see, there's no help for it. Cudjoe must put in the horses, as quietly as may be, about twelve o'clock, and I'll take her over; and then, to give color to the matter, he must carry me on to the next tavern, to take the stage for Columbus, that comes by about three or four, and so it will look as if I had had the carriage only for that. I shall get into business bright and early in the morning. But I'm thinking I shall feel rather cheap there, after all that's been said and done; but, hang it, I can't help it!"

"Your heart is better than your head, in this case, John," said the wife, laying her little white hand on his. "Could I ever have loved you, had I not known you better than you know yourself?" And the little woman looked so handsome, with the tears sparkling in her eyes, that the senator thought he must be a decidedly clever fellow, to get such a pretty creature into such a passionate admiration of him; and so, what could he do but walk off soberly, to see about the carriage. . . .

What a situation, now, for a patriotic senator, that had been all the week before spurring up the legislature of his native state to pass more stringent resolutions against escaping fugitives, their harborers and abettors!

Our good senator in his native state had not been exceeded by any of his brethren at Washington, in the sort of eloquence which has won for them immortal renown! How sublimely he had sat with his hands in his pockets, and scouted all sentimental weakness of those who would put the welfare of a few miserable fugitives before great state interests!

He was as bold as a lion about it, and "mightily convinced" not only himself, but everybody that heard him;—but then his idea of a fugitive was only an idea of the letters that spell the word,—or, at the most, the image of a little newspaper picture of a man with a stick and bundle, with "Ran away from the subscriber" under it. The magic of the real presence of distress,— the imploring human eye, the frail, trembling human hand, the despairing appeal of helpless agony,—these he had never tried. He had never thought that a fugitive might be a hapless mother, a defenceless child,—like that one which was now wearing his lost boy's little well-known cap; and so, as our poor senator was not stone or steel,—as he was a man, and a downright noble-hearted one, too,—he was, as everybody must see, in a sad case for his patriotism. And you need not exult over him, good brother of the Southern States; for we have some inklings that many of you, under similar circumstances, would not do much better. We have reason to know, in Kentucky, as in Mississippi, are noble and generous hearts, to whom never was tale of suffering told in vain. Ah, good brother! is it fair for you to expect of us services which your own brave, honorable heart would not allow you to render, were you in our place?

23. Thomas Wentworth Higginson: *Massachusetts in Mourning* (1854)

Thomas Wentworth Higginson, a theological disciple of Theodore Parker, served as a Unitarian minister in Newburyport and then assumed charge of Worcester's new Free Church. Simultaneously, through his sermons and his newspaper articles, he was something of a public figure. When he ran, unsuccessfully, as a Free-Soil candidate for Congress in 1850, he urged his constituents to disobey the Fugitive Slave Law but to "show [their] good citizenship by taking the legal consequences."[1] By 1854, however, his views had become more radical, and he led the abortive attack on the courthouse in Boston in which one deputy was killed as Higginson and his followers tried to rescue Anthony Burns before he could be sent back to slavery. Like Parker and Phillips, Higginson was arrested but freed when the indictments were dismissed on technical grounds.

As *Massachusetts in Mourning* shows, Higginson was hardly daunted by the raid's failure. In fact, as the decade wore on he saw abundant reason to give even freer rein to his continuing interest in the "manliness" of militant force. He went to Kansas with the free-soil riflemen; he gave money and moral support to John Brown. With the coming of the Civil War he became the colonel of the first authorized regiment of black soldiers.[2]

Reprinted from Thomas Wentworth Higginson, *Massachusetts in Mourning* (Boston: James Munroe, 1854), pp. 4–5, 8–15.

. . . Words are nothing—we have been surfeited with words for twenty years. I am thankful that this time there was action also ready for Freedom. God gave men bodies, to live and work in; the powers of those bodies are the first things to be consecrated to the Right. He gave us higher powers, also, for weapons, but, in using those, we must not forget to hold the lower ones also ready; else we miss our proper manly life on earth, and lay down our means of usefulness before we have outgrown them. "Render unto Caesar the things which are Caesar's and unto God the things which are God's." Our souls and bodies are both God's, and resistance to tyrants is obedience to Him.

If you meet men whose souls are contaminated, and have time enough to work on them, you can deal with them by the weapons of the soul alone; but if men array brute force against Freedom—pistols, clubs, drilled soldiers, and stone walls—then the body also has its part to do in resistance. You must hold yourself above men, I own, yet not too far above to reach them.

I do not like even to think of taking life, only of giving it; but physical force that is forcible enough, acts without bloodshed. They say that with twenty more men at hand, that Friday night, at the Boston Court House, the Slave might have been rescued without even the death of that one man—who was perhaps killed by his frightened companions, then and there. So you see force may not mean bloodshed; and calm, irresistible force, in a good cause, becomes sublime. The strokes on the door of that Court House that night for instance—they may perchance have disturbed some dreamy saint from his meditations, (if dreamy saints abound in Court Square,)—but I think they went echoing from town to town, from Boston to far New Orleans, like the first drum beat of the Revolution—and each reverberating throb was a blow upon the door of every Slave-prison of this guilty Republic.

. . . If the attack on the Court House had no greater effect than to send that Slave away under a guard of two thousand men, instead of two hundred, it was worth a dozen lives. If we are all Slaves indeed—if there is no law in Massachusetts except the telegraphic orders from Washington—if our own military are to be made Slave-catchers—if our Governor is a mere piece of State ceremony, permitted only to rise at a military dinner and thank his own soldiers for their readiness to shoot down his own constituents, without even the delay of a riot act—if Massachusetts is merely a conquered province and under martial law—*then I wish to know it*, and I am grateful for every additional gun and sabre that forces the truth deeper into our hearts. *Lower, Massachusetts, lower, kneel still lower!* Serve, Irish Marines! the kidnappers, your masters; down in the dust, citizen soldiery! before the Irish Marines. . . .

In view of these facts, what stands between us and a military despotism? "Sure guarantees," you say. So has every nation thought until its fall came. "The outward form of Roman institutions stood uninjured till long after Caligula had made his horse consul." What is your safeguard? Nothing but a parchment

Constitution, which has been riddled through and through whenever it pleased the Slave Power; which has not been able to preserve to you the oldest privileges of Freedom—Habeas Corpus and Trial by Jury! . . .

How simple the acts of our tragedy may be! Let another Fugitive Slave case occur, and more blood be spilt (as might happen another time;)—let Massachusetts be declared insurrectionary, and placed under martial law, (as it might;)—let the President be made Dictator, with absolute power; let him send his willing Attorney General to buy up officers of militia, (which would be easy,) and frighten Officers of State, (which would be easier;)— let him get half the press, and a quarter of the pulpits, to sustain his usurpation, under the name of "law and order";—let the flame spread from New England to New York, from New York to Ohio, from Ohio to Wisconsin;—and how long would it take for some future Franklin Pierce to stand where Louis Napoleon stands now? How much would the commercial leaders of the East resist, if an appeal were skilfully made to their pockets? —or the political demagogues of the West, if an appeal were made to their ambition? It seems inconceivable! Certainly—so did the *coup d'état* of Louis Napoleon, the day before it happened!

"Do not despair of the Republic," says some one, remembering the hopeful old Roman motto. But they had to despair of that one in the end,—and why not of this one also? Why, when we were going on, step by step, as older Republics have done, should we expect to stop just as we reach the brink of Niagara? The love of Liberty grows stronger every year, some think, in some places. Thirty years ago, it cost only $25 to restore a Fugitive Slave from Boston, and now it costs $100,000;—*but still the Slave is restored.* . . . We talk of the Anti-Slavery sentiment as being stronger; but in spite of your Free Soil votes, your Uncle Tom's Cabin, and your New York Tribunes, here is the simple fact: *the south beats us more and more easily every time.* . . .

No wonder that this excitement is turning Whigs and Democrats into Free Soilers, and Free Soilers into disunionists. But this is only the eddy, after all; the main current sets the wrong way. The nation is intoxicated and depraved. It takes all the things you count as influential,—all the "spirit of the age," and

the "moral sentiment of Christendom," and the best eloquence
and literature of the time,—to balance the demoralization of a
single term of Presidential patronage. Give the offices of the nation to be controlled by the Slave Power, and I tell you that there
is not one in ten, even of professed Anti-Slavery men, who can
stand the fire in the furnace of sin; and there is not a plot so
wicked but it will have, like all its predecessors, a sufficient majority when the time comes. . . .

For myself, I do not expect to live to see [the Fugitive Slave
Law] repealed by the votes of politicians at Washington. It can
only be repealed by ourselves, upon the soil of Massachusetts.
For one, I am glad to be deceived no longer. I am glad of the dis-
covery—(no hasty thing, but gradually dawning upon me for
ten years)—that I live under a despotism. I have lost the dream
that ours is a land of peace and order. I have looked thoroughly
through our "Fourth of July," and seen its hollowness; and I
advise you to petition your City Government to revoke their ap-
propriation for its celebration, (or give the same to the Nebraska
Emigration Society,) and only toll the bells in all the churches,
and hang the streets in black from end to end. O shall we hold
such ceremonies when only some statesman is gone, and omit
them over dead Freedom, whom all true statesmen only live to
serve!

At any rate my word of counsel to you is to learn this lesson
thoroughly—*a revolution is begun!* not a Reform, but a Revolution. If you take part in politics henceforward, let it be only to
bring nearer the crisis which will either save or sunder this nation—or perhaps save in sundering. I am not very hopeful, even
as regards you; I know the mass of men will not make great
sacrifices for Freedom, but there is more need of those who will.
I have lost faith forever in numbers; I have faith only in the con-
stancy and courage of a "forlorn hope." And for aught we know,
a case may arise, this week, in Massachusetts, which may not
end like the last one.

Let us speak the truth. Under the influence of Slavery, we
are rapidly relapsing into that state of barbarism in which every
man must rely on his own right hand for his protection. Let any
man yield to his instinct of Freedom, and resist oppression, and
his life is at the mercy of the first drunken officer who orders
his troops to fire. For myself, existence looks worthless under

such circumstances; and I can only make life worth living for, by becoming a revolutionist. The saying seems dangerous; but why not say it if one means it, as I certainly do. I respect law and order, but as the ancient Persian sage said, "*always* to obey the laws, virtue must relax much of her vigor." I see, now, that while Slavery is national, law and order must constantly be on the wrong side. I see that the case stands for me precisely as it stands for Kossuth and Mazzini, and I must take the consequences.

Do you say that ours is a Democratic Government, and there is a more peaceable remedy? I deny that we live under a Democracy. It is an oligarchy of Slaveholders, and I point to the history of a half century to prove it. Do you say, that oligarchy will be propitiated by submission? I deny it. It is the plea of the timid in all ages. Look at the experience of our own country. Which is most influential in Congress—South Carolina, which never submitted to anything, or Massachusetts, with thrice the white population, but which always submits to everything? . . . The way to make principles felt is to assert them—peaceably, if you can; forcibly, if you must. The way to promote Free Soil is to have your own soil free; to leave courts to settle constitutions, and to fall back (for your own part,) on first principles: then it will be seen that you mean something. How much free territory is there beneath the Stars and Stripes? I know of four places— Syracuse, Wilkesbarre, Milwaukie, and Chicago:* I remember no others. "Worcester," you say. Worcester has not yet been tried. If you think Worcester County is free, say so and act accordingly. Call a County Convention, and declare that you leave legal quibbles to lawyers, and parties to politicians, and plant yourselves on the simple truth that God never made a Slave, and that man shall neither make nor take one here! Over your own city, at least, you have power; but will you stand the test when it comes? Then do not try to avoid it. For one thing only I blush—that a Fugitive has ever fled from here to Canada. Let it not happen again, I charge you, if you are what you think you are. No longer conceal Fugitives and help them on, but show them and defend them. Let the Underground Railroad stop here! Say to the South that Worcester, though a part of a Repub-

---

*Scenes of successful rescues of fugitive slaves or other dramatic public opposition to the Fugitive Slave Law of 1850.—Ed.

lic, shall be as free as if ruled by a Queen! *Hear, O Richmond! and give ear, O Carolina! henceforth Worcester is Canada to the Slave!* And what will Worcester be to the kidnapper? I dare not tell; and I fear that the poor sinner himself, if once recognized in our streets, would scarcely get back to tell the tale.

I do not discourage more peaceable instrumentalities; would to God that no other were ever needful. Make laws, if you can, though you have State processes already, if you had officers to enforce them; and, indeed, what can any State process do, except to legalize nullification? Use politics, if you can make them worth using, though a coalition administration proved as powerless, in the Sims case, as a Whig administration has proved now. But the disease lies deeper than these remedies can reach. It is all idle to try to save men by law and order, merely, while the men themselves grow selfish and timid, and are only ready to talk of Liberty, and risk nothing for it. Our people have no active physical habits; their intellects are sharpened, but their bodies, and even their hearts, are left untrained; they learn only (as a French satirist once said,) the fear of God and the love of money; they are taught that they owe the world nothing, but that the world owes them a living, and so they make a living; but the fresh, strong spirit of Liberty droops and decays, and only makes a dying. I charge you, parents, do not be so easily satisfied; encourage nobler instincts in your children, and appeal to nobler principles; teach your daughter that life is something more than dress and show, and your son that there is some nobler aim in existence than a good bargain, and a fast horse, and an oyster supper. Let us have the brave, simple instincts of Circassian mountaineers, without their ignorance; and the unfaltering moral courage of the Puritans, without their superstition; so that we may show the world that a community may be educated in brain without becoming cowardly in body; and that a people without a standing army may yet rise as one man, when Freedom needs defenders.

May God help us so to redeem this oppressed and bleeding State, and to bring this people back to that simple love of Liberty, without which it must die amidst its luxuries, like the sad nations of the elder world. May we gain more iron in our souls, and have it in the right place;—have soft hearts and hard wills, not as now, soft wills and hard hearts. Then will the iron break the Northern iron and the steel no longer,* and "God save the Commonwealth of Massachusetts!" will be at last a hope fulfilled.

24. Henry David Thoreau: "Slavery in Massachusetts" (1854)

This speech, delivered and published in the summer of 1854, is in a different key from that of "Resistance to Civil Government." The events of the intervening years—the passage of the new Fugitive Slave Law; the return to slavery first of Thomas Sims and then of Anthony Burns from Massachusetts soil; the passage of the Kansas-Nebraska Bill, which opened to slavery large territories that had been closed to it—all these shocks have changed Thoreau's tone. One sign of his altered mood is the aggressiveness with which he contrasts (favorably) Higginson's raid on the Boston Courthouse both with the passivity of most of the state's citizens and with the Boston Tea Party. If the earlier essay is an argument and an exhortation, this one is a denunciation, almost an angry eulogy for a Massachusetts that no longer exists. Invective and a deep discouragement take turns in challenging Thoreau's previous serenity, his optimistic, romantic faith in the securely millenarian thrust of history. The prophecies that remain are muted: "the time *may* come when man's deeds will smell as sweet" as the white water lily. While in 1848 the moral acceptability of violence under some extreme circumstances is tacitly assumed in Thoreau's respectful references to the American Revolution, by 1854 the extreme circumstances have become actual, and a readiness for violence has become explicit in Thoreau's militant language.

Reprinted from Henry David Thoreau, *The Writings of Henry David Thoreau* (Cambridge, Mass.: Riverside Press, 1894), vol. 10, pp. 179–182, 186–192, 194–195.

Much has been said about American slavery, but I think that we do not even yet realize what slavery is. If I were seriously to propose to Congress to make mankind into sausages, I have no doubt that most of the members would smile at my proposition, and if any believed me to be in earnest, they would think that I

*Jeremiah 15:12.—Ed.

proposed something much worse than Congress had ever done. But if any of them will tell me that to make a man into a sausage would be much worse,—would be any worse,—than to make him into a slave,—than it was to enact the Fugitive Slave Law, —I will accuse him of foolishness, of intellectual incapacity, of making a distinction without a difference. The one is just as sensible a proposition as the other.

I hear a good deal said about trampling this law under foot. Why, one need not go out of his way to do that. This law rises not to the level of the head or the reason; its natural habitat is in the dirt. It was born and bred, and has its life, only in the dust and mire, on a level with the feet; and he who walks with freedom, and does not with Hindoo mercy avoid treading on every venomous reptile, will inevitably tread on it, and so trample it under foot,—and Webster, its maker, with it, like the dirt-bug and its ball. . . .

It is to some extent fatal to the courts, when the people are compelled to go behind them. I do not wish to believe that the courts were made for fair weather, and for very civil cases merely; but think of leaving it to any court in the land to decide whether more than three millions of people, in this case a sixth part of a nation, have a right to be freemen or not! But it has been left to the courts of *justice*, so called,—to the Supreme Court of the land,—and, as you all know, recognizing no authority but the Constitution, it has decided that the three millions are and shall continue to be slaves. Such judges as these are merely the inspectors of a pick-lock and murderer's tools, to tell him whether they are in working order or not, and there they think that their responsibility ends. There was a prior case on the docket, which they, as judges appointed by God, had no right to skip; which having been justly settled, they would have been saved from this humiliation. It was the case of the murderer himself.

The law will never make men free; it is men who have got to make the law free. They are the lovers of law and order who observe the law when the government breaks it.

Among human beings, the judge whose words seal the fate of a man furthest into eternity is not he who merely pronounces the verdict of the law, but he, whoever he may be, who, from a love of truth, and unprejudiced by any custom or enactment of men, utters a true opinion or *sentence* concerning him. He it is that *sentences* him. Whoever can discern truth has received his commission from a higher source than the chiefest justice in the world who can discern only law. He finds himself constituted judge of the judge. Strange that it should be necessary to state such simple truths! . . .

The majority of the men of the North, and of the South and East and West, are not men of principle. If they vote, they do not send men to Congress on errands of humanity; but while their brothers and sisters are being scourged and hung for loving liberty, while—I might here insert all that slavery implies and is—it is the mismanagement of wood and iron and stone and gold which concerns them. Do what you will, O Government, with my wife and children, my mother and brother, my father and sister, I will obey your commands to the letter. It will indeed grieve me if you hurt them, if you deliver them to overseers to be hunted by hounds or to be whipped to death; but, nevertheless, I will peaceably pursue my chosen calling on this fair earth, until perchance, one day, when I have put on mourning for them dead, I shall have persuaded you to relent. Such is the attitude, such are the words of Massachusetts.*

Rather than do thus, I need not say what match I would touch, what system endeavor to blow up; but as I love my life, I would side with the light, and let the dark earth roll from under me, calling my mother and my brother to follow.

I would remind my countrymen that they are to be men first, and Americans only at a late and convenient hour. No matter how valuable law may be to protect your property, even to keep soul and body together, if it do not keep you and humanity together.

I am sorry to say that I doubt if there is a judge in Massachusetts who is prepared to resign his office, and get his living innocently, whenever it is required of him to pass sentence under a law which is merely contrary to the law of God. I am compelled

---

*This is an ironic allusion to a famous—or notorious—speech by Orville Dewey, a leading Unitarian minister, in which Dewey insisted that he would prefer the enslavement of his brother, his son, or himself to the sacrifice of the Union.—Ed.

to see that they put themselves, or rather are by character, in this respect, exactly on a level with the marine who discharges his musket in any direction he is ordered to. They are just as much tools, and as little men. Certainly, they are not the more to be respected, because their master enslaves their understandings and consciences, instead of their bodies.

The judges and lawyers,—simply as such, I mean,—and all men of expediency, try this case by a very low and incompetent standard. They consider, not whether the Fugitive Slave Law is right, but whether it is what they call *constitutional*. Is virtue constitutional, or vice? Is equity constitutional, or iniquity? In important moral and vital questions, like this, it is just as impertinent to ask whether a law is constitutional or not, as to ask whether it is profitable or not. They persist in being the servants of the worst of men, and not the servants of humanity. The question is, not whether you or your grandfather, seventy years ago, did not enter into an agreement to serve the Devil, and that service is not accordingly now due; but whether you will not now, for once and at last, serve God,—in spite of your own past recreancy, or that of your ancestor,—by obeying that eternal and only just CONSTITUTION, which He, and not any Jefferson or Adams, has written in your being.

The amount of it is, if the majority vote the Devil to be God, the minority will live and behave accordingly,—and obey the successful candidate, trusting that, some time or other, by some Speaker's casting-vote, perhaps, they may reinstate God. This is the highest principle I can get out or invent for my neighbors. These men act as if they believed that they could safely slide down a hill a little way,—or a good way,—and would surely come to a place, by and by, where they could begin to slide up again. This is expediency, or choosing that course which offers the slightest obstacles to the feet, that is, a downhill one. But there is no such thing as accomplishing a righteous reform by the use of "expediency." There is no such thing as sliding up hill. In morals the only sliders are backsliders.

. . . What is wanted is men, not of policy, but of probity,— who recognize a higher law than the Constitution, or the decision of the majority. The fate of the country does not depend on how you vote at the polls,—the worst man is as strong as the best at that game; it does not depend on what kind of paper you drop into the ballot-box once a year, but on what kind of man you drop from your chamber into the street every morning.

What should concern Massachusetts is not the Nebraska Bill, nor the Fugitive Slave Bill, but her own slaveholding and servility. Let the State dissolve her union with the slaveholder. She may wriggle and hesitate, and ask leave to read the Constitution once more; but she can find no respectable law or precedent which sanctions the continuance of such a union for an instant.

Let each inhabitant of the State dissolve his union with her, as long as she delays to do her duty.

The events of the past month teach me to distrust Fame. I see that she does not finely discriminate, but coarsely hurrahs. She considers not the simple heroism of an action, but only as it is connected with its apparent consequences. She praises till she is hoarse the easy exploit of the Boston Tea Party, but will be comparatively silent about the braver and more disinterestedly heroic attack on the Boston Court-House, simply because it was unsuccessful!

Covered with disgrace, the State has sat down coolly to try for their lives and liberties the men who attempted to do its duty for it. And this is called *justice!* They who have shown that they can behave particularly well may perchance be put under bonds for *their good behavior.* They whom truth requires at present to plead guilty are, of all the inhabitants of the State, preëminently innocent. While the Governor, and the Mayor, and countless officers of the Commonwealth are at large, the champions of liberty are imprisoned.

Only they are guiltless who commit the crime of contempt of such a court. It behooves every man to see that his influence is on the side of justice, and let the courts make their own characters. My sympathies in this case are wholly with the accused, and wholly against their accusers and judges. Justice is sweet and musical; but injustice is harsh and discordant. The judge still sits grinding at his organ, but it yields no music, and we hear only the sound of the handle. He believes that all the music resides in the handle, and the crowd toss him their coppers the same as before. . . .

Show me a free state, and a court truly of justice, and I will fight for them, if need be; but show me Massachusetts, and I refuse her my allegiance, and express contempt for her courts.

. . . We have used up all our inherited freedom. If we would
save our lives, we must fight for them.

I walk toward one of our ponds; but what signifies the beauty
of nature when men are base? We walk to lakes to see our serenity reflected in them; when we are not serene, we go not to
them. Who can be serene in a country where both the rulers
and the ruled are without principle? The remembrance of my
country spoils my walk. My thoughts are murder to the State,
and involuntarily go plotting against her.

But it chanced the other day that I scented a white water-lily,
and a season I had waited for had arrived. It is the emblem of
purity. It bursts up so pure and fair to the eye, and so sweet to
the scent, as if to show us what purity and sweetness reside in,
and can be extracted from, the slime and muck of earth. I think
I have plucked the first one that has opened for a mile. What
confirmation of our hopes is in the fragrance of this flower! I
shall not so soon despair of the world for it, notwithstanding
slavery, and the cowardice and want of principle of Northern
men. It suggests what kind of laws have prevailed longest and
widest, and still prevail, and that the time may come when
man's deeds will smell as sweet. . . .

25. Lydia Maria Child: *The Duty of Disobedience to the Fugitive Slave Act* (1860)

During her twenties Maria Child established herself as an author of
historical novels and other books and as editor of the *Juvenile Miscellany.*
In 1833, however, when she was thirty-one, she published *An Appeal in
Favor of That Class of Americans called Africans,* a sober indictment of racism and segregation as well as of slavery. Though it influenced several
important contemporaries—among them Channing, Higginson, and
Phillips—on behalf of the antislavery movement, its appearance se-
verely damaged her standing as a popular author. In the years that followed she organized abolitionist fund-raising affairs,[1] edited for a time
the *National Anti-Slavery Standard,* and wrote columns for the *Boston
Courier* which were collected in book form as *Letters from New York* and
went through eleven editions. Despite this success and some others,

she and her husband, David (a lawyer, abolitionist, and Whig editorialist), endured a long period of economic insecurity and strain.[2]

Though by 1860 polemics against the Fugitive Slave Law had been appearing for a decade, Maria Child's tract was anything but old hat. Many northern citizens were still seeking accommodation with the South; in December forty-two of the pillars of Massachusetts society published an *Address to the People of Massachusetts* which urged their fellow citizens to press the legislature not to annul the Fugitive Slave Law but on the contrary to repeal the Personal Liberty Law, which had been passed five years before as a protest and a means of defense against the federal legislation. The *Address* characterized the Personal Liberty Law as flagrantly provocative and unconstitutional; it called for an affirmation of "our constitutional duty of surrendering fugitives from service." Among the signers were James Walker and Jared Sparks, former presidents of Harvard; Benjamin Robbins Curtis, a former justice of the United States Supreme Court; Lemuel Shaw, for more than thirty years the Chief Justice of Massachusetts; and George Ticknor, famed scholar and previously a preeminent Harvard professor of modern languages.[3] These men did not by this time speak for a majority; but in so divided a community Maria Child's passionate, ironic cry—"I beseech you to let me die on Free Soil!"—placed her as far from some of her most eminent neighbors as had her other appeal, nearly three decades earlier. Eighteen-sixty was also the year, however, in which her famous correspondence with the wife of Virginia's Senator James Mason (after John Brown's raid on Harpers Ferry) found an audience that had scarcely existed in 1833 and carried her antislavery arguments into hundreds of thousands of homes.

The Duty of Disobedience tells of several episodes of extreme suffering on the part of slaves and fugitive slaves; at times the author's sympathetic imagination becomes melodramatic. But the discourse is also energized by a fine, cutting irony and a fierce, righteous anger. The latter occasionally produces an invective that can seem either excessive or rousing, as when Mrs. Child refers to supporters of the Fugitive Slave Law as "the hounds of the United States, who use the constitution for their kennel."

Reprinted from L. Maria Child, *The Duty of Disobedience to the Fugitive Slave Act: An Appeal to the Legislators of Massachusetts* (Boston: American Anti-Slavery Society, 1860), pp. 3, 4–5, 12–13, 19–23.

I feel there is no need of apologizing to the Legislature of Massachusetts because a woman addresses them. Sir Walter Scott says: "The truth of Heaven was never committed to a tongue, however feeble, but it gave a right to that tongue to announce mercy, while it declared judgment." And in view of all that women have done, and are doing, intellectually and morally, for the advancement of the world, I presume no enlightened legislator will be disposed to deny that the "truth of Heaven" *is* often committed to them, and that they sometimes utter it with a degree of power that greatly influences the age in which they live.

I therefore offer no excuses on that score. But I do feel as if it required some apology to attempt to convince men of ordinary humanity and common sense that the Fugitive Slave Bill is utterly wicked, and consequently ought never to be obeyed. Yet Massachusetts consents to that law! Some shadow of justice she grants, inasmuch as her Legislature have passed what is called a Personal Liberty Bill, securing trial by jury to those claimed as slaves. Certainly it is *something* gained, especially for those who may get brown by working in the sunshine, to prevent our Southern masters from taking any of us, at a moment's notice, and dragging us off into perpetual bondage. It is *something* gained to require legal proof that a man is a slave, before he is given up to arbitrary torture and unrecompensed toil. But is *that* the measure of justice becoming the character of a free Commonwealth? "*Prove* that the man is property, according to *your* laws, and I will drive him into your cattle-pen with sword and bayonet," is what Massachusetts practically says to Southern tyrants. "Show me a Bill of Sale from the Almighty!" is what she *ought* to say. No other proof should be considered valid in a Christian country.

. . . Here, in the noon-day light of the nineteenth century, in a nation claiming to be the freest and most enlightened on the face of the globe, a portion of the population of fifteen States have thus agreed among themselves: "Other men shall work for us, without wages, while we smoke, and drink, and gamble, and race horses, and fight. We will have their wives and daughters for concubines, and sell their children in the market with horses and pigs. If they make any objection to this arrangement, we will break them into subjection with the cow-hide and the bucking-paddle. They shall not be permitted to read or write, because that would be likely to 'produce dissatisfaction in their minds.' If they attempt to run away from us, our blood-hounds shall tear the flesh from their bones, and any man who sees them may shoot them down like mad dogs. If they succeed in getting beyond our frontier, into States where it is the custom to pay men for their work, and to protect their wives and children from outrage, we will compel the people of those States to drive them back into the jaws of our blood-hounds."

And what do the people of the other eighteen States of that enlightened country answer to this monstrous demand? What says Massachusetts, with the free blood of the Puritans coursing in her veins, and with the sword uplifted in her right hand, to procure "peaceful repose under liberty"? Massachusetts answers: "O yes. We will be your blood-hounds, and pay our own expenses. Only prove to our satisfaction that the stranger who has taken refuge among us is one of the men you have agreed among yourselves to whip into working without wages, and we will hunt him back for you. Only prove to us that this woman, who has run away from your harem, was bought for a concubine, that you might get more drinking-money by the sale of the children she bears you, and our soldiers will hunt her back with alacrity."

Shame on my native State! Everlasting shame! Blot out the escutcheon of the brave old Commonwealth! Instead of the sword uplifted to protect liberty, let the slave-driver's whip be suspended over a blood-hound, and take for your motto, Obedience to tyrants is the highest law.

Legislators of Massachusetts, can it be that you really understand what Slavery *is*, and yet consent that a fugitive slave, who seeks protection here, shall be driven back to that dismal house of bondage? For sweet charity's sake, I must suppose that you have been too busy with your farms and your merchandise ever to have imagined yourself in the situation of a slave. . . .

All of you have doubtless read some accounts of what these unhappy men and women have dared and endured. Do you never put yourselves in their stead, and imagine how *you* would feel, under similar circumstances? Not long ago, a young man escaped from slavery by clinging night and day to the under part of a steamboat, drenched by water, and suffering for food. He was discovered and sent back. If the Constitution of the

United States sanctioned such an outrage upon *you*, what would *you* think of those who answered your entreaties and remonstrances by saying, "Our fathers made an agreement with the man who robs you of your wages and your freedom. It is law; and it is your duty to submit to it patiently"? I think you would *then* perceive the necessity of having the Constitution forthwith amended; and if it were not done very promptly, I apprehend you would appeal vociferously to a higher law. . . .

Many of you have heard of William and Ellen Craft, a pious and intelligent couple, who escaped from bondage some years ago. She disguised herself in male attire, and passed for a white gentleman, taking her darker colored husband with her as a servant. When the Fugitive Slave Act went into operation, they received warning that the hounds were on their track. They sought temporary refuge in the house of my noble-hearted friend, Ellis Gray Loring, who then resided in the vicinity of Boston. He and his family were absent for some days; but a lady in the house invited Mr. Craft to come in and stay till they returned. "No, I thank you," he replied. "There is a heavy fine for sheltering fugitives; and it would not be right to subject Mr. Loring to it without his consent." "But you know he is a true friend to the slaves," urged the lady. "If he were at home, I am sure he would not hesitate to incur the penalty." "Because he is such a good friend to my oppressed race, there is all the more reason why I should not implicate him in my affairs, without his knowledge," replied this nobleman of nature. His wife had slept but little the previous night, having been frightened by dreams of Daniel Webster chasing her husband, pistol in hand. The evening was stormy, and she asked him if they could not remain there till morning. "It would not be right, Ellen," he replied; and with tears in her eyes, they went forth into the darkness and rain. Was *that* a man to be treated like a chattel? How many white gentlemen are there, who, in circumstances as perilous, would have manifested such nicety of moral perception, such genuine delicacy of feeling? England has kindly received that worthy and persecuted couple. All who set foot on *her* soil are free. Would to God it were so in Massachusetts!

It is well known that Southerners have repeatedly declared they do not demand fugitives merely to recover articles of property, or for the sake of making an example of them, to inspire terror in other runaways; that they have a still stronger motive, which is, to humiliate the North; to make them feel that no latitude limits their mastership. Have we no honest pride, that we so tamely submit to this? What lethargic disease has fallen on Northern souls, that they dare not be as bold for Freedom as tyrants are for Slavery? . . .

What satisfactory reasons can be alleged for submitting to this degradation? . . . Suppose the descendants of Ham were ordained to be slaves to the end of time, for an offence committed thousands of years ago, by a progenitor they never heard of. Still, the greatest amount of theological research leaves it very uncertain who the descendants of Ham are, and where they are. I presume you would not consider the title even to one acre of land satisfactorily settled by evidence of such extremely dubious character; how much less, then, a man's ownership of himself! . . .

If you resort to the alleged legal obligation to return fugitives, it has more plausibility, but has it in reality any firm foundation? Americans boast of making their own laws, and of amending them whenever circumstances render it necessary. How, then, can they excuse themselves, or expect the civilized world to excuse them, for making, or sustaining, unjust and cruel laws? The Fugitive Slave Act has none of the attributes of law. If two highwaymen agreed between themselves to stand by each other in robbing helpless men, women and children, should we not find it hard work to "conquer our prejudices" so far as to dignify their bargain with the name of *law*? That is the light in which the compact between North and South presents itself to the minds of intelligent slaves, and we should view it in the same way, if we were in their position. . . . It commands what is wrong, and forbids what is right. It commands us to trample on the weak and defenceless, to persecute the oppressed, to be accomplices in defrauding honest laborers of their wages. It forbids us to shelter the homeless, to protect abused innocence, to feed the hungry, to "hide the outcast." Let theological casuists argue as they will, Christian hearts *will* shrink from thinking of Jesus as surrendering a fugitive slave; or of any of his apostles, unless it be Judas. Political casuists may exercise their skill in making the worse appear the better reason, still all honest minds have an intuitive perception that no human enactment which violates God's laws is worthy of respect. . . .

There is another consideration, which ought alone to have sufficient weight with us to deter us from attempting to carry out this tyrannical enactment. All history, and all experience, show it to be an immutable law of God, that whosoever injures another, injures himself in the process. These frequent scuffles between despotism and freedom, with despotism shielded by law, cannot otherwise than demoralize our people. They unsettle the popular mind concerning eternal principles of justice. They harden the heart by familiarity with violence. They accustom people to the idea that it is right for Capital to own Labor; and thus the reverence for Liberty, which we inherited from our fathers, will gradually die out in the souls of our children. We are compelled to disobey our own consciences, and repress all our humane feelings, or else to disobey the law. It is a grievous wrong done to the people to place them between these alternatives. The inevitable result is to destroy the sanctity of law. The doctrine that "might makes right," which our rulers consent to teach the people, in order to pacify slaveholders, will come out in unexpected forms to disturb our own peace and safety. There is "even-handed justice" in the fact that men cannot aid in enslaving others, and themselves remain free; that they cannot assist in robbing others, without endangering their own security.

Moreover, there is wrong done, even to the humblest individual, when he is compelled to be ashamed of his country. . . . The tears of a secluded woman, who has no vote to give, may appear to you of little consequence. But assuredly it is not well with any Commonwealth, when her daughters weep over her degeneracy and disgrace.

In the name of oppressed humanity, of violated religion, of desecrated law, of tarnished honor, of our own freedom endangered, of the moral sense of our people degraded by these evil influences, I respectfully, but most urgently, entreat you to annul this infamous enactment, so far as the jurisdiction of Massachusetts extends. Our old Commonwealth has been first and foremost in many good works; let her lead in this also. And deem it not presumptuous, if I ask it likewise for my own sake.

I am a humble member of the community; but I am deeply interested in the welfare and reputation of my native State, and that gives me some claim to be heard. I am growing old; and on this great question of equal rights I have toiled for years, sometimes with a heart sickened by "hope deferred." I beseech you to let me die on Free Soil! . . .

If you cannot be induced to reform this great wickedness, for the sake of outraged justice and humanity, then do it for the honor of the State, for the political welfare of our own people, for the moral character of our posterity. For, as sure as there is a Righteous Ruler in the heavens, if you continue to be accomplices in violence and fraud, God will *not* "save the Commonwealth of Massachusetts."

IV DISOBEDIENT FEMINISTS

We do not wish to make any plea before this court. We do not consider ourselves subject to this court, since as an unenfranchised class we have nothing to do with the making of the laws which have put us in this position.

—Alice Paul, 1917

26. Elizabeth Cady Stanton, Lucretia Mott, and others: "Declaration of Sentiments and Resolutions of the First Woman's Rights Convention" (1848)

The organizers of the first Woman's Rights Convention, held in Seneca Falls, New York, in July 1848, had epochal objectives. "The Declaration and resolutions in the very first convention," the *History of Woman Suffrage* observes, "demanded all [that] the most radical friends of the movement have since claimed"; and Frederick Douglass told the readers of his *North Star* that the declaration was "to be regarded as the basis of a grand movement for attaining the civil, social, political, and religious rights of women."[1] The scope of the enterprise was reflected in the choice of the Declaration of Independence as the rhetorical model for the convention's manifesto.

Yet the moment had its ironies—among them the women's installation of James Mott, Lucretia's husband, as the convention's presiding officer—and though the sustained allusion to Jefferson's Declaration provided a revolutionary idiom for revolutionary aspirations, still the program the convention envisioned was largely political and reformist. The only one of the resolutions to be contested was the one espousing woman suffrage; it was adopted by a narrow majority over the dissent of Mrs. Mott and others, who feared that its radicalism would discredit the entire occasion.

The propositions that historically have proved to be the most enduringly difficult and controversial were adopted unanimously. Prominent among them are the first two resolutions, which provide a theoretical touchstone for the later challenges to law of Susan B. Anthony and Abby Smith. They also have kinship with the natural-rights logic of disobedience argued by Theodore Parker,[2] and with the thought of Martin Luther King, Jr., whose definition of an unjust law as one in which "difference is made legal" is very close in spirit to the positions that the Seneca Falls convention affirmed.

❀ Reprinted from Elizabeth Cady Stanton, Susan B. Anthony, and Matilda Joslyn Gage, eds., *History of Woman Suffrage* (New York: Fowler & Wells, 1881), vol. 1, pp. 70–73.

Declaration of Sentiments

When, in the course of human events, it becomes necessary for one portion of the family of man to assume among the people of the earth a position different from that which they have hitherto occupied, but one to which the laws of nature and of nature's God entitle them, a decent respect to the opinions of mankind requires that they should declare the causes that impel them to such a course.

We hold these truths to be self-evident: that all men and women are created equal; that they are endowed by their Creator with certain inalienable rights; that among these are life, liberty, and the pursuit of happiness; that to secure these rights governments are instituted, deriving their just powers from the consent of the governed. Whenever any form of government becomes destructive of these ends, it is the right of those who suffer from it to refuse allegiance to it, and to insist upon the institution of a new government, laying its foundation on such principles, and organizing its powers in such form, as to them shall seem most likely to effect their safety and happiness. Prudence, indeed, will dictate that governments long established should not be changed for light and transient causes; and accordingly all experience hath shown that mankind are more disposed to suffer, while evils are sufferable, than to right themselves by abolishing the forms to which they were accustomed. But when a long train of abuses and usurpations, pursuing invariably the same object evinces a design to reduce them under absolute despotism, it is their duty to throw off such government, and to provide new guards for their future security. Such has been the patient sufferance of the women under this government, and such is now the necessity which constrains them to demand the equal station to which they are entitled.

The history of mankind is a history of repeated injuries and usurpations on the part of man toward woman, having in direct object the establishment of an absolute tyranny over her. To prove this, let facts be submitted to a candid world.

He has never permitted her to exercise her inalienable right to the elective franchise.

He has compelled her to submit to laws, in the formation of which she had no voice.

He has withheld from her rights which are given to the most ignorant and degraded men—both natives and foreigners.

Having deprived her of this first right of a citizen, the elective franchise, thereby leaving her without representation in the halls of legislation, he has oppressed her on all sides.

He has made her, if married, in the eye of the law, civilly dead.

He has taken from her all right in property, even to the wages she earns.

He has made her, morally, an irresponsible being, as she can commit many crimes with impunity, provided they be done in the presence of her husband. In the covenant of marriage, she is compelled to promise obedience to her husband, he becoming, to all intents and purposes, her master—the law giving him power to deprive her of her liberty, and to administer chastisement.

He has so framed the laws of divorce, as to what shall be the proper causes, and in case of separation, to whom the guardianship of the children shall be given, as to be wholly regardless of the happiness of women—the law, in all cases, going upon a false supposition of the supremacy of man, and giving all power into his hands.

After depriving her of all rights as a married woman, if single, and the owner of property, he has taxed her to support a government which recognizes her only when her property can be made profitable to it.

He has monopolized nearly all the profitable employments, and from those she is permitted to follow, she receives but a scanty remuneration. He closes against her all the avenues to wealth and distinction which he considers most honorable to himself. As a teacher of theology, medicine, or law, she is not known.

He has denied her the facilities for obtaining a thorough education, all colleges being closed against her.

He allows her in Church, as well as State, but a subordinate position, claiming Apostolic authority for her exclusion from the ministry, and, with some exceptions, from any public participation in the affairs of the Church.

He has created a false public sentiment by giving to the world a different code of morals for men and women, by which moral delinquencies which exclude women from society, are not only tolerated, but deemed of little account in man.

He has usurped the prerogative of Jehovah himself, claiming it as his right to assign for her a sphere of action, when that belongs to her conscience and to her God.

He has endeavored, in every way that he could, to destroy her confidence in her own powers, to lessen her self-respect, and to make her willing to lead a dependent and abject life.

Now, in view of this entire disfranchisement of one-half the people of this country, their social and religious degradation—in view of the unjust laws above mentioned, and because women do feel themselves aggrieved, oppressed, and fraudulently deprived of their most sacred rights, we insist that they have immediate admission to all the rights and privileges which belong to them as citizens of the United States.

In entering upon the great work before us, we anticipate no small amount of misconception, misrepresentation, and ridicule; but we shall use every instrumentality within our power to effect our object. We shall employ agents, circulate tracts, petition the State and National legislatures, and endeavor to enlist the pulpit and the press in our behalf. We hope this Convention will be followed by a series of Conventions embracing every part of the country.

Resolutions

WHEREAS, The great precept of nature is conceded to be, that "man shall pursue his own true and substantial happiness." Blackstone in his Commentaries remarks, that this law of Nature being coeval with mankind, and dictated by God himself, is of course superior in obligation to any other. It is binding over all the globe, in all countries and at all times; no human laws are of any validity if contrary to this, and such of them as are valid, derive all their force, and all their validity, and all their authority, mediately and immediately, from this original; therefore,

Resolved, That such laws as conflict, in any way, with the true and substantial happiness of woman, are contrary to the great precept of nature and of no validity, for this is "superior in obligation to any other."

Resolved, That all laws which prevent woman from occupying such a station in society as her conscience shall dictate, or which place her in a position inferior to that of man, are contrary to the great precept of nature, and therefore of no force or authority.

Resolved, That woman is man's equal—was intended to be so by the Creator, and the highest good of the race demands that she should be recognized as such.

Resolved, That the women of this country ought to be enlightened in regard to the laws under which they live, that they may no longer publish their degradation by declaring themselves satisfied with their present position, nor their ignorance, by asserting that they have all the rights they want.

Resolved, That inasmuch as man, while claiming for himself intellectual superiority, does accord to woman moral superiority, it is pre-eminently his duty to encourage her to speak and teach, as she has an opportunity, in all religious assemblies.

Resolved, That the same amount of virtue, delicacy, and refinement of behavior that is required of woman in the social state, should also be required of man, and the same transgressions should be visited with equal severity on both man and woman.

Resolved, That the objection of indelicacy and impropriety, which is so often brought against woman when she addresses a public audience, comes with a very ill-grace from those who encourage, by their attendance, her appearance on the stage, in the concert, or in feats of the circus.

Resolved, That woman has too long rested satisfied in the circumscribed limits which corrupt customs and a perverted application of the Scriptures have marked out for her, and that it is time she should move in the enlarged sphere which her great Creator has assigned her.

Resolved, That it is the duty of the women of this country to secure to themselves their sacred right to the elective franchise.

Resolved, That the equality of human rights results necessarily from the fact of the identity of the race in capabilities and responsibilities.

Resolved, therefore, That, being invested by the Creator with the same capabilities, and the same consciousness of responsibility for their exercise, it is demonstrably the right and duty of woman, equally with man, to promote every righteous cause by every righteous means; and especially in regard to the great subjects of morals and religion, it is self-evidently her right to participate with her brother in teaching them, both in private and in public, by writing and by speaking, by any instrumentalities proper to be used, and in any assemblies proper to be held; and this being a self-evident truth growing out of the divinely implanted principles of human nature, any custom or authority adverse to it, whether modern or wearing the hoary sanction of antiquity, is to be regarded as a self-evident falsehood, and at war with mankind.

Resolved, That the speedy success of our cause depends upon the zealous and untiring efforts of both men and women, for the overthrow of the monopoly of the pulpit, and for the securing to woman an equal participation with men in the various trades, professions, and commerce.

27. Susan B. Anthony: Statement to the Court (1873)

From 1871 until a decisively adverse ruling by the Supreme Court in 1875, the National Woman Suffrage Association maintained the position that no new constitutional amendment was necessary to achieve the vote for women—that they were already enfranchised under the Fourteenth Amendment.[1] The association therefore urged its members and other women to attempt to register to vote, and if possible to vote, in the expectation that denials by registrars and election officials could lead to lawsuits that might secure favorable action in the courts.[2] With this strategy in mind, and also in the passionate conviction that as citizens American women were indeed entitled to vote, Susan B. Anthony and fourteen other women in Rochester, New York, succeeded in registering and voting in the election of 1872—whereupon a criminal indictment was handed down on the grounds that they "did knowingly, wrongfully and unlawfully vote . . . without having a lawful right to vote."[3] After a bitterly contested trial in which several dubious rulings were made by an apparently prejudiced judge (among other things he effectively usurped the jury's role of rendering a verdict in a criminal case), Susan Anthony was convicted and fined $100 plus costs. She never paid the fine, however, refusing to acquiesce in what her followers called "an example of authority overriding law." [4]

Since Susan Anthony's counsel argued throughout her trial that her actions had all been entirely law-abiding (at least in intention), she will seem at first not to be an advocate of civil disobedience at all. Yet the language of her statement to the court (reprinted here) implies her support for such disobedience. Her exercise of the franchise was an act of principle that transcended all legal and constitutional strategies. For one thing, she refused to post bail because she was "determined not to recognize the right of the courts to interfere with her exercise of the franchise," [5] and in any case her approach to the issues of her trial contains a large measure of ambiguity and contingency. Her view that the Fourteenth Amendment had already enfranchised her was based on the principle that "'anything for human rights is constitutional, everything against human rights unconstitutional'" [6]—a position that needless to say can easily lead (as it did in her case) to private assessments of a statute's validity at odds with those of the Supreme Court. Her argument thus points toward lawbreaking that is simultaneously a constitutional appeal and a symbolic protest. Her use in her statement at the trial of "unjust" and "unconstitutional" as all but synonymous terms is a corollary of this argument; in adopting it Susan Anthony essentially left to the courts the practical judgment whether she had acted lawfully or disobediently, at the same time that she continued to insist that whatever the courts did, her own position and behavior were securely rooted in equity and justice. She is therefore one of a large company of Americans who, in placing themselves in conflict with the police and the courts, have insisted that at least in principle the law was on their side—conscientious lawbreakers convinced that the true disobedients were the holders and abusers of power. [7]

Reprinted from Elizabeth Cady Stanton, Susan B. Anthony, and Matilda Joslyn Gage, eds., *History of Woman Suffrage* (New York: Fowler & Wells, 1881), vol. 2, pp. 687–689.

THE COURT: The prisoner will stand up. Has the prisoner anything to say why sentence shall not be pronounced?

MISS ANTHONY: Yes, your honor, I have many things to say; for in your ordered verdict of guilty, you have trampled underfoot, every vital principle of our government. My natural rights, my civil rights, my political rights, are all alike ignored. Robbed of the fundamental privilege of citizenship, I am degraded from the status of a citizen to that of a subject; and not only myself individually, but all of my sex, are, by your honor's verdict, doomed to political subjection under this so-called republican government.

JUDGE HUNT: The Court can not listen to a rehearsal of arguments the prisoner's counsel has already consumed three hours in presenting.

MISS ANTHONY: May it please your honor, I am not arguing the question, but simply stating the reasons why sentence can not, in justice, be pronounced against me. Your denial of my citizen's right to vote is the denial of my right of consent as one of the governed, the denial of my right of representation as one of the taxed, the denial of my right to a trial by a jury of my peers as an offender against law, therefore, the denial of my sacred rights to life, liberty, property, and—

JUDGE HUNT: The Court can not allow the prisoner to go on.

MISS ANTHONY: But your honor will not deny me this one and only poor privilege of protest against this high-handed outrage upon my citizen's rights. May it please the Court to remember that since the day of my arrest last November, this is the first time that either myself or any person of my disfranchised class has been allowed a word of defense before judge or jury—

JUDGE HUNT: The prisoner must sit down; the Court can not allow it.

MISS ANTHONY: Of all my prosecutors, from the 8th Ward corner grocery politician, who entered the complaint, to the United States Marshal, Commissioner, District Attorney, District Judge, your honor on the bench, not one is my peer, but each and all are my political sovereigns; and had your honor submitted my case to the jury, as was clearly your duty, even then I should have had just cause of protest, for not one of those men was my peer; but, native or foreign, white or black, rich or poor, educated or ignorant, awake or asleep, sober or drunk, each and every man of them was my political superior; hence, in no sense, my peer. Even, under such circumstances, a commoner of England tried before a jury of lords, would have far less cause to complain than [have] I, a woman, tried before a jury of men. Even my counsel, the Hon. Henry R. Selden, who has argued my cause so ably, so earnestly, so unanswerably before your honor, is my political sovereign. Precisely as no disfranchised person is entitled to sit upon a jury, and no woman is entitled to the franchise, so, none but a regularly admitted lawyer is allowed to practice in the courts, and no woman can gain admission to the bar—hence, jury, judge, counsel, must all be of the superior class.

JUDGE HUNT: The Court must insist—the prisoner has been tried according to the established forms of law.

MISS ANTHONY: Yes, your honor, but by forms of law all made by men, interpreted by men, administered by men, in favor of men, and against women; and hence, your honor's ordered verdict of guilty, against a United States citizen for the exercise of "that citizen's right to vote," simply because that citizen was a woman and not a man. But, yesterday, the same man-made forms of law declared it a crime punishable with $1,000 fine and six months' imprisonment, for you, or me, or any of us, to give a cup of cold water, a crust of bread, or a night's shelter to a panting fugitive as he was tracking his way to Canada. And every man or woman in whose veins coursed a drop of human sympathy violated that wicked law, reckless of consequences, and was justified in so doing. As then the slaves who got their freedom [had to] take it over, or under, or through the unjust forms of law, precisely so now must women, to get their right to a voice in this Government, take it; and I have taken mine, and mean to take it at every possible opportunity.

JUDGE HUNT: The Court orders the prisoner to sit down. It will not allow another word.

MISS ANTHONY: When I was brought before your honor for trial, I hoped for a broad and liberal interpretation of the Constitution and its recent amendments, that should declare all United States citizens under its protecting aegis—that should declare equality of rights the national guarantee to all persons born or naturalized in the United States. But failing to get this justice— failing, even, to get a trial by a jury *not* of my peers—I ask not leniency at your hands—but rather the full rigors of the law.

JUDGE HUNT: The Court must insist— (Here the prisoner sat down.)

JUDGE HUNT: The prisoner will stand up. (Here Miss Anthony arose again.) The sentence of the Court is that you pay a fine of one hundred dollars and the costs of the prosecution.

MISS ANTHONY: May it please your honor, I shall never pay a dollar of your unjust penalty. All the stock in trade I possess is a $10,000 debt, incurred by publishing my paper—*The Revolution*—four years ago, the sole object of which was to educate all women to do precisely as I have done, rebel against your man-made, unjust, unconstitutional forms of law, that tax, fine, imprison, and hang women, while they deny them the right of representation in the Government; and I shall work on with might and main to pay every dollar of that honest debt, but not a penny shall go to this unjust claim. And I shall earnestly and persistently continue to urge all women to the practical recognition of the old revolutionary maxim, that "Resistance to tyranny is obedience to God."

28. Abby Smith: Speeches and Letters (1873–1874)

Abby and Julia Smith were raised on their family's farm in Glastonbury, Connecticut, by parents given to religious independence and abolitionism; but they were in their seventies and eighties when they became determined (and famous) activists. Abby apparently began to attend suffrage meetings in 1869; four years later, when she was seventy-six, she went to New York to a woman's congress, came home, and the next month refused to pay her property taxes unless she was given a vote in the town meeting. Together with her more diffident sister Julia, she maintained this resistance for the rest of her life, refusing to be deterred by forced sales of her cattle (which she bought back at auction) and land.[1]

Abby Smith's determination had been spurred in part by the decision of the Glastonbury tax assessor in 1872 to raise a few tax bills but not others, all of the increases being levied against women. The following year Julia was still inclined not to resist, but she was won over:

> My sister who has the most courage of the two, and seemed to think almost the whole of our native town friendly to us, declared she was not going to be so unjustly used, without tell-

ing of it. I warned her of the consequences, and as we had so short a time to stay here, we had better submit; and asked how she would do it? She said, when the men met in town meeting. I at last consented to go with her to the town hall, she having written better than I thought possible.[2]

Julia kept a scrapbook record of their contest, which she eventually published in 1877, the year after she brought out her translation of the Bible from Latin, Greek, and Hebrew. By then the sisters (and their cows) were more or less national figures, attracting some inevitable amusement even among their sympathizers but having won a respectful following as well. Julia herself was not blind to the incongruous aspects of their situation. In Washington in 1876, at a meeting of men and women who supported woman suffrage, Julia, then eighty-three, spoke dryly of their two remaining cows, Taxey, who was aggressive and insistent, and Votey, who though "quiet and shy . . . is growing more docile and domesticated every day"; "and it is my opinion, that in a very short time, wherever you find Taxey there Votey will be also."[3]

Reprinted from Julia Smith, *Abby Smith and Her Cows, with a Report of the Law Case Decided Contrary to Law* (Hartford, Conn., 1877), pp. 9–11, 32–33.

It is not without due deliberation that we have been willing to attend this meeting, but we had no other way of coming before the men of the town. Others, our neighbours, can complain more effectually than we can, without speaking a word, when they think those who rule over them rule with injustice; but we are not put under the laws of the land as they are—we are wholly in the power of those we have come to address. You have the power over our property to take it from us whenever you choose, and we can have no voice in the matter whatever, not even to say what shall be done with it, and no power to appeal to; we are perfectly defenseless. Can you wonder, then, we should wish to speak with you? People do not generally hold power without exercising it, and those who exercise it do not appear to have the least idea of its injustice. The Southern slaveholder only possessed the same power that you have to rule over us. "Happy dog," he would say of his slave, "I have given him everything; I am the slave, and he the master; does he complain? give him ten lashes." The slaveholders really thought they had done so much for their slaves they would not leave them, when the great consideration was, the slave wanted the control of his own earnings; and so does every human being of what rightfully belongs to him. We do not suppose the men of the town think they have done so much for us that they have a right to take our money when they please. But then there is always excuse enough where there is power. They say all the property of the town should be taxed for the expenses of the town, according to its valuation, and as taxation without representation is wrong, they give permission to a part of these owners to say what valuation shall be made, and how the money can best be applied for their benefit. They meet together to consult who among them shall have the offices of the town and what salary they will give them. All this is done without ever consulting or alluding to the other part of the owners of this property. But they tax the other owners and take from them just what amount they please. We had two hundred dollars taken from us in this way the past year, by the same power the robber takes his money, because we are defenceless and cannot resist. But the robber would have the whole community against him, and he would not be apt to come but once; but from the men of our town we are never safe—they can come in and take our money from us just when they choose. Now, we cannot see any justice, any right, or any reason in this thing. . . . Is it any more just to take a woman's property without her consent, than it is to take a man's property without his consent? Those whom the town put over us are the very dregs of society, those who are making the town and their families continual expense and trouble, for which we are liable, and the authorities make the town pay the expense of meeting to take off their poll tax, for they can't pay a dollar; and they have taken some from the insane retreat and kept them in a barn over night to vote the next day. Now all these things clearly prove how much more these lawless men are valued by the town than such citizens as we are, who never make it the least trouble or expense. Such men as these are set over us and can vote away our property; indeed, our property is liable for their support. Now all we ask of the town is to put us on an equality with these men, not to rule over them as they rule over us, but to be put on an equality with them. Is this an unreasonable request? Do we not stand on an equality with them, and every man in this assembly, before the law of God? God is a God of justice; men and women stand alike in his sight; he has but one law for both. And why should man [not] have but one law for both, to which both shall be accountable alike? Let each rise if they can by their own ability, and put no obstructions in their way. Is it right because men are the strongest, that they should go into the women's houses and take their money from them, knowing they cannot resist? It is not physical strength that makes a town prosper; it is mind; it is capability to guide the physical strength and put its resources to the best possible advantage. You are rejecting just half of the very element you need. . . . No woman concerns herself about the government of the town; being placed under the men, instead of being placed under the laws, their whole business is to please the men as the slave's business is to please his master, because their living comes from the men; the laws are such that they can get it in no other way. The motto of our government is "Proclaim liberty to all the inhabitants of the land," and here where liberty is so highly extolled and gloried by every man in it, one-half the inhabitants are not put under her laws, but are ruled over by the other half, who can by their own laws, not hers, take from the other half all they possess. How is Liberty pleased with such worship? Would she not be apt to think of her own sex?

This assembly have put such men as Judge Hunt over us, to fine a woman one hundred dollars for doing what is an honor for a man to do, and denied us a trial by jury. This is the highest court in the land made by your votes. . . . Money . . . is taken from us and every other woman in the place, to strengthen the power of those that rule over us. It is taken to pay the men for making laws to govern us, by which they themselves would not be governed under any consideration. Neither would we, if we could help it. Some of it is given to buy votes which add to their power. A man's wife told me they gave her husband four dollars, which kept him drunk a long time to abuse his family. His wife said if she could vote, her vote would be as good as her husband's, and the men which came after him to carry him to the polls would treat her as well as they treated him. Her hard earnings could not be taken for his drams. . . .

.   .   .

. . . The roads make the most complaint to every woman that owns property; they all know as well as we do, that they would not be made as they are before their houses if they could vote. . . .

Why should we be outlawed? We should be glad to stay in our homestead where we were born and have always lived, the little time we have to stay, and to be buried with our family and ancestors, but its pleasantness is gone, for we know we do not hold it in security as our neighbors hold theirs; that it is liable to be taken from us whenever the town sees fit.

The town collector called for our taxes on Monday at sunset—the last day and hour he could call. We told him we would prefer to wait till we had been heard by the town, for if they gave us no hopes of voting, we wanted them to sell our farm for the taxes, for it was but reasonable, if they owned it, to get the taxes from it, we could not; and we wished they would begin at the east end and come into the street, for we wanted to save our homestead while we lived, and thought it would last us. He said he hoped he should not be the collector then. He agreed to all the injustice of which we complained. . . . [He] said, as many do, he thought women that had property ought to vote. We said those that had none needed it more. . . .

.   .   .

We come before you, gentlemen, in no spirit of defiance, but as fellow-citizens with you of the same place, having the [same] interests with yourselves and the same love for the prosperity of the town. We wanted to see you and to reason with you, desiring that the difficulty which has arisen between us might be settled among ourselves, as brethren and sisters of the same family, to the satisfaction of both. We shall agree that towns should be regulated as families are regulated, that a natural feeling of affinity may exist among all that compose the household. If we are all of one family, would it not be well to look to our own individual families, to see how its members are dealt by?

The first thing you will observe among them is, that each claims his or her own things, with which the other is not allowed to meddle. Unless this right is accorded to every one, there will be no peace among them, there will be no living together. The first thing a child says is "It is mine!" and will scream and fight to have it taken away from him by violence, though he will give it up by persuasion. There is no difference between boys and girls in this respect; the girls will yield their things no sooner than the boys. There is the same mind in both, for, being born of the same parents, they must have the same mind,—like produces like throughout the world. It is the mind we value. One is as necessary to the welfare of the whole family as the other; their advice and counsel must both be sought, for both are equally interested. What do we say of those young men that forsake the society of their sisters, and counsel together without them? We all know their way leads to ruin. But what should we say if the brothers should by agreement, without consulting their sisters, take their sisters' property from them whenever they chose, and as much as they chose, alleging as an excuse, they had made a law among themselves they would do it. Are their sisters bound by such a law? Are *we* bound by such a law? The case is precisely the same. You all know it is not just. It is not doing as you would be done by, and as you are done by. We are perfectly willing to share the expenses of this large family equally with you, but as unwilling as you are, to be ruled over and have our property taken from us by force.

We have had sad experience of this power that rules over us to take whatever we own from us, and as much as it chooses to take. We have had sad experience of being under no law but the irresponsible will of the men of the town, whose interest it is to take our property. We thought they would allow us to own our cows, that we had raised with our own hands. But they tied up those young animals seven days and seven nights in a close place, seven of them,—having never been tied before,—without hay or water, near by, and whether they were supplied with either could not be known by those that put them there, living several miles off, and at last driven to the sign-post to be sold to the highest bidder. All this was more trying to our feelings than any act that was ever done to us. And to whom was it done? To two lone women, standing by themselves,—the last of their family, among the town's oldest inhabitants, having no relatives to take their part, and none to stand up for them. And by whom was it done? By their natural protectors (they having had no brothers), into whose hands they were paying more in money, as appears by the collector's books, than any other of the town's three thousand inhabitants were paying—and these men knew, when doing it, there could be no redress for us, and no appeal. And for what was it done? Because we refused to give them any more money till they allowed us to stand on an equality with themselves. No such deed as this has ever been done, to our knowledge, since the declaration of independence, making that instrument a nullity.

And how was it looked upon by the men of the nation?—to say nothing of the women—men who possess the same power that you have; for this case has gone from Maine to California and to Oregon, throughout the land, and the men have shown the same spirit of our forefathers of 100 years ago, when they declared on a like occasion that "resistance to tyrants is obedience to God." They have shown their belief in that doctrine by not only assisting us at once, but giving us every assurance to stand by us "to the bitter end." For we are standing, they say, on the foundation on which all our liberties are built that "taxation without representation is tyranny," and "governments derive their just powers from the consent of the governed." Will this spirit ever be put down? It was not put down, one hundred years ago, and there is no probability it can ever be done at this time. To make a distinction between mankind and womankind, when one cannot exist without the other, that man should take all the great privileges and allow her no share, but her money must be taken to pay all the expenses of these privileges, though she must never enjoy them. The government of this town is supported by her money, while it allows her no pay from the emoluments of its offices. These the men take. Is it not wholly contrary to any idea of honor that men profess, to say nothing of honesty, for the men to take the women's money to spend without her participation?—depriving her of every honored

right that they would give up their lives rather than lose themselves! Can any low-lived plunder be equal to this?

We pray you, brethren,—for our natural affection still remains,—leave off this plunder, and give unto us our rights,—
those rights we have inherited, together with you, "from nature
and nature's God,"—the right to the same liberty that you possess, the right to stand on the same platform, to partake with
you of the same privileges. We have the same minds, the same
intellect. It is intellect that rules the world. Give unto us the
comfort of replying to those who offer to speak for us to the
king, "We dwell among our own people." God's laws are fulfilled by love,—let man's be so impartial that they can be fulfilled in the same way.

29. Militant Suffragists Picket President Wilson (1917)

In the first years of Woodrow Wilson's presidency, suffragists of
the Congressional Union for Woman Suffrage and the Woman's Party,
led by Alice Paul, succeeded in making the passage of the National
Suffrage Amendment a live issue in Congress.[1] Their methods, though
they were pursued with rare energy and persistence, were more or less
traditional ones—deputations, petitions, lobbying, political organizing
in the states where women already had the vote, demonstrations. By
the beginning of Wilson's second term, however, convinced that only a
strong exercise of presidential power could overcome congressional
resistance and that Wilson himself did not wish to make such a commitment, militant suffragists began a new program of increasingly
dramatic forms of symbolic protest. Throughout most of 1917 they
picketed the White House, carrying banners that read, "Mr. President!
How long must women wait for liberty?"[2]

Such methods were at first unsettling but not intolerable. The picketers were criticized not only by antisuffragists but by prosuffrage senators and by the moderate leadership of the National American Woman
Suffrage Association. In the press and elsewhere they were described
as politically naive, as "unwomanly," "unsexed," and "shameless";
their banners were "an insult to the President."[3] Still, even after the

United States declared war on Germany early in April, the picketing was allowed to continue.

But by early summer the banners had become more provocative: "Kaiser Wilson! Have you forgotten how you sympathized with the poor Germans because they were not self-governed? 20,000,000 American women are not self-governed. Take the beam out of your own eye."[4] Whatever their effect on the president himself, such taunts led to considerable roughness from onlookers, many of whom were servicemen. Banners were grabbed away and destroyed; picketers were knocked down and bruised; police protection was negligible or nil, or worse. The entire situation became too aggravated to ignore. In the next several months hundreds of women were arrested (on arbitrary charges of "obstructing traffic") and scores jailed. Owing to conditions of imprisonment that may be charitably described as substandard, the sentences (most were for thirty or sixty days) were more severe than they may sound. But the militants were not deterred: those in prison went on hunger strikes, and the picketing continued. Eventually the women began to hold public burnings of Wilson's speeches about democracy, believing them to be hypocritical in the light of continued congressional opposition to the amendment; on at least one occasion the president was burned in effigy. Except for a hiatus of several months following passage of the amendment by the House in January 1918, the militants continued their protests almost until final congressional passage in the spring of 1919. (Ratification followed, not easily, fourteen months later.)[5]

The suffragists who had kept on returning to the picket lines in the face of certain arrest and probable imprisonment had no stake in the concept of civil disobedience and no intention of breaking the law. In their eyes (and not only in their eyes) their opponents were perverting and exploiting the machinery of the law for purposes of political repression. "The pickets," Eleanor Flexner has pointed out, "were actually among the earliest victims in this country of the abrogation of civil liberties in wartime."[6] In this important sense they were not committing civil disobedience at all, and in fact their position was upheld the following year in the District of Columbia Court of Appeals.[7]

Nonetheless, as determined activists who were prepared to persist in behavior that had been *called* illegal by the police and the lower courts, they occupy a position that resembles in significant ways those of many modern disobedient demonstrators for civil rights, of Susan B. Anthony, and of the signers of the *Flushing Remonstrance*, among others. Though in theory they were perfectly law-abiding, in practice the suffragists too had to confront the organized power of the state on issues of principle and then take their chances, merely hoping that ultimately the lawfulness as well as the justice of their actions would be vindicated.

❀   Reprinted from Doris Stevens, *Jailed for Freedom* (New York: Boni & Liveright, 1920), pp. 93–95, 96, 99–104, 111.

. . . The Chief of Police, Major Pullman, was detailed to "request" us to stop "picketing" and to tell us that if we continued to picket, we would be arrested.

"We have picketed for six months without interference," said Miss Paul. *"Has the law been changed?"*

"No," was the reply, "but you must stop it."

"But, Major Pullman, we have consulted our lawyers and know we have a legal right to picket."

"I warn you, you will be arrested if you attempt to picket again."

The following day Miss Lucy Burns and Miss Katherine Morey of Boston carried to the White House gates "We shall fight for the things we have always held nearest our hearts, for democracy, for the right of those who submit to authority to have a voice in their own government," and were arrested.

News had spread through the city that the pickets were to be arrested. A moderately large crowd had gathered to see the "fun." One has only to come into conflict with prevailing authority, whether rightly or wrongly, to find friendly hosts vanishing with lightning speed. To know that we were no longer wanted at the gates of the White House and that the police were no longer our "friends" was enough for the mob mind.

Some members of the crowd made sport of the women. Others hurled cheap and childish epithets at them. Small boys were allowed to capture souvenirs, shreds of the banners torn from non-resistant women, as trophies of the sport.

Thinking they had been mistaken in believing the pickets were to be arrested, and having grown weary of their strenuous sport, the crowd moved on its way. Two solitary figures remained, standing on the sidewalk, flanked by the vast Pennsylvania Avenue, looking quite abandoned and alone, when suddenly without any warrant in law, they were arrested on a completely deserted avenue.

Miss Burns and Miss Morey upon arriving at the police station, insisted to the great surprise of all the officials, upon knowing the charge against them. Major Pullman and his entire staff were utterly at a loss to know what to answer. The Administration had looked ahead only as far as threatening arrest. They doubtless thought this was all they would have to do. People could not be arrested for picketing. Picketing is a guaranteed right under the Clayton Act of Congress. Disorderly conduct? There had been no disorderly conduct. Inciting to riot? Impossible! The women had stood as silent sentinels holding the President's own eloquent words.

Doors opened and closed mysteriously. Officials and subofficials passed hurriedly to and fro. Whispered conversations were heard. The book on rules and regulations was hopefully thumbed. Hours passed. Finally the two prisoners were pompously told that they had "obstructed the traffic" on Pennsylvania Avenue, were dismissed on their own recognizance, and never brought to trial.

The following day, June 23rd, more arrests were made; two women at the White House, two at the Capitol. All carried banners with the same words of the President. There was no hesitation this time. They were promptly arrested for "obstructing the traffic." They, too, were dismissed and their cases never tried. It seemed clear that the Administration hoped to suppress picketing merely by arrests. When, however, women continued to picket in the face of arrest, the Administration quickened its advance into the venture of suppression. It decided to bring the offenders to trial.

On June 26, six American women were tried, judged guilty on the technical charge of "obstructing the traffic," warned by the court of their "unpatriotic, almost treasonable behavior," and sentenced to pay a fine of twenty-five dollars or serve three days in jail.

"Not a dollar of your fine will we pay," was the answer of the women. "To pay a fine would be an admission of guilt. We are innocent."

.   .   .

Independence Day, July 4, 1917, is the occasion for two demonstrations in the name of liberty. Champ Clark, late Democratic speaker of the House, is declaiming to a cheering crowd behind the White House, "Governments derive their just powers from the consent of the governed." In front of the White House thirteen silent sentinels with banners bearing the same words, are arrested. It would have been exceedingly droll if it had not been so tragic. Champ Clark and his throng were not molested. The women with practically a deserted street were arrested and served jail terms for "obstructing traffic."

.   .   .

It is Bastille Day, July fourteenth. Inspiring scenes and tragic sacrifices for liberty come to our minds. Sixteen women march in single file to take their own "Liberty, Equality, Fraternity" to the White House gates. It is the middle of a hot afternoon. A thin line of curious spectators is seen in the park opposite the suffrage headquarters. The police assemble from obscure spots; some afoot, others on bicycles. They close in on the women and follow them to the gates.

The proud banner is scarcely at the gates when the leader is placed under arrest. Her place is taken by another. She is taken. Another, and still another steps into the breach and is arrested.

Meanwhile, the crowd grows, attracted to the spot by the presence of the police and the patrol wagon. Applause is heard. There are cries of "shame" for the police, who, I must say, did not always act as if they relished carrying out what they termed "orders from higher up." An occasional hoot from a small boy served to make the mood of the hostile ones a bit gayer. But for the most part an intense silence fell upon the watchers, as they saw not only younger women, but white-haired grandmothers hoisted before the public gaze into the crowded patrol, their heads erect, their eyes a little moist and their frail hands holding tightly to the banner until wrested from them by superior brute force. . . .

The stuffy court room is packed to overflowing. . . . An aged government clerk, grown infirm in the service, takes the stand and the government attorney proves through him that there is a White House; that it has a side-walk in front of it, and a pavement, and a hundred other overwhelming facts. The pathetic clerk shakes his dusty frame and slinks off the stand. The prose-cuting attorney now elaborately proves that we walked, that we carried banners, that we were arrested by the aforesaid officers while attempting to hold our banners at the White House gates.

Each woman speaks briefly in her own defense. She de-nounces the government's policy with hot defiance. The blame is placed squarely at the door of the Administration, and in un-mistakable terms. Miss Anne Martin opens for the defense:

"This is what we are doing with our banners before the White House, petitioning the most powerful representative of the gov-ernment, the President of the United States, for a redress of grievances; we are asking him to use his great power to secure the passage of the national suffrage amendment.

"As long as the government and the representatives of the government prefer to send women to jail on petty and technical charges, we will go to jail. Persecution has always advanced the cause of justice. The right of American women to work for de-mocracy must be maintained. . . . We would hinder, not help, the whole cause of freedom for women, if we weakly submitted to persecution now. Our work for the passage of the amend-ment must go on. It *will* go on."

Mrs. John Rogers, Jr., descendant of Roger Sherman, one of the signers of the Declaration of Independence, speaks: "We are not guilty of any offence, not even of infringing a police regula-tion. We know full well that we stand here because the Presi-dent of the United States refuses to give liberty to American women. We believe, your Honor, that the wrong persons are before the bar in this Court. . . ."

"I object, your Honor, to this woman making such a state-ment here in Court," says the District Attorney.

"We believe the President is the guilty one and that we are innocent."

"Your Honor, I object," shouts the Government's attorney.

The prisoner continues calmly: "There are votes enough and there is time enough to pass the national suffrage amendment through Congress at this session. More than two hundred votes in the House and more than fifty in the Senate are pledged to this amendment. The President puts his power behind all mea-sures in which he takes a genuine interest. If he will say one frank word advocating this measure it will pass as a piece of war emergency legislation."

Mrs. Florence Bayard Hilles speaks in her own defense: "For generations the men of my family have given their services to their country. For myself, my training from childhood has been with a father who believed in democracy and who belonged to the Democratic Party. By inheritance and connection I am a Democrat, and to a Democratic President I went with my appeal. . . . What a spectacle it must be to the thinking people of this country to see us urged to go to war for democracy in a foreign land, and to see women thrown into prison who plead for that same cause at home.

"I stand here to affirm my innocence of the charge against me. This court has not proven that I obstructed traffic. My presence at the White House gate was under the constitutional right of petitioning the government for freedom or for any other cause. During the months of January, February, March, April and May picketing was legal. In June it suddenly becomes illegal. . . .

"My services as an American woman are being conscripted by order of the President of the United States to help win the world war for democracy, . . . 'for the right of those who submit to authority to have a voice in their own government.' I shall continue to plead for the political liberty of American women—and especially do I plead to the President, since he is the one person who . . . can end the struggles of American women to take their proper places in a true democracy."

There is continuous objection from the prosecutor, eager advice from the judge, "you had better keep to the charge of obstructing traffic." But round on round of applause comes from the intent audience, whenever a defiant note is struck by the prisoners, and in spite of the sharp rapping of the gavel confusion reigns. And how utterly puny the "charge" is ! If it were true that the prisoners actually obstructed the traffic, how grotesque that would be. The importance of their demand, the purity of their reasoning, the nobility and gentle quality of the prisoners at the bar; all conspire to make the charge against them, and the attorney who makes it, and the judge who hears it, petty and ridiculous.

But justice must proceed.

Mrs. Gilson Gardner of Washington, D.C., a member of the Executive Committee of the National Woman's party, and the wife of Gilson Gardner, a well-known Liberal and journalist, speaks:

"It is impossible for me to believe that we were arrested because we were obstructing traffic or blocking the public highway.

"We have been carrying on activities of a distinctly political nature, and these political activities have seemingly disturbed certain powerful influences. Arrests followed. I submit that these arrests are purely political and that the charge of an unlawful assemblage and of obstructing traffic is a political subterfuge. Even should I be sent to jail which, I could not, your Honor, anticipate, I would be in jail, not because I obstructed traffic, but because I have offended politically, because I have demanded of this government freedom for women."

.   .   .

Telegrams poured in from all over the country. The press printed headlines which could not but arouse the sympathy of thousands. Even people who did not approve of picketing the White House said, "After all, what these women have done is certainly not 'bad' enough to merit such drastic punishment."

And women protested. From coast to coast there poured in at our headquarters copies of telegrams sent to Administration leaders. Of course not all women by any means had approved this method of agitation. But the government's action had done more than we had been able to do for them. It had made them feel sex-conscious. Women were being unjustly treated. Regardless of their feelings about this particular procedure, they stood up and objected.

For the first time, I believe, our form of agitation began to seem a little more respectable than the Administration's handling of it. But the Administration did not know this fact yet.

V CIVIL DISOBEDIENCE FOR CIVIL RIGHTS

*Most Americans are more interested in order than in law,
more interested in law than in justice.*

—*Bayard Rustin*

30. A. Philip Randolph vs. Wayne Morse (1948)

Asa Philip Randolph first achieved preeminence among black public figures in the United States through his successful leadership of the Brotherhood of Railroad Porters in its long fight for recognition by the Pullman Company. In 1941, four years after the porters' victory, Randolph's determination and firmness as head of the March on Washington Movement won from Franklin Roosevelt an executive order—the first such order to deal with race relations since the Emancipation Proclamation[1]—which declared as national policy "that there shall be no discrimination in the employment of workers in defense industries or government because of race, creed, color, or national origin."[2]

In 1948, as treasurer of the Committee against Jimcrow in Military Service and Training, Randolph sought from Harry Truman another epochal executive order. Congress was moving toward the enactment of a peacetime draft law, and both civilian and military leaders had made clear their intention of maintaining racial segregation in the armed forces under the new legislation. Randolph and others therefore urged Truman to act decisively on behalf of the Negroes who would soon be conscripted under a democratic banner. When the president refused, Randolph went into the hearing rooms of Congress and the streets of Harlem to argue for mass refusals of induction into a segregated army.[3] In July, Truman, responding to other political pressures as well as to Randolph's campaign, signed an executive order prohibiting discrimination and segregation in the armed forces. As in the case of Roosevelt's order seven years before, implementation was scarcely instantaneous, but the two cases helped to establish the political possibility of federal intervention on behalf of minority rights.[4]

Randolph's support of civil disobedience had been shaped long before. In World War I he had been arrested for a similar public espousal of draft resistance. (The judge, apparently in the paternalistic belief that Randolph's writings in the *Messenger* were really the work of white Socialists, released him.)[5] And during the March on Washington Movement, Randolph had envisioned mass civil disobedience as one of several valuable political tactics. "Government," he said in 1943, "is an accommodative and repressive organism which is constantly balancing pressures from conflicting social forces in the local and national communities, and without regard to the question of right or wrong, it inevitably moves in the direction of the pressure of the greatest challenge." Only techniques that were "revolutionary, unusual, extraordinary, dramatic, and drastic" held any realistic promise for "placing the cause of a minority into the mainstream of national and international public opinion."[6] Civil disobedience, he observed, met these criteria. The revolution Randolph sought, however, was social rather than political. Though he had drawn inspiration from the example of Gandhi, Randolph carefully distinguished between the Indian and the American Negro movements: "The March on Washington Movement does not seek to bring about any transition of governmental power from the hands of the white people to the Negro people. There is no desire to see the collapse of American civil government. Negroes are not seeking independence as a racial unit. On the contrary we want to maintain American civil government because wherever it ceases to function, mob law reigns and Negroes are the victims."[7]

Draft refusal made sense to many more black Americans in 1948 than it had in 1918,[8] and Randolph's personal prestige now made his advocacy of mass civil disobedience a potent political force. One of those who were distressed by Randolph's campaign and resisted its pressure was Senator Wayne Morse of Oregon, a leading liberal voice in Congress and a member of the board of directors of the National Association for the Advancement of Colored People. Morse argued that "our constitutional guarantees are the rights of every citizen" but that "we have to be realists in the political field" and that "we [cannot] make progress in this country in a great many fields of social legislation by way of a social avalanche. The test should be the test of progress. Are we moving ahead?"[9] Morse was unsettled both by Randolph's radical proposal and by the ambiguous response to it of Walter White, the secretary of the NAACP, who telegraphed Morse that while the NAACP would not advocate resistance to law, "there is sympathy in many hearts for the Randolph point of view. The remedy is not to threaten treason trials, but to give these loyal citizens the democracy they are expected and asked to defend."[10] In response Morse threatened to resign from the NAACP board unless the organization repudiated Randolph's position unequivocally.[11] His cross-examination of Randolph before the Senate Armed Services Committee provides a classic illustration of the divergence between liberal and radical approaches to change and recalls the antislavery debate between gradualists and immediatists a century before.[12]

Reprinted from the *Congressional Record*, vol. 94, pp. 4312–4313 (80th Congress, 2d sess., Senate, April 12, 1948).

SENATOR MORSE: Mr. Randolph, I want to question you a bit on your proposal for civil disobedience. Up until now refusal to serve in the military forces of this country in time of national emergency has been limited, as far as one's psychological attitudes are concerned, to conscientious objections to war, the participating in war.

It is based upon the legal theory of freedom of religion in this country, that if one's religious scruples are such that in good conscience he cannot bring himself to participate in war, which involves the taking of human life, our Government has protected him in that religious belief, and we have our so-called exemption on the ground of conscientious objection.

Now, this proposal of yours—I am not one to minimize your testimony—your proposal is not based upon conscientious objection in the sense that the American law has recognized it to date; am I not right about that?

MR. RANDOLPH: That is correct.

SENATOR MORSE: But your proposal, and put me straight on this, your proposal is really based upon conviction that because your Government has not given you certain social, economic, and race protection from discrimination because of race, color, or creed, you feel that even in a time of national emergency, when your Government and the country itself may be at stake, you are justified in saying to any segment of our populace— whether it is the colored group or, as you say in your statement, the white group with like sympathies—that under those circumstances you would be justified then in saying, "Do not shoulder arms in protection of your country in this national emergency"?

MR. RANDOLPH: That is a correct statement, Mr. Senator. I may add that it is my deep conviction that in taking such a position we are doing our country a great service. Our country has come out before the world as the moral leader of democracy, and it is preparing its defense forces and aggressive forces upon the theory that it must do this to protect democracy in the world.

Well, now, I consider that if this country does not develop the democratic process at home and make the democratic process work by giving the very people whom they propose to draft in the Army to fight for them democracy, democracy then is not the type of democracy that ought to be fought for, and, as a matter of fact, the policy of segregation in the armed forces and in other avenues of our life is the greatest single propaganda and political weapon in the hands of Russia and international communism today.

SENATOR MORSE: . . . Let us assume this hypothetical. A country proceeds to attack the United States or commits acts which make it perfectly clear that our choice is only the choice of war. Would you take the position then that unless our Government granted the demands which are set out in your testimony, or most of the demands set out in your testimony, that you would recommend a course of civil disobedience to our Government?

MR. RANDOLPH: In answer to that question, the Government now has time to change its policy on segregation and discrimination and if the Government does not change its policy on segregation and discrimination in the interests of the very democracy it is fighting for, I would advocate that Negroes take no part in the Army. . . .

SENATOR MORSE: . . . I understand your answer to be that under those circumstances, even though it was perfectly clear that we would have to fight then to exist as a country, you would still recommend the program of civil disobedience?

MR. RANDOLPH: Because I would believe that that is in the interest of the soul of our country and I unhesitatingly and very adamantly hold that that is the only way by which we are going to be able to make America wake up and realize that we do not have democracy here as long as one black man is denied all of the rights enjoyed by all the white men in this country.

SENATOR MORSE: Now, fᴀcing realistically that hypothetical situation and the assumption that it has come to pass, do you have any doubt then that this Government as presently constituted under the Constitution that governs us would necessarily follow a legal course of action of applying the legal doctrine of treason to that conduct? . . .

MR. RANDOLPH: I would anticipate nationwide terrorism against Negroes who refused to participate in the armed forces, but I believe that that is the price we have to pay for democracy that we want. In other words, if there are sacrifices and sufferings, terrorism, concentration camps, whatever they may be, if that is the only way by which Negroes can get their democratic rights, I unhesitatingly say that we have to face it.

SENATOR MORSE: But on the basis of the law as it now exists, going back to my premise that you and I know of no legal exemption from participation in military service in the defense of our country other than that of conscientious objection on religious grounds, not on the grounds in which you place your civil disobedience, that then the doctrine of treason would be applied to those people participating in that disobedience?

MR. RANDOLPH: Exactly. I would be willing to face that doctrine on the theory and on the grounds that we are serving a higher law than the law which applies the act of treason to us when we are attempting to win democracy in this country and to make the soul of America democratic. I would contend that we are serving a higher law than that law with its legal technicalities. . . .

SENATOR MORSE: But you would fully expect that because the law of treason in this country relates to certain specific overt acts on the part of the individual irrespective of what he considers to be his spiritual or moral motivation in justification, that there would not be any other course of action for our Government to follow but indictments for treason? . . .

MR. RANDOLPH: Let me add here in connection with that that we would participate in no overt acts against our Government, no overt acts of any kind. In other words, ours would be one of nonresistance. Ours would be one of noncooperation; ours would be one of nonparticipation in the military forces of the country.

I want you to know that we would be willing to absorb the violence, to absorb the terrorism, to face the music and to take whatever comes and we, as a matter of fact, consider that we are more loyal to our country than the people who perpetrate segregation and discrimination upon Negroes because of color or race.

I want it thoroughly understood that we would certainly not be guilty of any kind of overt act against the country but we would not participate in any military operation as segregation and Jim Crow slaves in the Army.

SENATOR MORSE: I think you will agree with me that this is

not the time and place for you and me to argue the legal meaning of aiding and abetting the enemy but if you refresh your memory of treason cases, as I have been doing, sitting here this morning, I would only point out to you most kindly that the legal concepts of aiding and abetting are flexible concepts that can be applied to the behavior of individuals which in effect serve the enemy in time of war to the endangerment of the rest of the people of our country.

Furthermore, and I know you are aware of the fact, any such program as you outline would not be a passive program but would be one that would be bound to result in all sorts of overt actions you could not possibly control, but for which you who sponsored it would, as a matter of law, be fixed with the proximate cause of the conduct and, therefore, would be legally responsible for it.

MR. RANDOLPH: I recognize that fact just as for instance a union may call a strike. The union does not promote the violence but the forces that are opposed to the union may create the violence.

Well now, in this instance we are definitely opposed to violence of any kind; we are definitely opposed to any overt acts that would be construed in the form of violence but, nevertheless, we would relentlessly wage a warfare against the Jim Crow armed forces program and against the Negroes and others participating in that program. That is our position. . . . However the law may be construed we would be willing to face it on the grounds that our actions would be in obedience and in conformity with the higher law of righteousness than that set forth in the so-called law of treason.

SENATOR MORSE: . . . I agree that both parties too frequently have been guilty of political professings rather than political action in support of the principles of Constitutional rights. [But] I do want to say with all the sincerity that I possess that I do not think the proposal you offer is the way to establish full civil rights in America.

31. Martin Luther King, Jr.:
Three Statements on
Civil Disobedience (1961–1968)

Civil disobedience did not become an integral part of Martin Luther King's program of nonviolent direct action until the latter part of his life. In Montgomery, for instance, the protestors' strategy was not at first conceived of as illegal: it was almost three months after the initiation of the bus boycott that the city government invoked an old law prohibiting organized boycotts that had no "just cause or legal excuse."[1] Even in Birmingham, where the marchers violated a court injunction for the first time, King argued that their civil disobedience was based not only on justice but on law: the Alabama courts were being used in "a maliciously effective, pseudo-legal way" to deprive the demonstrators of their constitutional right to engage in peaceable assembly.[2] Though in 1967 the Supreme Court upheld King's Birmingham conviction, other decisions by the Court made essential contributions to the success of the Montgomery and Birmingham campaigns, and for more than a decade after the epochal *Brown vs. Board of Education* decision in 1954, the civil rights movement regarded the whole machinery of federal law as one of its critical allies. "Nonviolent action," King said, ". . . was the way to supplement—not replace—the process of change through legal recourse."[3] King never did defy a *federal* court injunction, though he was on the verge of doing so when he was killed.[4]

For most of King's adult life, then, he accepted civil disobedience as simply a logical and righteous response to the statutes and ordinances by which the South institutionalized its system of racial discrimination; lawbreaking remained a distinctly subordinate aspect of his program of nonviolent resistance. In the last months of his life, however, King began to envision civil disobedience in a new way, one that would bring it to bear not just on the humiliation of discrimination but on poverty itself. "Our idea," he said in a piece published shortly after his death, "is to dramatize the whole economic problem of the poor."[5]

In his search for a strategy that would be applicable to northern as well as southern conditions and that would be credible as a nonviolent alternative to revolutionary and quasi-revolutionary forms of militancy, he began to see "mass civil disobedience as a new stage of struggle" which could "transmute the deep rage of the ghetto into a constructive and creative force." Since, as James Bevel dryly observed, "there's nothing unconstitutional about children starving to death,"[6] this new approach could not seek to subject Jim Crow ordinances to the constitutional scrutiny of higher courts; instead it would have to aim at challenging the institutional arrangements and social priorities of the country as a whole. Though it would remain nonviolent and open, and though its practitioners would retain their willingness to bear witness in jail, it would seek a "key point" at which to "interrupt the functioning" of the larger society and thus to compel Congress to take action on a scale that would begin to make fundamental changes in the lives of poor people generally.

The evolution of King's conception of civil disobedience is traced in the three statements that follow.

"Love, Law, and Civil Disobedience" (1961)

I would say that the first point or the first principle in the movement is the idea that means must be as pure as the end. This movement is based on the philosophy that ends and means must cohere. Now this has been one of the long struggles in history, the whole idea of means and ends. Great philosophers have grappled with it, and sometimes they have emerged with the idea, from Machiavelli on down, that the end justifies the means. There is a great system of thought in our world today, known as Communism. And I think that with all of the weaknesses and tragedies of Communism, we find its greatest tragedy right here, that it goes under the philosophy that the end justifies the means that are used in the process. So we can read or we can hear the Lenins say that lying, deceit, or violence, that many of these things [are justified by] the ends of the classless society.

This is where the student movement and the non-violent movement that is taking place in our nation would break with

Communism and any other system that would argue that the end justifies the means. For in the long run, we must see that the [means] represents the [end] in process and the ideal in the making. In other words, we cannot believe, or we cannot go with the idea that the end justifies the means because the end is pre-existent in the means. So the idea of non-violent resistance, the philosophy of non-violent resistance, is the philosophy which says that the means must be as pure as the end, that in the long run of history, immoral destructive means cannot bring about moral and constructive ends.

. . . This is the whole idea, that the individual who is engaged in a non-violent struggle must never inflict injury upon another. Now this has an external aspect and it has an internal one. From the external point of view it means that the individuals involved must avoid external physical violence. So they don't have guns, they don't retaliate with physical violence. If they are hit in the process, they avoid external physical violence at every point. But it also means that they avoid internal violence of spirit. This is why the love ethic stands so high in the student movement. . . .

. . . When one rises to love on this level, he loves men not because he likes them, not because their ways appeal to him, but he loves every man because God loves him. And he rises to the point of loving the person who does an evil deed while hating the deed that the person does. I think this is what Jesus meant when he said "love your enemies." I'm very happy that he didn't say like your enemies, because it is pretty difficult to like some people. Like is sentimental, and it is pretty difficult to like someone bombing your home; it is pretty difficult to like somebody threatening your children; it is difficult to like congressmen who spend all of their time trying to defeat civil rights. But Jesus says love them, and love is greater than like. Love is understanding, redemptive, creative, good will for all men. And it is this idea, it is this whole ethic of love which is the idea standing at the basis of the student movement.

There is something else: that one seeks to defeat the unjust system, rather than individuals who are caught in that system. And that one goes on believing that somehow this is the important thing, to get rid of the evil system and not the individual who happens to be misguided, who happens to be misled, who was taught wrong. The thing to do is to get rid of the system and thereby create a moral balance within society.

Another thing that stands at the center of this movement is another idea: that suffering can be a most creative and powerful social force. Suffering has certain moral attributes involved, but it can be a powerful and creative social force. Now, it is very interesting at this point to notice that both violence and non-violence agree that suffering can be a very powerful social force. But there is this difference: violence says that suffering can be a powerful social force by inflicting the suffering on somebody else; so this is what we do in war, this is what we do in the whole violent thrust of the violent movement. It believes that you achieve some end by inflicting suffering on another. The non-violent say that suffering becomes a powerful social force when you willingly accept that violence on yourself, so that self-suffering stands at the center of the non-violent movement and the individuals involved are able to suffer in a creative manner, feeling that unearned suffering is redemptive, and that suffering may serve to transform the social situation.

. . . Man has the capacity to be good, man has the capacity to be evil.

And so the non-violent resister never lets this idea go, that there is something within human nature that can respond to goodness. So that a Jesus of Nazareth or a Mohandas Gandhi can appeal to human beings and appeal to that element of goodness within them, and a Hitler can appeal to the element of evil within them. But we must never forget that there is something within human nature that can respond to goodness, that man is not totally depraved, to put it in theological terms, the image of God is never totally gone. And so the individuals who believe in this movement and who believe in non-violence and our struggle in the South somehow believe that even the worst segregationist can become an integrationist. Now sometimes it is hard to believe that this is what this movement says, and it believes it firmly, that there is something within human nature that can be changed, and this stands at the top of the whole philosophy of the student movement and the philosophy of non-violence.

It says something else. It says that it is as much a moral obligation to refuse to cooperate with evil as it is to cooperate with good. Non-cooperation with evil is as much a moral obligation as the cooperation with good. So that the student movement is willing to stand up courageously on the idea of civil disobedience. Now I think this is the part of the student movement that is probably misunderstood more than anything else. And it is a difficult aspect, because on the one hand the students would say, and I would say, and all the people who believe in civil rights would say, obey the Supreme Court's decision of 1954 and at the same time, we would disobey certain laws that exist on the statutes of the South today.

This brings in the whole question of how can you be logically consistent when you advocate obeying some laws and disobeying other laws. Well, I think one would have to see the whole meaning of this movement at this point by seeing that the students recognize that there are two types of laws. There are just laws and there are unjust laws. And they would be the first to say obey the just laws, they would be the first to say that men and women have a moral obligation to obey just and right laws. And they would go on to say that we must see that there are unjust laws. Now the question comes into being, what is the difference, and who determines the difference, what is the difference between a just and an unjust law?

Well, a just law is a law that squares with a moral law. It is a law that squares with that which is right, so that any law that uplifts human personality is a just law. Whereas that law which is out of harmony with the moral is a law which does not square with the moral law of the universe. It does not square with the law of God, so for that reason it is unjust and any law that degrades the human personality is an unjust law.

Well, somebody says that that does not mean anything to me; first, I don't believe in these abstract things called moral laws and I'm not too religious, so I don't believe in the law of God; you have to get a little more concrete, and more practical. What do you mean when you say that a law is unjust, and a law is just? Well, I would go on to say in more concrete terms that an unjust law is a code that the majority inflicts on the minority that is not binding on itself. So that this becomes difference made legal. Another thing that we can say is that an unjust law is a code which the majority inflicts upon the minority, which that minority had no part in enacting or creating, because that minority had no right to vote in many instances, so that the leggislative bodies that made these laws were not democratically elected. Who could ever say that the legislative body of Mississippi was democratically elected, or the legislative body of Alabama was democratically elected, or the legislative body even of Georgia has been democratically elected, when there are people in Terrell County and in other counties because of the color of their skin who cannot vote? They confront reprisals and threats and all of that; so that an unjust law is a law that individuals did not have a part in creating or enacting because they were denied the right to vote.

Now the same token of just law would be just the opposite. A just law becomes sameness made legal. It is a code that the majority, who happen to believe in that code, compel the minority, who don't believe in it, to follow, because they are willing to follow it themselves, so it is sameness made legal. Therefore the individuals who stand up on the basis of civil disobedience realize that they are following something that says that there are just laws and there are unjust laws. Now, they are not anarchists. They believe that there are laws which must be followed; they do not seek to defy the law, they do not seek to evade the law. For many individuals who would call themselves segregationists and who would hold on to segregation at any cost seek to defy the law, they seek to evade the law, and their process can lead on into anarchy. They seek in the final analysis to follow a way of uncivil disobedience, not civil disobedience. And I submit that the individual who disobeys the law, whose conscience tells him it is unjust and who is willing to accept the penalty by staying in jail until that law is altered, is expressing at the moment the very highest respect for law.

This is what the students have followed in their movement. Of course there is nothing new about this, they feel that they are in good company and rightly so. We go back and read the Apology and the Crito, and you see Socrates practicing civil disobedience. And to a degree academic freedom is a reality today because Socrates practiced civil disobedience. The early Christians practiced civil disobedience in a superb manner, to a point where they were willing to be thrown to the lions. They were willing to face all kinds of suffering in order to stand up for what they knew was right even though they knew it was against the laws of the Roman Empire.

We could come up to our own day and we see it in many instances. We must never forget that everything that Hitler did in Germany was "legal." It was illegal to aid and comfort a Jew, in the days of Hitler's Germany. But I believe that if I had the same attitude then as I have now I would publicly aid and comfort my Jewish brothers in Germany if Hitler were alive today calling this an illegal process. If I lived in South Africa today in the midst of the white supremacy law in South Africa, I would join Chief Luthuli and others in saying break these unjust laws. And even let us come up to America. Our nation in a sense came into being through a massive act of civil disobedience, for the Boston Tea Party was nothing but a massive act of civil disobedience. Those who stood up against the slave laws, the abolitionists, by and large practiced civil disobedience. So I think these students are in good company, and they feel that by practicing civil disobedience they are in line with men and women through the ages who have stood up for something that is morally right.

Now there are one or two other things that I want to say about this student movement, moving out of the philosophy of nonviolence, something about what it is a revolt against. On the one hand it is a revolt against the negative peace that has encompassed the South for many years. I remember when I was in Montgomery, Ala., one of the white citizens came to me one day and said—and I think he was very sincere about this—that in Montgomery for all of these years we have been such a peaceful community, we have had so much harmony in race relations and then you people have started this movement and boycott, and it has done so much to disturb race relations, and we just don't love the Negro like we used to love them, because you have destroyed the harmony and the peace that we once had in race relations. And I said to him, in the best way I could say and I tried to say it in non-violent terms, we have never had peace in Montgomery, Ala., we have never had peace in the South. We have had a negative peace, which is merely the absence of tension; we've had a negative peace in which the Negro patiently accepted his situation and his plight, but we've never had true peace, we've never had positive peace, and what we're seeking now is to develop this positive peace. For we must come to see that peace is not merely the absence of some negative force, it is the presence of a positive force. True peace is not merely the absence of tension, but it is the presence of justice and brotherhood. I think this is what Jesus meant when he said, I come not to bring peace but a sword. Now Jesus didn't mean he came to start war, to bring a physical sword, and he didn't mean, I come not to bring positive peace. But I think what Jesus was saying in substance was this, that I come not to bring an old negative peace, which makes for stagnant passivity and deadening complacency, I come to bring something different, and whenever I come, a conflict is precipitated, between the old and the new, whenever I come a struggle takes place between justice and injustice, between the forces of light and the forces of darkness. I come not to bring a negative peace, but a positive peace, which is brotherhood, which is justice, which is the Kingdom of God.

And I think this is what we are seeking to do today, and this movement is a revolt against a negative peace and a struggle to bring into being a positive peace, which makes for true brotherhood, true integration, true person-to-person relationships. This movement is also revolt against what is often called tokenism. Here again many people do not understand this, they feel that in this struggle the Negro will be satisfied with tokens of integration, just a few students and a few schools here and there and a few doors open here and there. But this isn't the meaning of the movement and I think that honesty impels me to admit it everywhere I have an opportunity, that the Negro's aim is to bring about complete integration in American life. And he has come to see that token integration is little more than token democracy, which ends up with many new evasive schemes and it ends up with new discrimination, covered up with such niceties of complexity. It is very interesting to discover that the movement has thrived in many communities that had token integration. So this reveals that the movement is based on a principle that integration must become real and complete, not just token integration.

It is also a revolt against what I often call the myth of time. We hear this quite often, that only time can solve this problem. That if we will only be patient, and only pray—which we must do, we must be patient and we must pray—but there are those who say just do these things and wait for time, and time will solve this problem. Well, the people who argue this do not themselves realize that time is neutral, that it can be used constructively or destructively. At points the people of ill will, the segregationists, have used time much more effectively than the people of good will. So individuals in the struggle must come to realize that it is necessary to aid time, that without this kind of aid, time itself will become an ally of the insurgent and primitive forces of social stagnation. Therefore, this movement is a revolt against the myth of time.

There is a final thing that I would like to say to you, this movement is a movement based on faith in the future. . . . There is something in this student movement which says to us, that we shall overcome. Before the victory is won some may have to get scarred up, but we shall overcome. Before the victory of brotherhood is achieved, some will maybe face physical death, but we shall overcome. Before the victory is won, some will lose jobs, some will be called Communists, and reds, merely because they believe in brotherhood, some will be dismissed as dangerous rabblerousers and agitators merely because they're standing up for what is right, but we shall overcome. That is the basis of this movement. . . .

"Address to the American Jewish Committee" (1965)

In the past several years it has become clear that the technique of mass nonviolent direct action has not only become the accepted method of the civil rights movement but beyond that, the vast majority of all Americans now support and approve it. What began as a limited expression of protest ten years ago in Montgomery, Alabama, to integrate a bus line has grown into a national phenomenon. As history spiraled over a decade, the movement returned to Montgomery and involved in direct action nuns and priests, rabbis, Protestant ministers, and laity of every race, social class, and age.

Many observers have been surprised and even shocked by these methods. The enemies of the civil rights movement have been quick and vocal to denounce them as undemocratic pressure tactics and even un-American in philosophy. Yet the truth is that no one can scorn nonviolent direct action or civil disobedience without canceling out American history. The first nonviolent direct action did not occur in Montgomery. Its roots go back to the American Revolution and the boycott against British tea culminating in the Boston Tea Party. It was the favorite weapon of the suffragette movement when women had to fight for their right to vote. It was a technique the trade unions employed to organize the mass production industries. Many here tonight can recall the events of the thirties, when federal court injunctions crippled and stifled union organization. Even a Wagner Act could not facilitate a breakthrough. When the now historic sit-down strikes burst forth in 1937, a new national attitude congealed. Through the Congress of Industrial Organizations a new major movement was born. Then too the nation was warned that the profit system was the target of this new form of struggle. Nearly three decades later we are able to see that the profit system was not only unimpaired but became significantly strengthened.

If there is some confusion about the origins of nonviolent direct action, there is even more about civil disobedience. The two methods are not synonymous. Civil disobedience in its true sense has not been employed by Negroes in their struggle. To utilize civil disobedience in its authentic historical form involves defiance of fundamental national law. For example, when Antigone insisted upon her right to follow her individual conscience and religious convictions to bury her brother, she was defying the king and the unqualified majesty of his law. When the Quakers refused to return runaway slaves, they were defying the Supreme Court. . . . When Thoreau refused to pay taxes in protest against the Mexican War, he was breaking a fundamental legislative enactment and opposing the declaration of war of the Congress. And certainly we all understand this and

I heartily approve of civil disobedience in a creative sense in many instances.

But we must see that the Negro today, when he marches in the streets, is not practicing civil disobedience because he is not challenging the Constitution, the Supreme Court, or the enactments of Congress. Instead he seeks to uphold them. He may be violating local municipal ordinances or state laws, but it is these laws which [contradict] basic national law. Negroes by their direct action are exposing the contradiction. The civil disobedience—or I should say uncivil disobedience in this situation, resting on unjust foundations—is that of the segregationists. Negroes have not willfully and frivolously violated the law. Many goodhearted people believe they do exactly that and forgive them on grounds that they endured appalling grievances. Yet these people forgive them for misdeeds they are not committing. The truly unsocial lawbreaker disregards law because he as an individual is seeking a personal advantage. Negroes have never forgotten, even under the crushing burdens of injustice, that they are connected with the larger society, and that the roads they may obstruct and the public buildings they picket are used in common by all citizens.

For that reason, before a protest can be approved by a responsible leadership, they must answer the following questions. One, do we have a just grievance, or is our purpose merely to create confusion for its own sake as a form of revenge? Two, have we first used every form of normal means to eliminate the problem by negotiation, petition, and appropriate appeals to authority? Three, having found these channels useless or forcibly closed to us, and we embark on any type of lawbreaking, are we prepared to accept the consequences society will inflict, and to maintain even under punishment a sense of brotherhood? Four, do we have a clear program to relieve injustice which does not inflict injustice upon others, and is that program reasonable and grounded in the ethics and best traditions of our society?

In establishing these prerequisite conditions before employing direct action, the civil rights movement meets its responsibility to society and fulfills its obligations to democratic principles. Even after the movement embarks upon a program of nonviolent direct action or civil disobedience, its purposes are not narrowly confined, to obtain benefits exclusively for the Negro. It is an axiom of nonviolent action and democracy that when any group struggles properly and justly to achieve its own rights, it enlarges the rights of all. This element is what makes both democracy and nonviolent action self-renewing and creative. . . .

The Trumpet of Conscience (1968)

I am still convinced that a solution of nonviolence remains possible. However, nonviolence must be adapted to urban conditions and urban moods. The effectiveness of street marches in cities is limited because the normal turbulence of city life absorbs them as mere transitory drama quite common in the ordinary movement of masses. In the South, a march was a social earthquake; in the North, it is a faint, brief exclamation of protest.

Nonviolent protest must now mature to a new level to correspond to heightened black impatience and stiffened white resistance. This higher level is mass civil disobedience. There must be more than a statement to the larger society; there must be a force that interrupts its functioning at some key point. That interruption must not, however, be clandestine or surreptitious. It is not necessary to invest it with guerrilla romanticism. It must be open and, above all, conducted by large masses without violence. If the jails are filled to thwart it, its meaning will become even clearer.

The Negro will be saying, "I am not avoiding penalties for breaking the law—I am willing to endure all your punishment because your society will not be able to endure the stigma of violently and publicly oppressing its minority to preserve injustice."

Mass civil disobedience as a new stage of struggle can transmute the deep rage of the ghetto into a constructive and creative force. To dislocate the functioning of a city without destroying it can be more effective than a riot because it can be longer-lasting, costly to the larger society, but not wantonly destructive. Finally, it is a device of social action that is more difficult for the government to quell by superior force.

The limitation of riots, moral questions aside, is that they cannot win and their participants know it. Hence, rioting is not revolutionary but reactionary because it invites defeat. It involves an emotional catharsis, but it must be followed by a sense of futility.

. . . Many people believe that the urban Negro is too angry and too sophisticated to be nonviolent. Those same people dismiss the nonviolent marches in the South and try to describe them as processions of pious elderly ladies. The fact is that in all the marches we have organized some men of very violent tendencies have been involved. It was routine for us to collect hundreds of knives from our own ranks before the demonstrations, in case of momentary weakness. And in Chicago last year we saw some of the most violent individuals accepting nonviolent discipline. Day after day during those Chicago marches I walked in our lines and I never saw anyone retaliate with violence. There were lots of provocations, not only the screaming white hoodlums lining the sidewalks, but also groups of Negro militants talking about guerrilla warfare. We had some gang leaders and members marching with us. I remember walking with the Blackstone Rangers while bottles were flying from the sidelines, and I saw their noses being broken and blood flowing from their wounds; and I saw them continue and not retaliate, not one of them, with violence. I am convinced that even very violent temperaments can be channeled through nonviolent discipline, if the movement is moving, if they can act constructively and express through an effective channel their very legitimate anger.

But even if nonviolence can be valid, psychologically, for the protesters who want change, is it going to be effective, strategically, against a government and a status quo that have so far resisted this summer's demands on the grounds that "we must not reward the rioters"? Far from rewarding the rioters, far from even giving a hearing to their just and urgent demands, the administration has ignored its responsibility for the causes of the riots, and instead has used the negative aspects of them to justify continued inaction on the underlying issues. The administration's only concrete response was to initiate a study and call for a day of prayer. As a minister, I take prayer too seriously to use it as an excuse for avoiding work and responsibility. When a government commands more wealth and power than has ever been known in the history of the world, and offers no more than this, it is worse than blind, it is provocative. It is paradoxical but fair to say that Negro terrorism is incited less on ghetto street corners than in the halls of Congress.

I intended to show that nonviolence will be effective, but not until it has achieved the massive dimensions, the disciplined planning, and the intense commitment of a sustained, direct-action movement of civil disobedience on the national scale.

The dispossessed of this nation—the poor, both white and Negro—live in a cruelly unjust society. They must organize a revolution against that injustice, not against the lives of the persons who are their fellow citizens, but against the structures through which the society is refusing to take means which have been called for, and which are at hand, to lift the load of poverty.

The only real revolutionary, people say, is a man who has nothing to lose. There are millions of poor people in this country who have very little, or even nothing, to lose. If they can be helped to take action together, they will do so with a freedom and a power that will be a new and unsettling force in our complacent national life. Beginning in the New Year, we will be recruiting three thousand of the poorest citizens from ten different urban and rural areas to initiate and lead a sustained, massive, direct-action movement in Washington. Those who choose to join this initial three thousand, this nonviolent army, this "freedom church" of the poor, will work with us for three months to develop nonviolent action skills. Then we will move on Washington, determined to stay there until the legislative and executive branches of the government take serious and adequate action on jobs and income. A delegation of poor people can walk into a high official's office with a carefully, collectively prepared list of demands. (If you're poor, if you're unemployed anyway, you can choose to stay in Washington as long as the struggle needs you.) And if that official says, "But Congress would have to approve this," or, "But the President would have to be consulted on that," you can say, "All right, we'll wait." And you can settle down in his office for as long a stay as necessary. If you are, let's say, from rural Mississippi, and have never had medical attention, and your children are undernourished and unhealthy, you can take those little children into the Washington hospitals and stay with them there until the medical workers cope with their needs, and in showing it your children you will have shown this country a sight that will make it stop in its busy tracks and think hard about what it has done. The many people who will come and join this three thousand, from all groups in the country's life, will play a supportive role, deciding to be poor for a time along with the dispossessed who are asking for their right to jobs or income—jobs, income, the demolition of slums, and the rebuilding by the people who live there of new communities in their place; in fact, a new economic deal for the poor.

Why camp in Washington to demand these things? Because only the federal Congress and administration can decide to use the billions of dollars we need for a real war on poverty. We need, not a new law, but a massive, new national program.

32. Stokely Carmichael: "Black Power" (1966)

Born in Trinidad in 1941, Stokely Carmichael came to the United States in 1952 and received his academic education at the Bronx High School of Science and Howard University. He made his first momentous political commitments while he was still in college: in 1961 he went on a freedom ride to Mississippi, was arrested, and spent seven weeks in the state penitentiary. For the next several years he was active in the Student Nonviolent Coordinating Committee; he did field organizing in such places as Lowndes County, Alabama, where few or no blacks were registered to vote (in Lowndes blacks made up 80 percent of the population) and where other civil rights workers had been assassinated. By the spring of 1966 he had been jailed more than twenty times for his roles in various demonstrations. In May of that year he became SNCC's national chairman, having identified himself with a movement within the organization which opposed having whites in policy-making roles, though it did not rule out the possibility of other sorts of interracial alliances.[1]

In late 1966 and 1967 Carmichael attracted national attention by declaring his determination not to serve in the armed forces during the Vietnam war even if he were drafted (he was eventually classified 4-F) and by urging others, especially blacks, to refuse induction. One of his principal arguments for this disobedience was an extension of the one A. Philip Randolph had pressed two decades before—that it made no sense for blacks to fight abroad in the name of democracy when democratic rights were denied to them at home. The armed forces were of course generally integrated by this time, but Carmichael used a broader definition of democracy, noting, for instance, the continuing inability of blacks to live where they wished because of white resistance to open housing.[2]

During this period Carmichael's ideas and rhetoric began to move beyond militance to belligerence. Speaking to an audience of 10,000 at a rally sponsored by Students for a Democratic Society at Berkeley in October 1966, he argued that "there's a higher law than a racist named [Robert] McNamara, a fool named [Dean] Rusk, and a buffoon named [Lyndon] Johnson."[3] The following month he spoke again at Berkeley. His words on this occasion provide an ambiguous bridge between his early experience in the civil rights movement and what was to come later. In August of 1967 he was in Havana, advocating an armed revolution that would overthrow "the imperialist, capitalist and racialist structure of the United States."[4]

❀   Reprinted from Joanne Grant, ed., *Black Protest: History, Documents, and Analyses, 1619 to the Present* (New York: Fawcett World Library, 1968), pp. 459–466. Copyright © 1968 by Joanne Grant. By permission of Joan Daves.

. . . It seems to me that the institutions that function in this country are clearly racist, and that they're built upon racism. And the question then is, how can black people inside this country move? And then how can white people, who say they're not a part of those institutions, begin to move, and how then do we begin to clear away the obstacles that we have in this society that keep us from living like human beings. How can we begin to build institutions that will allow people to relate with each other as human beings? This country has never done that. Especially around the concept of white or black.

Now . . . some Negroes have been walking down a dream street talking about sitting next to white people. . . . That does not begin to solve the problem. When we went to Mississippi, we did not go to sit next to [Governor] Ross Barnett; we did not go to sit next to [Sheriff] Jim Clark; we went to get them out of our way, and people ought to understand that. We were never fighting for the right to integrate, we were fighting against white supremacy. . . .

Now we are engaged in a psychological struggle in this country and that struggle is whether or not black people have the right to use the words they want to use without white people giving their sanction to it. We maintain, whether they like it or not, we gon' use the word "black power" and let them address themselves to that. We are not gonna wait for white people to sanction black power. We're tired of waiting. . . .

We are oppressed as a group because we are black, not because we are lazy, not because we're apathetic, not because we're stupid, not because we smell, not because we eat watermelon and have good rhythm. We are oppressed because we are black, and in order to get out of that oppression, one must feel the group power that one has. . . .

The political parties in this country do not meet the needs of the people on a day-to-day basis. The question is, how can we build new political institutions that will become the political expressions of people on a day-to-day basis. The question is, how can you build political institutions that will begin to meet the needs of Oakland, California; and the needs of Oakland, California is not 1,000 policemen with submachine guns. They don't need that. They need that least of all. The question is, how can we build institutions where those people can begin to function on a day-to-day basis, where they can get decent jobs, where they can get decent housing, and where they can begin to participate in the policy and major decisions that affect their lives. That's what they need. Not Gestapo troops. Because this is not 1942. And if you play like Nazis, we're playing back with you this time around. Get hip to that.

The question then is, how can white people move to start making the major institutions that they have in this country function the way they are supposed to function? That is the real question. And can white people move inside their own community and start tearing down racism where, in fact, it does exist? It is you who live in Cicero and stop us from living there. It is white people who stop us from moving into Grenada. It is white people who make sure that we live in the ghettos of this country. It is white institutions that do that. They must change. In order for America to really live on a basic principle of human relationships, a new society must be born. Racism must die, and the economic exploitation of this country, of non-white people around the world, must also die. . . .

I maintain, as we have in SNCC, that the war in Vietnam is an illegal and immoral war. And the question is, what can we do to stop that war. What can we do to stop the people who, in the name of our country, are killing babies, women and children. What can we do to stop that? And I maintain that we do not have the power in our hands to change that institution, to begin to recreate it so that they learn to leave the Vietnamese people alone, and that the only power we have is the power to say "Hell, no!" to the draft. . . . There isn't one organization that has begun to meet our stand on the war in Vietnam. Because we not only say we are against the war in Vietnam; *we are against the draft*. We are against the draft. No man has the right to take a man for two years and train him to be a killer. . . .

We need new political institutions in this country. And any time Lyndon Baines Johnson can head a party which has in it Bobby Kennedy, Wayne Morse, [James] Eastland, [George] Wallace and all those other supposedly liberal cats, there's something wrong with that party. They're moving politically, not morally. And if that party refuses to seat black people from Mississippi and goes ahead and seats racists like Eastland and his clique, then it is clear to me that they're moving politically and that one cannot begin to talk morality to people like that. We must begin to think politically and see if we can have the power to impose and keep the moral values that we hold high. We must question the values of this society. And I maintain that black people are the best people to do that because we have been excluded from that society and the question is, we ought to think whether or not we want to become a part of that society. . . .

We have grown up and we are the generation that has found this country to be a world power, that has found this country to be the wealthiest country in the world. We must question how she got her wealth. That's what we're questioning. And whether or not we want this country to continue being the wealthiest country in the world at the price of raping everybody across the world. That's what we must begin to question. And because black people are saying we do not now want to become a part of you, we are called reverse racists. Ain't that a gas? . . .

This country knows what power is and knows it very well. And knows what black power is because it's deprived black people of it for 400 years. So it knows what black power is. But the question is, why do white people in this country associate black power with violence? Because of their own inability to deal with blackness. If we had said Negro power, nobody would get scared. Everybody would support it. And if we had said power for colored people, everybody would be for that. But it is the word 'black,' it is the word 'black' that bothers people in this country, and that's their problem, not mine. . . .

And the question is, how will white people who call themselves activists get ready to start moving into the white communities on two counts? On building new political institutions, to destroy the old ones that we have, and to move around the concept of white youth refusing to go into the army. So that we can start then to build a new world.

It is ironic to talk about civilization in this country. This country is uncivilized. It needs to be civilized. We must begin to raise those questions of civilization. What it is, and we'll do it. And so we must urge you to fight now to be the leaders of today, not tomorrow. We've got to be the leaders of today. This country is a nation of thieves. It stands on the brink of becoming a nation of murderers. We must stop it. *We* must stop it.

And then, in a larger sense, there is the question of black people. We are on the move for our liberation. We have been tired of trying to prove things to white people. We are tired of trying to explain to white people that we're not going to hurt them. We are concerned with getting the things we want, the things that we have to have to be able to function. The question is, can white people allow for that in this country? The question is, will white people overcome their racism and allow for that to happen in this country? If that does not happen, brothers and sisters, we have no choice, but to say very clearly, move on over, or we're going to move on over you.

VI CONSCIENTIOUS RESISTANCE TO WAR IN THE TWENTIETH CENTURY

A statute which is contrary to a precept of the natural law has no moral force. . . . Such an enactment is not law at all, but, as St. Thomas calls it, "a species of violence."
—John A. Ryan, Catholic World *(1921)*

33. John Haynes Holmes, "A Statement to My People on the Eve of War" (1917)

John Haynes Holmes, minister of the Community Church of New York (at first the Church of the Messiah) from 1907 to 1949, was an outspoken advocate of civil liberties, social justice, and pacifism; he was a founder and leader of the NAACP, the American Civil Liberties Union, the International Fellowship of Reconciliation, and the War Resisters League.

Unlike Einstein, who suspended his pacifism in the face of the menace of the Third Reich, Holmes reaffirmed his unwavering opposition to all wars even in the immediate aftermath of Pearl Harbor. In 1941 as in 1917, the trustees of his church were nearly unanimous in disavowing his antiwar positions, but they were also firm in their defense of freedom of the pulpit, and Holmes's ministry was not threatened in either case. In 1917, however, a sizable minority of his parishioners left the church rather than sustain a pastoral relation with a preacher of such doctrine. The patriotic fever of the time was expressed in more sinister ways as well: the Secret Service had agents in the congregation to hear each of Holmes's sermons during the war, and in April 1918 the American Unitarian Association (to which Holmes belonged) formally reaffirmed its loyalty to the government and resolved "that any society which employs a minister who is not a willing, earnest and outspoken supporter of the United States in the vigorous and resolute prosecution of the war cannot be considered eligible for aid from the Association." [1]

That he revered both Theodore Parker and Gandhi suggests the tension in Holmes's preaching (especially in the sermon presented here) between uncompromising and aggressive attacks on what he believed to be wrong and a catholicity of feeling that earnestly sought grounds of common humanity and fellowship with his opponents. While the "Statement to My People" unequivocally condemns America's imminent entry into World War I and affirms Holmes's support for draft resistance, it also expresses his respect and affection for friends and parishioners who believed that the war was just and intended to fight in it. During the same week in which the sermon was preached, Holmes publicly announced his dissociation from the Anti-Enlistment League, expressing his wish to "give my blessing and best wishes to the young men of my church who go to the front." [2]

Nonetheless, Holmes insisted that "the whole fabric of democracy is threatened" by war, by conscription, and by the national war fever that inevitably attends them: "Already we are in the midst of such an orgy of bigotry, intolerance, and persecution for opinions' sake, as America has not seen since the days of the Salem witches."[3] He did not exaggerate in observing that "statements of this kind [i.e., like his sermon], made on the eve of war, seem to many persons to be treasonable."[4] In his search for reconciliation without compromise, he thought and spoke his heresies in a language of traditional and powerful affirmation, conceiving of radical dissent and even draft resistance as a deeply patriotic vocation. In this spirit he sought to assimilate the notion of America as a chosen nation to a vision of international brotherhood in which nationalism would have no place.

Reprinted from *The Messiah Pulpit*, May 1917, pp. 4–5, 6, 8–9, 10–12, 15–16, by permission of Donald Szantho Harrington for The Community Church of New York.

. . . You have a right to know what I shall say and do in the event of war, upon what road of doctrine I shall set my feet, into what hazards of pain and peril I shall lead this church. The pew is always entitled to the full confession of the pulpit, but never so urgently as at the time when such confession touches the deep issues of life and death. If there be any here who is tempted to question the wisdom or the sincerity of what I am now doing, let him think for a moment of how easy it would have been for me to keep silent, avoid the questions which are to-day setting the son "at variance against his father, the daughter against her mother, the daughter-in-law against her mother-in-law," and trust to the kindly sentiments of personal affection, conceived, nourished, and matured through ten years of labor in this parish, to sustain the relationship between minister and people unbroken, till happier times should come again to earth. The easiest way, however, in this instance as in all instances, would have been dishonorable, and, in the long run, disastrous. The only honest, the only safe way, is for me to ask you to look me in the face this day—to "search me and know my heart, try me and know my thoughts"—and then to determine whether my God is your God, and we can worship and work together in war as in peace. Therefore, before the bugles sing and the flags are lifted high, I ask you to hear me. My purpose is not

to argue or persuade. I would not even exhort or plead, much
less instruct. I propose simply to speak my whole mind on the
present crisis, and then leave with you my fate.

. . . War is in open and utter violation of Christianity. If war
is right, then Christianity is wrong, false, a lie. If Christianity
is right, then war is wrong, false, a lie. The God revealed by
Jesus, and by every great spiritual leader of the race, is no God
of battles. He lifts no sword—he asks no sacrifice of blood. He is
the Father of all men, Jew and Gentile, bond and free. His spirit
is love, his rule is peace, his method of persuasion is forgiveness. His law, as interpreted and promulgated by the Nazarene,
is "love one another," "resist not evil with evil," "forgive seventy times seven," "overcome evil with good," "love your enemies, bless them that curse you, do good to them that hate you,
pray for them which despitefully use you and persecute you."
Such a God and such a law, others may reconcile with war, if
they can. I cannot—and what I cannot do, I will not profess
to do.

But I must go farther—I must speak not only of war in general, but of this war in particular. Most persons are quite ready
to agree, especially in the piping times of peace, that war is
wrong. But let a war cloud no bigger than a man's hand, appear
on the horizon of the nation's life, and they straightway begin
to qualify their judgment, and if the war cloud grow until it
covers all the heavens, they finally reverse it. This brings the
curious situation of all war being wrong in general, and each
war being right in particular. . . . If you say that this is a war of
defense against wanton and intolerable aggression, I must reply
that every blow which we have endured has been primarily a
blow directed not against ourselves but against England, and
that it has yet to be proved that Germany has any intention or
desire of attacking us. If you say that this war is a life-and-death
struggle for the preservation of civilization against barbarism, I
must ask you why we remained neutral when Belgium was
raped, and were at last aroused to action not by the cries of the
stricken abroad, but by our own losses in men and money? If
you say that this war is a last resort in a situation which every
other method, patiently tried, has failed to meet, I must answer
that this is not true—that other ways and means of action, tried

by experience and justified by success, have been laid before the administration and wilfully rejected.

In its ultimate causes, this war is the natural product and expression of our unchristian civilization. Its armed men are grown from the dragon's teeth of secret diplomacy, imperialistic ambitions, dynastic pride, greedy commercialism, economic exploitation at home and abroad. In the sowing of these teeth, America has had her part; and it is therefore only proper, perhaps, that she should have her part also in the reaping of the dreadful harvest. In its more immediate causes, this war is the direct result of unwarrantable, cruel, but none the less inevitable interferences with our commercial relations with one group of the belligerents. Our participation in the war, therefore, like the war itself, is political and economic, not ethical, in its character. Any honor, dignity, or beauty which there may be in our impending action, is to be found in the impulses, pure and undefiled, which are actuating many patriotic hearts to-day, and not at all in the real facts of the situation. The war itself is wrong. Its prosecution will be a crime. There is not a question raised, an issue involved, a cause at stake, which is worth the life of one blue-jacket on the sea or one khaki-coat in the trenches. I question the sincerity of no man who supports this war—I salute the devotion of every man who proposes to sustain it with his money or his blood. But I say to you that when, years hence, the whole of this story has been told, it will be found that we have been tragically deceived, and all our sacrifices been made in vain.

. . . Nothing that America can do, can quench my passion for her beauty, or divert my loyalty from her service. She is the only country I have, or shall ever have, and I propose that she shall be mine forever, in war or peace, in storm or calm, in evil or good. In this impending crisis with Germany, I believe that she is wrong. She seems to me to be faithless to her own supreme calling among the nations of the earth, disloyal to high interests of humanity long since committed to her care, guilty for a selfish motive of a grievous fault. But her infidelity shall not shake my faith, her disloyalty shall not change my loyalty, her guilt shall not discharge my obligation. I shall decline to become, or to be made, "a man without a country." America has committed wrongs in the past, and she will undoubtedly commit other wrongs in the future. But she is mine, as Hosea's adulterous wife, Gomer, was his; and I will love her, dream of her, hope for her, serve her, without ceasing. "I will betroth thee unto me forever; yea, I will betroth thee unto me in righteousness, in loving kindness and in tender mercy. I will even betroth thee unto me in faithfulness, until thou shalt know the Lord."

And how shall I, a pacifist, serve my country in time of war?

When hostilities begin, it is universally assumed that there is but a single service which a loyal citizen can render to the state —that of bearing arms and killing the enemy. Will you understand me if I say, humbly and regretfully, that this I cannot, and will not, do. If any man or boy in this church answers the call to arms, I shall bless him as he marches to the front. When he lies in the trenches, or watches on the lonely sentinel post, or fights in the charge, I shall follow him with my prayers. If he is brought back dead from hospital or battlefield, I shall bury him with all the honors not of war but of religion. He will have obeyed his conscience and thus performed his whole duty as a man. But I also have a conscience, and that conscience I also must obey. When, therefore, there comes a call for volunteers, I shall have to refuse to heed. When, or if, the system of conscription is adopted, I shall have to decline to serve. If this means a fine, I will pay my fine. If this means imprisonment, I will serve my term. If this means persecution, I will carry my cross. No order of president or governor, no law of nation or state, no loss of reputation, freedom or life, will persuade me or force me to this business of killing. On this issue, for me at least, there is "no compromise." Mistaken, foolish, fanatical, I may be; I will not deny the charge. But false to my own soul I will not be. Therefore here I stand. God help me! I cannot do other!

And this resolution applies, let me now be careful to state, quite as much to my professional as to my personal life. Once war is here, the churches will be called upon to enlist, as will every other social institution. Therefore would I make it plain that, so long as I am your minister, the Church of the Messiah will answer no military summons. Other pulpits may preach recruiting sermons; mine will not. Other parish houses may be turned into drill halls and rifle ranges; ours will not. Other clergymen may pray to God for victory for our arms; I will not. In this church, if nowhere else in all America, the Germans will still be included in the family of God's children. No word of hatred shall be spoken against them—no evil fate shall be desired upon them. War may beat upon our portals, like storm waves on the granite crags; rumors of war may thrill the atmosphere of this sanctuary, as lightning the still air of a summer night. But so long as I am priest, this altar shall be consecrated to human brotherhood, and before it shall be offered worship only to that one God and Father of us all, "who hath made of one blood all nations of men for to dwell together on the face of the earth."

. . . [The] necessity of living together cannot be escaped. . . . To discover terms of reconciliation, to work out methods of co-operation, to soften hate and dispell suspicion, to spread abroad sweet influences of confidence and healing—this is a task as beneficent as it is prodigious. Before she herself became a belligerent, this was the task appointed as by the fiat of God for America. But now that she has cast away this sacred charge, it remains for us who cannot take up arms at her behest, to keep it in her stead. How better can we serve our country than by restoring to her, or fulfilling for her, that high mission of peacemaking, which is so uniquely and divinely hers! . . .

No nation is worthy the allegiance of even the meanest of her citizenry, which is not dedicated to the establishment of that larger and more inclusive life of universal association, which is the glad promise of mankind. America, for more than a hundred years, has been first among the countries of the world, in recognition and service of this ideal. She has been a gathering place of all the tribes of earth—a melting-pot into which the ingredients of every race, religion and nationality have been poured. And out of it has come not so much a new nation as a new idea —the idea of brotherhood. This idea has stamped our people as a chosen people. It has set our land apart as a holy land. It has exalted our destiny as a divine destiny. And now, with the plunge into the welter of contending European nationalities, all this is gone. Gone, at least, if those of us who see not today's quarrel but tomorrow's prophecy, do not dedicate ourselves unfalteringly to the forgotten vision! This I am resolved to do. . . .

34. Carl Haessler, Maurice Hess, and Roger Baldwin: Statements by Conscientious Objectors (1918)

During 1917 and 1918 the Army inducted more than twenty thousand men who had filed claims to be classified as conscientious objectors. Of these about four thousand at first refused to cooperate by accepting noncombatant status, but most of this group eventually served in the Medical Corps or other noncombatant branches of the army, or else accepted agricultural furloughs. Several hundred, however, some of whom were religious and some political objectors, refused all forms of alternative service and were court-martialed and sentenced to prison, some for very long terms. Other men had declined even to register for the draft and so were tried and sentenced by civil courts.[1] Three of the objectors' statements are given here. Carl Haessler was a Rhodes scholar and a professor of philosophy; Maurice Hess later also became a college professor; Roger Baldwin was director of the Civil Liberties Bureau, the precursor of the American Civil Liberties Union.

The Judge Mack referred to in Haessler's statement was a member of the presidential board of inquiry charged with distinguishing between "sincere" and "insincere" conscientious objectors. At stake was often the difference between a civilian furlough to do work in agriculture or in the Red Cross, on the one hand, and a military court-martial on the other.[2]

Reprinted from Norman M. Thomas, *The Conscientious Objector in America* (New York: B. W. Huebsch, 1923), pp. 23–28, by permission of Evan W. Thomas and John W. Gates.

The Statement of Carl Haessler

I, Carl Haessler, Recruit, Machine Gun Company, 46th Infantry, respectfully submit the following statement in extenuation in connection with my proposed plea of guilty to the charge of violation of the 64th Article of War, the offense having been committed June 22, 1918, in Camp Sheridan, Ala.

The offense was not committed from private, secret, personal, impulsive, religious, pacifist or pro-German grounds. An admixture of quasi-personal motives is admitted, but they were in no sense the guiding or controlling factors. I have evidence for each of these assertions, should it be required.

The willful disobedience of my Captain's and of my Lieutenant-Colonel's orders to report in military uniform arose from a conviction which I hesitate to express before my country's military officers but which I nevertheless am at present unable to shake off, namely, that America's participation in the World War was unnecessary, of doubtful benefit (if any) to the country and to humanity, and accomplished largely, though not exclusively, through the pressure of the Allied and American commercial imperialists.

Holding this conviction, I conceived my part as a citizen to be opposition to the war before it was declared, active efforts for a peace without victory after the declaration, and a determination so far as possible to do nothing in aid of the war while its character seemed to remain what I thought it was. I hoped in this way to help bring the war to an earlier close and to help make similar future wars less probable in this country.

I further believe that I shall be rendering the country a service by helping to set an example for other citizens to follow in the matter of fearlessly acting on unpopular convictions instead of forgetting them in time of stress. The crumbling of American radicalism under pressure in 1917 has only been equalled by that of the majority of German socialist leaders in August, 1914.

Looking at my case from the point of view of the administration and of this court, I readily admit the necessity of exemplary punishment. I regret that I have been forced to make myself a nuisance and I grant that this war could not be carried on if objections like mine were recognized by those conducting the war. My respect for the administration has been greatly increased by the courteous and forbearing treatment accorded me since having been drafted, but my view of international politics and diplomacy, acquired during my three years of graduate study in England, has not altered since June, 1917, when I formally declared that I could not accept service if drafted. Although officers have on three occasions offered me noncombatant service if I would put on the uniform, I have regretfully refused each time on the ground that "bomb-proof" service on my part would give the lie to my sincerity (which was freely granted by Judge Julian Mack when he and his colleagues examined me at Camp Gordon). If I am to render any war services, I shall not ask for special privileges.

I wish to conclude this long statement by reiterating that I am not a pacifist or pro-German, not a religious or private objector, but regard myself as a patriotic political objector, acting largely from public and social grounds.

I regret that, while my present view of this war continues, I cannot freely render any service in aid of the war. I shall not complain about the punishment that this court may see fit to mete out to me.

The Statement of Maurice Hess

I do not believe that I am seeking martyrdom. As a young man, life and its hopes and freedom and opportunities for service are sweet to me. I want to go out into the world and make use of what little talent I may have acquired by long and laborious study.

But I know that I dare not purchase these things at the price of eternal condemnation. I know the teaching of Christ, my Savior. He taught us to resist not evil, to love our enemies, to bless them that curse us, and do good to them that hate us. Not only did he teach this, but he also practiced it in Gethsemane, before Pilate, and on Calvary. We would indeed be hypocrites and base traitors to our profession if we would be unwilling to bear the taunts and jeers of a sinful world, and its imprisonment, and torture or death, rather than to participate in war and military service. We know that obedience to Christ will gain for us the glorious prize of eternal life. We cannot yield, we cannot compromise, we must suffer.

Two centuries ago our people were driven out of Germany by religious persecution, and they accepted the invitation of William Penn to come to his colony where they might enjoy the blessing of religious liberty which he promised them. This religious liberty was later confirmed by the Constitution of Pennsylvania, and the Constitution of the United States.

If the authorities now see fit to change those fundamental documents and take away our privilege of living in accordance with the teaching of the scriptures of God, then we have no course but to endure persecution as true soldiers of Christ.

If I have committed anything worthy of bonds or death, I do not refuse to suffer or to die.

I pray God for strength to remain faithful.

The Statement of Roger Baldwin

The compelling motive for refusing to comply with the draft act is my uncompromising opposition to the principle of conscription of life by the state for any purpose whatever, in time of war or peace. I not only refuse to obey the present conscription law, but I would in future refuse to obey any similar statute which attempts to direct my choice of service and ideals. I regard the principle of conscription of life as a flat contradiction of all our cherished ideals of individual freedom, democratic liberty, and Christian teaching.

I am the more opposed to the present act, because it is for the purpose of conducting war. I am opposed to this and all other wars. I do not believe in the use of physical force as a method of achieving any end, however good. . . .

I am not complaining for myself or others. I am merely advising the court that I understand full well the penalty of my heresy, and am prepared to pay it. The conflict with conscription is irreconcilable. Even the liberalism of the President and Secretary of War in dealing with objectors leads those of us who are "absolutists" to a punishment longer and severer than that of desperate criminals.

But I believe most of us are prepared even to die for our faith, just as our brothers in France are dying for theirs. To them we are comrades in spirit—we understand one another's motives, though our methods are wide apart. We both share deeply the common experience of living up to the truth as we see it, whatever the price.

Though at the moment I am of a tiny minority, I feel myself just one protest in a great revolt surging up from among the people—the struggle of the masses against the rule of the world by the few—profoundly intensified by the war. It is a struggle against the political state itself, against exploitation, militarism, imperialism, authority in all forms. . . .

Having arrived at the state of mind in which those views mean the dearest things in life to me, I cannot consistently, with self-respect, do other than I have, namely, to deliberately violate an act which seems to me to be a denial of everything which ideally and in practice I hold sacred.

35. Albert Einstein: The Two Percent Speech (1930)

For much of the period between World War I and Hitler's assumption of power early in 1933, Einstein was a major, militant figure in international pacifism. During the latter part of this era he made many public statements in favor of the refusal of military service, lending the immense prestige of his unparalleled scientific reputation to the support of this radical position. His thinking about draft refusal had two major aspects. One was that in moral terms any war was murder organized on a mass scale and that a conscientious individual ought to refuse to participate in it. "No one," he said, "has the moral right to call himself a Christian or a Jew if he is prepared to commit murder upon the instruction of a given authority."[1] The other was that modern warfare threatened the progress and even the existence of civilization and that war resistance—public refusal to accept conscription—was a uniquely promising method of insisting on the need for new approaches to the resolution of international conflicts. Since compulsory military service was a prop to militarism and a precursor of war, draft refusal struck at one of the root causes of any future armed conflict.[2]

Ultimately, Einstein believed, war could be eliminated only through the creation of a supranational organization with broad support from the community of nations and with the power to enforce its arbitrations of international disputes. But in the meantime war resistance was a crucial means of embodying pacifism in "concrete actions" that would have real political impact.[3] It would, he felt, make pacifism more dramatic (and thus more effective) "because it will inevitably create a conflict by providing a direct challenge to our opponents."[4] He hailed the "young men in twelve countries who are resisting conscription" as "the pioneers of a warless world."[5] One of his best expositions of these views was given in a speech before the New History Society in New York on December 14, 1930, and is reprinted here.

Einstein's prediction that resistance by only 2 percent of the eligible manpower of a modern nation would politically incapacitate it for war is reminiscent of Thoreau's argument that "if one thousand, if one hundred, if ten men whom I could name—if ten *honest* men only—ay, if *one Honest* man, in this State of Massachusetts," were to be jailed for tax refusal, slavery would effectively be abolished by that action. But Einstein's conception relies more directly on political pressure than does that of Thoreau, whose dependence is not on numbers but on the spiritual force inherent in right actions. At the peak of World War II the United States had 11,000,000 men in service; 2 percent of that force would have been 220,000—a formidable number of resisters, needless to say. Even at much lower levels of military preparedness, 2 percent of the American armed forces would be a difficult number of men to prosecute and imprison. Nonetheless, Einstein was clear about at least some of the limitations of his proposal. In 1932 he conceded that in Russia and some other totalitarian countries even 10 percent of the prospective soldiery could simply be eliminated and warmaking go on as before; but he held to the view that if the obstruction were achieved in all the countries where it could work, war would be well on the way to disappearance.[6]

The perfervid militarism and persecutions of the Third Reich, however, changed Einstein's mind on these questions. Though he continued to respect individual acts of conscientious draft resistance, he himself came to feel very quickly that Hitler had decisively altered the circumstances in which such decisions had to be made. By the fall of 1933 he was writing to pacifists in several nations of his new conviction that to embrace pacifism in the face of Hitler's armies was to give up "the defense of culture."[7]

To many pacifists this shift in Einstein's posture was an acute disappointment, an embarrassment, even an outrage.[8] But he was now convinced that military preparedness was the only hope to preserve "the last remnants of personal freedom on the continent of Europe": "To prevent the greater evil, it is necessary that the lesser evil—the hated military—be accepted for the time being. Should German armed might prevail, life will not be worth living anywhere in Europe. . . . In the present circumstances, realistic pacifists should no longer advocate the destruction of military power; rather, they should strive for its internationalization."[9]

Einstein could in any case argue that his change in views was not an inconsistency. He had long since admitted that in some exceptional circumstances war resistance was not a reasonable choice, and now Hitler had brought such conditions to Europe. Still, the "Two Percent Speech" turned out to mark a preliminary stage in Einstein's social and political thought, one that he himself would later call "primitive." [10]

Einstein delivered the "Two Percent Speech" en route from his home in Berlin to the California Institute of Technology, where he was to spend several weeks as a visiting lecturer. He spoke extemporaneously in German, but a translator was present and his remarks were widely reported and quoted in the American press. By the end of 1933 he had left Germany for Princeton and had been declared an "enemy of the state" by the Nazis. In 1940 he became an American citizen.

Reprinted from Otto Nathan and Heinz Norden, eds., *Einstein on Peace* (New York: Simon & Schuster, 1960), pp. 116–118, by permission of Otto Nathan, trustee, Estate of Albert Einstein.

When those who are bound together by pacifist ideals hold a meeting they are usually consorting only with their own kind. They are like sheep huddled together while wolves wait outside. I believe that pacifist speakers face this difficulty: they ordinarily reach only their own group, people who are pacifists anyhow and hardly need to be convinced. The sheep's voice does not reach beyond this circle and is, therefore, ineffectual. That is the real weakness of the pacifist movement.

Genuine pacifists, those whose heads are not in the clouds but who think in realistic terms, must fearlessly endeavor to act in a manner which is of practical value to the cause rather than remain content merely to espouse the ideals of pacifism. Deeds, not words, are needed; mere words get pacifists nowhere. They must initiate action and begin with what can be achieved now.

As to what our next step should be, I should like you to realize that under the present military system every man is compelled to commit the crime of killing for his country. The aim of all pacifists must be to convince others of the immorality of war and rid the world of the shameful slavery of military service. I wish to suggest two ways to achieve that aim.

The first has already been put into practice: uncompromising war resistance and refusal to do military service under any circumstances. In countries where conscription exists, the true pacifist must refuse military duty. Already, a considerable number of pacifists in many countries have refused and are refusing, at great personal sacrifice, to serve a military term in peacetime. By doing so, it becomes manifest that they will not fight in the event of war.

In countries where compulsory service does not exist, true pacifists must publicly declare in time of peace that they will not take up arms under any circumstances. This, too, is an effective method of war resistance. I earnestly urge you to try to convince people all over the world of the justice of this position. The timid may say, "What is the use? We shall be sent to prison." To them I would reply: Even if only two per cent of those assigned to perform military service should announce their refusal to fight, as well as urge means other than war of settling international disputes, governments would be powerless, they would not dare send such a large number of people to jail.

A second line of action for war resisters, which I suggest, is a policy which would not involve personal involvement with the law. That is, to try to establish through international legislation the right to refuse military service in peacetime. Those who are unwilling to accept such a position might prefer to advocate legislation which would permit them, in place of military service, to do some strenuous or even dangerous work, in the interest of their own country or of mankind as a whole. They would thereby prove that their war resistance is unselfish and merely a logical consequence of the belief that international differences can be settled in ways other than fighting; it would further prove that their opposition to war could not be attributed to cowardice or the desire for personal comfort or unwillingness to serve their country or humanity. If we declare our willingness to accept work of a dangerous nature, we shall have advanced far on the road to a more peaceful world.

I further suggest that pacifists of all countries start raising funds to support those who would want to refuse military service but who cannot actually do so for lack of financial means. I, therefore, advocate the establishment of an international organization and an international pacifist fund to support the active war resisters of our day.

In conclusion, may I say that the serious pacifists who want to accomplish peace must have the courage to initiate and to carry on these aims; only then will the world be obliged to take notice.

Pacifists will then be heard by people who are not already pacifists; and once they are listened to, their message is bound to
be effective. If they are too restrained, their voices will continue
to reach only those in their own circle. They will remain sheep,
pacifist sheep.

36. Jessie Wallace Hughan: *The Beginnings of War Resistance* (1935)

Jessie Wallace Hughan was educated at Barnard and Columbia (where
she received a Ph.D. from the School of Political Science in 1911) and
then entered on a long career as an English teacher and an administrator in New York City high schools.[1] Her second vocation—as a prominent pacifist and Socialist—affected her first one: for more than a decade before, during, and after World War I she was at odds with an
educational hierarchy that feared and disapproved of her radicalism.
There were disputes over loyalty oaths (Miss Hughan insisted on add-
ing the phrase "in so far as the dictates of my conscience permit" to her
declaration of allegiance to the state and federal constitutions);[2] the
Board of Superintendents delayed her promotion for years because of
her politics.[3] In 1919 she was publicly named by a Senate committee
as one of sixty-two well-known "men and women who have been re-
corded as active in movements which did not help the United States
when the country was fighting the Central Powers."[4]
Her views were unwavering, however. She organized the Anti-
Enlistment League, was the principal founder of the War Resisters
League, was active in the Fellowship of Reconciliation, and ran on the
Socialist ticket for lieutenant governor, for congressman, for senator,
and for several lesser offices. In 1918, as the Socialist candidate for secretary of state of New York, she received nearly 100,000 votes in New
York City alone, but none of her campaigns approached an electoral
victory.
Miss Hughan wrote or edited more than a dozen books and pamphlets; the major ones, especially *The Facts of Socialism* (1913) and
A Study of International Government (1923), received considerable notice
and respectful reviews. Her long support of draft refusal (and related
actions) as a pacifist principle and tactic is perhaps best expressed in
The Beginnings of War Resistance, a pamphlet written for the War Resisters League in 1935. Chiefly a concise history of radical pacifism in the

United States and Europe from 1914 to 1935, it supports radical war resistance as an organized political tactic. (Miss Hughan expresses disappointment in less aggressive measures, including individual refusals of conscription which proceed solely from motives of private conscience.) She held to her radical pacifist position even after Pearl Harbor, believing (in the words of one historian) that even "German military defeats would in turn exact reprisals upon the Jewish scapegoat."[5]

❀   Reprinted from Jessie Wallace Hughan, *The Beginnings of War Resistance* (New York: War Resisters League, 1935).

There existed [in the United States] after the Armistice . . . no organization comparable to the war-time No-Conscription Fellowship in Great Britain which should enroll men and women of differing political and religious beliefs under the refusal to give support to war. Pacifists of the liberal type were inclined to place their hopes in the League of Nations, those of the Radical Wing in the Soviet Republic. To the absolutist minority conscientious objection was still more or less of an individual "soul-saving" affair, of a class with one's personal creed. With only a few did the growing reliance of the Soviets upon violence and of the League upon the militarist powers, strengthen the conviction that the war regime would not end until substantial numbers in each nation should make clear in advance their unconditional refusal to engage in the next suicidal folly at government bidding. . . .

How great a number is needed in order to be effective? No one knows, but this much is clear. Every belligerent government in the World War poured out millions in the effort to produce at least the semblance of 100% support on the part of the nation. It is certain that any administration would be hampered by the necessity of jailing even ten thousand and thus advertising its lack of popular support. . . .

[So] the War Resisters League has continued its work, the enrollment under the following declaration of men and women who for any reason whatsoever are uncompromisingly opposed to all war:

War is a crime against humanity. I, therefore, am determined not to support any kind of war, international or civil, and to strive for the removal of all the causes of war.

With no endowment and no large contributors, officered by persons whose energies are already taxed with other responsibilities in work for a better world, it has increased its enrollment from 985 in 1928 to 2,115 in 1931 and 9,562 in April, 1935. . . . In New York it has three times initiated a *No More War* Parade, held under the auspices of a joint committee. The first parade numbered three hundred marchers, the second, 3,000, the third, 10,000. While the League welcomes all efforts to lessen the power of militarism through disarmament and world organization, it makes these no part of its work, leaving them to the liberal peace groups in whose province they naturally fall. On the other hand, it rejects all suggestions to modify its refusal in favor of either "civil"* or "defensive" war, though it could obviously multiply its membership many times by these concessions.

In estimating the strength of War Resistance in the United States, we must add to the numbers of the War Resisters League those of the Fellowship of Reconciliation, at least equally large, and of the Women's Peace Union.

We must take into account, moreover, the thousands of persons who have registered their determination to take no part in war, but have not allied themselves definitely with war resistance groups: the 13,000 ministers listed in the questionnaire sent out by Kirby Page, editor of *The World Tomorrow*; the members of the Socialist Party, committed to internationalism; the 13,500 signers of Peace Letters and other declarations to the President circulated by the War Resisters League; and perhaps most significant of all, the hosts of students throughout the country who have declared in no uncertain terms their refusal to offer themselves as a sacrifice to government ineptitude. In the recent poll of students taken by the *Literary Digest* 89,765 or 82.18% registered their refusal to serve in any war outside the territory of the U.S., and 17,951 or 16.46% registered their refusal to bear arms even in case the U.S. should be invaded. The Committee for Student Enrollment of the WRL, organized by Frank Olmstead, has played no small part in preparing students for this significant vote. Although a number of student protesters must be counted among the Communist anti-imperialists,

---

*I.e., wars of revolution. Many militants, especially Communists, would refuse to sign the WRL's pledge unless it contained such an exemption.—Ed.

the returns from the colleges indicate with certainty a growing consciousness on the part of youth that declarations of war are scraps of paper to the extent that men refuse to fight. We are fairly safe in assuming the 15,000 enrolled war resisters in the U.S. to represent perhaps ten times as many men and women who have determined for themselves never to support another war. In time of trial—and the trial will be no child's play—there will be many who yield to fear and herd pressure; on the other hand, there are strong spirits whose defiance will be awakened by the crisis itself, as in the World War, when C.O.'s sprang up in quarters untouched by peace propaganda. . . .

The story of these pages . . . has shown a definite turning of the radical peace movement toward the personal and immediate boycott of war.* It marks a clear trend toward realism resulting from the disillusionment of 1914–1918. A generation of polite peace lobbying culminated in the most savage war of history. Four years of liberal proposals for a just settlement were scrapped in favor of the iniquities of Versailles. Governments not yet recovered from one futile tragedy are now proceeding to rush blindly along the pathway to the next.

The old-line peace advocates continue to request militarist powers to give up their respective advantages in land, sea, and air armament and to yield a portion of their sovereignty to the world state. The war resistance movement has lost faith in these requests. It demands, and puts force into its demands,—the force of the strike, of standing with hands folded, the force of withholding supplies which brought King John and King Charles to submission and compelled Louis XVI to convoke the Estates-General. The movement is still in its infancy, counting to thousands where hundreds of thousands are required. But in its twenty years of existence it has stirred to bitter persecution the war departments of the powers, which only smile tolerantly at the efforts of peace liberals. It has worried into a growl the war monster who has been growing in strength and savagery for twenty centuries.

---

* "Personal" here refers to public refusals of conscription undertaken by individuals acting in concert with others, as opposed to more moderate positions that do not explicitly commit the pacifist to a potentially lawbreaking course. Merely individual acts of war resistance are not of concern to Miss Hughan in this passage, since she regards them as apolitical.—Ed.

37. Leon Thomson, Donald Benedict, David Dellinger, and others: *Why We Refused to Register* (1941)

While the draft law of World War I had required conscientious objectors to perform noncombatant military service, the 1940 Burke-Wadsworth legislation offered them a nonmilitary alternative under the Civilian Public Service. Since the new law still required them to register with the Selective Service and then to perform their obligatory labor as a sort of adjunct to the military manpower system, however, some objectors felt that cooperation with it would be a form of complicity in the draft itself. Some of them saw this complicity in secular terms, as a personal partnership in militarism or imperialism; others viewed it as a compromise of their Christian pacifism. The statements that follow explain why their authors chose trial and imprisonment over the civilian employment that was available to them.

Leon Thomson was a Kansan who was serving on the field staff of the National Council for Prevention of War. Donald Benedict, Joseph J. Bevilacqua, Meredith Dallas, David Dellinger, George M. Houser, William H. Lovell, Howard E. Spragg, and Richard J. Wichlei were students at Union Theological Seminary in New York; they belonged to several Protestant denominations. In November 1940 they were sentenced to a year and a day in federal prison.[1]

❧ Reprinted from *Why We Refused to Register*, published jointly by the Fellowship of Reconciliation, the Keep America Out of War Congress, the National Council for Prevention of War, the Young People's Socialist League, and the War Resisters League (New York [1941?]), pp. 3, 5–7, from a copy in the Swarthmore College Peace Collection.

The Statement of Leon Thomson

On this day of deep personal regret that my beloved America should ever initiate conscription, I find that the proposal for me to participate in this system is in direct conflict with my fundamental religious convictions.

Conscription has always been abhorrent to free men because it is, in effect, a seizure of a man's body, time, and service by force and under threat of heavy penalty. This I regard as violence, just as the ultimate conscription aim of military operations is violence. . . .

The law states that a person who is "conscientiously opposed to war in any form" must nonetheless accept the specified forms of either army or labor service. This I regard as misleading to the pacifist who means that he finds "any form" beyond his convictions. The draft provides for the conscientious soldier as it does for the non-combatant and civilian worker, but it makes no mention of individuals who disbelieve in conscription for any purpose. . . .

The cleavage between my loyalty to God and to the State is at stake. I grant the right of the State to conscript property, under due process of law. . . . The State is an instrument for the socialization of property; I am eager that law should abound in that arena. The State may even forcibly restrain my physical body. But the United States Government did not create me; God did that. I must account to God for the real me, since man is a spiritual being. . . .

We have a huge task in our country—to defend our civil liberties; to put our unemployed to work at productive labor; to put an end to the disabilities under which Negroes and other minorities suffer; to organize the vast resources and energies of this nation so as to provide the material basis of the good life for all our people; to feed the starving and heal the wounded of Europe and Asia; to be ready to throw our full energies into the rehabilitation of war-torn nations. Were we to perform this task, our example of a "democracy that worked" would rob dictatorship of its arguments, and the power of democratic demonstration would constitute a far more sure defense than bombers and battleships. It is to these constructive labors that I desire to devote myself. . . .

If we go on with wars, what will remain of the America I love? Some will say that armed forces will "protect" me while I hew to my peace convictions, but I wish with all my heart that they, too, would not use destruction, and I deny that by so doing they "protect" me. I regard war as an eminent producer of more confusion rather than a solution of fearful problems. And although I am sure a sincere soldier must go to war if that is his highest devotion, yet I am simultaneously sure that the values I cherish will be corrupted by his actions, and that the soldier stands an awful chance of being betrayed in his idealism. . . .

I have never been more certain of anything in my life than in my present course. God beckons me to a far more significant life than war can offer. Aware of my own imperfection and the shortcomings of my testimony, I wish to follow this Truth wherever it may lead. . . .

The joint statement of Donald Benedict, Joseph J. Bevilacqua, Meredith Dallas, David Dellinger, George M. Houser, William H. Lovell, Howard E. Spragg, and Richard J. Wichlei

It is impossible for us to think of the conscription law without at the same time thinking of the whole war system, because it is clear to us that conscription is definitely a part of the institution of war. . . .

To us, the war system is an evil part of our social order, and we declare that we cannot cooperate with it in any way. War is an evil because it is in violation of the Way of Love as seen in God through Christ. It is a concentration and accentuation of all the evils of our society. War consists of mass murder, deliberate starvation, vandalism, and similar evils. Physical destruction and moral disintegration are the inevitable result. The war method perpetuates and compounds the evils it purports to overcome. It is impossible, as history reveals, to overcome evil with evil. The last World War is a notorious case of the failure of the war system, and there is no evidence to believe that this war will be any different. It is our positive proclamation as followers of Jesus Christ that we must overcome evil with good. We seek in our daily living to reconcile that separation of man from man and man from God which produces war.

We have also been led to our conclusion on the conscription law in the light of its totalitarian nature. It is a totalitarian move when our government insists that the manpower of the nation take a year of military training. It is a totalitarian move for the President of the nation to be able to conscript industry to produce certain materials which are deemed necessary for national defense without considering the actual physical needs of the people. We believe, therefore, that by opposing the Selective Service law, we will be striking at the heart of totalitarianism as well as war. . . .

We feel a deep bond of unity with those who decide to register as conscientious objectors, but our own decision must be different for the following reasons:

If we register under the act, even as conscientious objectors, we are becoming part of the act. The fact that we as conscientious objectors may gain personal exemption from the most crassly un-Christian requirements of the act does not compensate for the fact that we are complying with it and accepting its protection. If a policeman (or a group of vigilantes) stops us on the street, our possession of the government's card shows that we are 'all right'—we have complied with the act for the militarization of Ameria. If that does not hurt our Christian consciences, what will? If we try to rationalize on the theory that we must go along with the act in order to fight the fascism and militarism of which it is a part, it seems to us that we are doing that very thing which all pacifist Christians abhor: we are consciously employing bad means on the theory that to do so will contribute to a good end. . . .

In similar vein, it is urged that great concessions have been won for religious pacifists and that we endanger these by our refusal to accept them. Fascism, as it gradually supplanted democracy in Germany, was aided by the decision of Christians and leftists to accept a partial fascism rather than to endanger those democratic concessions which still remained. It is not alone for our own exemption from fighting that we work—it is for freedom of the American people from fascism and militarism.

Partial exemption of conscientious objectors has come about partly through the work of influential pacifists and partly through the open-mindedness of certain non-pacifists. But it has also been granted because of the fear of the government that, without such a provision, public opposition to war would be too great to handle. In particular, it seems to us that one of the reasons the government has granted exemption to ministers and theological students is to gain a religious sanction for its diabolical war. Where actual support could not be gained, it hoped to soothe their consciences so that they could provide no real opposition.

We do not contend that the American people maliciously choose the vicious instrument of war. In a very perplexing situation, they lack the imagination, the religious faith, and the precedents to respond in a different manner. This makes it all the more urgent to build in this country and throughout the world a group trained in the techniques of non-violent opposition to the encroachments of militarism and fascism. Until we build such a movement, it will be impossible to stall the war machine at home. When we do build such a movement, we will have forged the only weapon which can ever give effective answer to foreign invasion. Thus in learning to fight American Hitlerism we will show an increasing group of war-disillusioned Americans how to resist foreign Hitlers as well.

For these reasons we hereby register our refusal to comply in any way with the Selective Training and Service Act. We do not expect to stem the war forces today; but we are helping to build the movement that will conquer in the future.

38. Albert Bigelow: "Why I Am Sailing into the Pacific Bomb-Test Area" (1958)

In the spring of 1958, under the auspices of a coordinating committee known as Non-Violent Action against Nuclear Weapons, Albert Bigelow and three crew members attempted to sail the *Golden Rule*, a thirty-foot ketch, into the area of the Pacific where the United States government was carrying out tests of the hydrogen bomb. Though the *Golden Rule* herself was stopped in Hawaii, where the crew was arrested and jailed for violating a court injunction, another vessel, the *Phoenix*, succeeded in sailing into the test area itself (where its master, Earle Reynolds, was also arrested).

Bigelow and the others on the *Golden Rule* wanted to perform a powerfully symbolic act in opposition to the nuclear tests, but they did not seek a conflict with the law. Indeed, they would have preferred to avoid the entanglements and distractions of hearings and trials, especially when these proceedings kept them from reaching their destination. Their Gandhian perspectives, however, accommodated civil disobedience as well as nonviolent direct action. Shortly before they set sail, Bigelow published the following statement of their purposes and values.

Albert Bigelow is a painter and architect who has participated in many peace vigils, marches, and demonstrations. He is a Quaker. On

August 6, 1957, the twelfth anniversary of the bombing of Hiroshima, he was arrested in Nevada during a nonviolent protest against atomic tests that were being conducted there. In 1961 he took part in a Freedom Ride from Washington, D.C., to Alabama. In 1969 he was arrested for reading the names of Vietnam war dead on the steps of the Capitol.[1]

Reprinted from Albert Bigelow, *The Voyage of the "Golden Rule": An Experiment with Truth* (New York: Doubleday, 1959), pp. 44–47, by permission of Albert Bigelow and *Liberation* magazine.

My friend Bill Huntington and I are planning to sail a small vessel westward into the Pacific H-bomb test area. By April we expect to reach the nuclear testing grounds at Eniwetok. We will remain there as long as the tests of H-bombs continue. With us will be two other volunteers.

Why?

Why do I feel under compulsion, under moral orders, as it were, to do this?

The answer to such questions, at least in part, has to do with my experience as a Naval officer during World War II. . . .

The Turkey Shoot

From March to October of 1943 I was in command of a subchaser in the Solomon Islands. It was during this period that more than one hundred Japanese planes were shot down in one day. This was called "the turkey shoot." The insensitivity which decent men must develop in such situations is appalling. I remember that the corpse of a Japanese airman who had been shot down was floating bolt upright in one of the coves, a position resulting from the structure of the Japanese life belts, which were different from our Mae Wests. Each day as we passed the cove we saw this figure, his face growing blacker under the terrific sun. We laughingly called him Smiling Jack. As a matter of fact, I think I gave him that name myself and felt rather proud of my wit.

Later in World War II, I was Captain of the destroyer escort *Dale W. Peterson*—DE 337—and I was on her bridge as we approached Pearl Harbor from San Diego when the first news arrived of the explosion of an atomic bomb over Hiroshima. Although I had no way of understanding what an atom bomb was I was absolutely awe-struck, as I suppose all men were for a moment. Intuitively it was then that I realized for the first time that morally war is impossible.

I think also that deep down somewhere in me, and in all men at all times, there is a realization that the pattern of violence meeting violence makes no sense, and that war violates something central in the human heart—"that of God," as we Quakers sometimes say. For example, later, when each of us at the trial in Nevada had told why we were committing civil disobedience against nuclear tests, our attorney, Francis Heisler, said: "There isn't one of us in this courtroom who doesn't wish that he had walked into the testing grounds with these people this morning." Everybody, including the police and court officers, nodded assent.

Society of Friends

However, I am ahead of my story. At the close of the war, in spite of what I had felt on the bridge of that destroyer, I did not break away from my habitual attitudes. For a time I was Housing Commissioner of Massachusetts. Like many other people who had been through the war, I was seeking some sort of unified life-philosophy or religion. I did a good deal of religious "window-shopping." I became impressed by the fact that in one way or another the saints, the wise men, those who seemed to me truly experienced, all pointed in one direction—toward nonviolence, truth, love; toward a way and a goal that could not be reconciled with war. For quite a while, to use a phrase of Alan Watts', I "sucked the finger instead of going where it pointed." But finally I realized that I did have to move in that direction, and in 1952 I resigned my commission in the Naval Reserve. It was promptly and courteously accepted. I felt a bit proud of doing it a month before I would have become eligible for a pension. Such little things we pride ourselves on!

I worshiped often with the Quakers, the Society of Friends. My wife Sylvia had already joined the Society in 1948. As late as 1955 I was still fighting off joining the Society, which seemed to me to involve a great, awesome commitment. I suppose I was like the man in Bernard Shaw's play *Androcles and the Lion* who wanted "to be a Christian—but not yet."

I was not yet ready; ready as 17-year-old Betsy Gurney had written in her journal in 1798, "I know now what the mountain is I have to climb. I am to be a Quaker."

The Hiroshima Maidens

Then came the experience of having in our home, for more than a year, two of the Hiroshima maidens who had been injured and disfigured in the bombing of August 6, 1945. Norman Cousins and other wonderful people brought them to this country for plastic surgery. There were two things about these girls that hit me very hard and forced me to see that I had no choice but to make the commitment to live, as best I could, a life of nonviolence and reconciliation. One was the fact that when they were bombed in 1945 the two girls in our home were seven and thirteen years old. What earthly thing could they have done to give some semblance of what we call justice to the ordeal inflicted upon them and hundreds like them? What possible good could come out of human action—war—which bore such fruits? Is it not utter blasphemy to think that there is anything moral or Christian about such behavior?

The other thing that struck me was that these young women found it difficult to believe that we, who were not members of their families, could love them. But they loved us; they harbored no resentment against us or other Americans. How are you going to respond to that kind of attitude? The newly elected president of the National Council of Churches, Edwin T. Dahlberg, said in his inaugural talk that instead of "massive retaliation" the business of Christians is to practice "massive reconciliation." Well, these Hiroshima girls practiced "massive reconciliation" on us, on me, who had laughed derisively at "Smiling Jack." What response can one make to this other than to give oneself utterly to destroying the evil, war, that dealt so shamefully with them and try to live in the spirit of sensitivity and reconciliation which they displayed?

I was now ready.

I Am Going Because . . .

I am going because, as Shakespeare said, "Action is eloquence." Without some such direct action, ordinary citizens lack the power any longer to be seen or heard by their government.

I am going because it is time to do something about peace, not just talk about peace.

I am going because, like all men, in my heart I know that all nuclear explosions are monstrous, evil, unworthy of human beings.

I am going because war is no longer a feudal jousting match; it is an unthinkable catastrophe for all men.

I am going because it is now the little children, and, most of all, the as yet unborn who are the front-line troops. It is my duty to stand between them and this horrible danger.

I am going because it is cowardly and degrading for me to stand by any longer, to consent, and thus to collaborate in atrocities.

I am going because I cannot say that the end justifies the means. A Quaker, William Penn, said, "A good end cannot sanctify evil means; nor must we ever do evil that good may come of it." A Communist, Milovan Djilas, says, "As soon as means which would ensure an end are shown to be evil, the end will show itself as unrealizable."

I am going because, as Gandhi said, "God sits in the man opposite me; therefore to injure him is to injure God himself."

I am going to witness to the deep inward truth we all know, "Force can subdue, but love gains."

I am going because however mistaken, unrighteous, and unrepentant governments may seem, I still believe all men are really good at heart, and that my act will speak to them.

I am going in the hope of helping change the hearts and minds of men in government. If necessary I am willing to give my life to help change a policy of fear, force, and destruction to one of trust, kindness, and help.

I am going in order to say, "Quit this waste, this arms race. Turn instead to a disarmament race. Stop competing for evil, compete for good."

I am going because I have to—if I am to call myself a human being.

When you see something horrible happening, your instinct is to do something about it. You can freeze in fearful apathy or you can even talk yourself into saying that it isn't horrible. I can't do that. I have to act. This is too horrible. We know it. Let's all act.

39. Charlotte E. Keyes: "'Suppose They Gave a War and No One Came'" (1966)

For the act of civil disobedience chronicled in this article Gene Keyes was sentenced to three years in jail. He served thirteen months in federal prisons in Oklahoma and Missouri, and was paroled. Subsequently he worked for two years for a bookplate company in Ohio and then resumed his formal education, receiving his bachelor's and master's degrees in government from Southern Illinois University. He is now working on his doctoral dissertation at York University in Ontario.[1]

The publication of "'Suppose They Gave a War and No One Came'" in *McCall's* in the fall of 1966 carried support for antiwar civil disobedience into the pages of a mass-circulation magazine at a time when most Americans still supported the country's military involvement in Southeast Asia. The article was reprinted and distributed by several peace organizations and was used by draft counselors to help the parents of resisters understand their sons' ideas and attitudes. Its modest account of the gradual disappearance of one mother's opposition to her son's lawbreaking implicitly invited the reader to undergo the same shift in perspective. The unpretentiousness and self-deprecation of its tone, the fact that the author did not herself commit civil disobedience, and *McCall's* imprimatur all combined to create a rhetoric capable of swaying a vast audience beyond the reach of more polemical voices.

Mrs. Keyes has remained active in the Women's International League for Peace and Freedom and in the peace movement generally, working for complete amnesty for draft resisters and for reductions in the defense budget.[2]

Reprinted from *McCall's*, October 1966, pp. 26, 187–191. Abridged by permission of the author and McIntosh & Otis, Inc.

Carl Sandburg once told of a little girl who, after hearing his description of a Civil War battle, observed, "Suppose they gave a war and no one came."

Our son Gene has committed himself to that goal—to the day no one will come to war. The cost for him is high. He once told my husband and me, to our exasperation, "Jail is my destiny." And he has indeed been imprisoned four times. His last sentence was three years in a federal penitentiary for refusing induction into the armed services. At the trial, he explained why: "There is no moral validity to any part of any law whose purpose is to train people to kill one another."

What kind of oddball is our son, who decided against applying for alternative service as a conscientious objector because "that was selfish—to try to exempt just myself from military duty. It's the fact that my country, and every other country, teaches all of us that murder is right, when we know it's wrong, that I must witness against"?

Who are all of these "nonviolent agitators," these "peaceniks," these draft-card burners, who are often taunted for not working daily from nine to five, but who many times put in seven days a week, from dawn to midnight, on their chosen work?

We see them on television, picketing the White House or the Pentagon or a missile base, carrying signs and solemnly marching, in silence or gaily singing. Some of them are bearded, and the camera focuses on these and the long-haired ones, although the great majority have neatly trimmed hair and clean-shaven faces.

The peaceniks these days are legion—they are ninety years old and fifteen, heads of families and housewives with babies, students, young people who have gone back to tilling the soil in their search for basic realities. But a good many, as in the civil-rights movement, are young and unmarried, temporarily school dropouts. The radical pacifists among them are usually living a life of voluntary poverty, in order to be free to work for the kingdom of heaven or a truly great society.

No one of them can be called typical. They are very much individualists. But the one I know best, of course, is my own son. Perhaps if we follow his career, we can get behind the bearded stereotype fed to us by newspaper, movie, cartoon and comic strip.

What is Gene like? At twenty-five, he has been in jail; has been publicly condemned in resolutions passed by veterans' organizations in his Midwestern home town, as well as by the County Board of Supervisors; has postponed indefinitely all thought of any career except working for peace, because he is convinced that unless a wholly committed effort is made by him and many others, our world will soon be destroyed by nuclear catastrophe.

Is he a nut? Doesn't he think about his parents at all? How must we feel to have such a rebel for a son? Doesn't it humiliate us in our community—a university town, where my husband teaches?

To be quite honest, we have run the gamut from shock, disagreement, anger to "patient" (we always thought) explanation of why he was wrong, on to pride and finally to learning from him and changing our own lives.

Over the years, since Gene left college, we have tried to find the seeds of his present way of life and have more than once been taken aback to realize that we ourselves had planted some of them. One friend told us, "What else could you expect Gene to do, the way he's been brought up?"

Well, we parents don't realize—do we?—when we inculcate our moral standards, that the children may try really to live by them. Many of the American soldiers in World War II were not able to "pull the trigger" in combat, because at home and church they'd been taught "Thou shalt not kill." The Army had to change its training methods drastically before the young boys could be made into effective killers.

In Gene's case, he grew up in a home part Quaker (Scott, my husband, born to another denomination, is now, by choice, a Quaker); part Jewish (me); all pacifist, but "respectably" pacifist. Scott and I had been antimilitarists in the 'thirties and had indeed worked hard upholding our beliefs, but never with the total commitment that is our son's way. When World War II began, we regretfully felt that Hitlerism had to be fought with violence. It was not until 1945, four years after Gene was born, that we were drawn to learn more of the Quakers, because they knew no enemy and helped all with equal compassion.

How did Gene come to translate our peaceful ways into such uncompromising action? Was he always a rebel? people ask us. Yes, he was always a rebel, though a quiet and thoughtful one, from his schoolboy days. He was a fairly good student, interested in baseball, the high-school paper, dramatics and space travel. He always had friends—not a big circle, but warm and enduring ones. . . .

Gene was always a worrier. He worried, from the time he was a very little boy, about the ants and flies and spiders I killed as I cleaned house. I laughed at him at first, until I remembered how Albert Schweitzer had lived with just such reverence for life, even to squeezing grapefruit juice on the floor for the ants to eat. I made the mistake of telling this to Gene, and sure enough, every morning, there was the ants' juice, squeezed for them on the kitchen floor.

By the time Gene reached college, he was ready to take on the world's problems. This was in an era when students were still called the silent generation. His letters from college and vacation tales of his life there were normal enough. True, he picketed a Boston store whose Southern branch did not serve Negroes at its lunch counter, taught Spanish at a nearby jail, explored every student liberal group. All through school he'd been interested in so many things that he'd never been an honor student—usually a good, sturdy B with an occasional A. Then he began dropping to Cs and Ds.

As I reread my letters to Gene, at times they make me glow and at times make me blush. It's a salutary thing to read a correspondence one has had with one's son. I learned I was no Lady Chesterfield. Instead, I jumped around like a hen on a hot griddle, now approving and admiring, then suddenly growing alarmed and veering to waspish criticism. And it was this written advice I'd expected would steer him into the calm waters of living like everybody else. I suppose I still feel that some of my points were well taken; but it's fortunate that though his father's letters were few and sometimes as inconsistent as mine, they were all sober, calm and just.

We must have confused Gene by our changes in tone, because during his first year at Harvard, when we thought he was safely stashed away, our words were generally admiring. In the early months, we kept commending the causes he was taking up.

Later, writing about a theme he sent us, for which he'd received a lower grade than he had hoped for, I went further. "Life is too full of other things right now for you to sweat over every word of a theme—too full of wrongs to be righted, picket lines to be walked. So your theme was the best you could do in the pattern of your life and of what you think is important."

In February, the tone of the letters began to change. The Christmas holidays had been filled with long talks and with much advice from us elders about Gene's use of time and his slipping grades. He had a scholarship, and although his first year's average had been mediocre, Harvard had given him the benefit of the doubt and renewed the scholarship. Now his marks were worse than they were before.

His problem came, of course, from the immense amount of time he spent in such outside activities as campaigning for a peace-minded Congressman, leafleting about nuclear bombs, picketing for civil rights and working for social betterment with his Friends Meeting and student liberal groups. At Christmas, the three of us had carefully listed everything, including class attendance, class preparation, term papers, examinations, cafeteria job, eating, sleeping and recreation. Something had to go, and that something had to be outside activities.

We thought Gene had agreed to this. In fact, he *had* agreed. But though he tried, when he returned to college, to practice what we preached, spirit was having trouble following reason's sage advice.

Scott wrote him: "In regard to your single-mindedness—which, I take it, is peace these days—if you want to be in a position to exert real leverage, you should guard against dissipating your efforts and energies at this time. . . . How will you best serve the cause of peace: By throwing yourself into the fight now, in what may be exciting but relatively minor engagements, at the expense of your studies? Or by turning in a creditable performance at school, and on the basis of that performance getting yourself set for more strategic roles where you take part in heavier engagements? Well, maybe all this is just well-meaning but misguided moralizing. Who knows? Do what you have to do, and we will be behind you."

Already crossing ours in the mail that month of February came Gene's letter that threw the bombshell, if a pacifist will excuse the expression. It began with: "Page for page, this letter has more news than any I've ever written, so take it slowly, and perhaps read it twice. . . . I've been persuaded of the effectiveness of outright nonviolent civil disobedience. I'm not the first college student to join this movement full-time, and those who have are yelling for more. The more who give up the works to join all the way, the more physically effective this thing is going to be. . . .

"This won't be a glamorous business like running away to sea, although that's what I'm doing as it were, and it will have all the drudgery that starry-eyed lads found when they did so. The business of Polaris Action is mostly leafleting, speaking, clerical, canvassing, with infrequent melodramatic and physically dangerous moments of submarine boarding. (It's the Gandhian idea of lying across the railroad tracks, except we're lying across the Polaris Submarines.) Polaris efforts are just like any politicking, about the same proportion of glamour and lots of tedium, about 1 to 20 maybe.

"The decision is not a sudden one, but fourteen months in the making and fourteen years indirectly. I understand fully the enormity of this departure and its counter considerations. Without exaggeration, that is the outcome of every hour of sixty weeks of direct meditation on the problem. Most importantly, I have tried to *know thyself,* and to the best of my knowledge, I think this course of action is most consistent and true to myself.

". . . I'm returning the money you sent me this month. I've joined Polaris Action with the understanding that I'll be self-sufficient. It runs on voluntary contributions, voluntary poverty, and part-time work by participants, who live on a farm in an 'intentional community.' Two adults, Marge and Bob Swann, live there with their four children, and are the directors of the project."

. . . Gene's dedication was growing ever deeper. At each next drastic step, this pattern evolved: his decision and gentle explanations to us; our counseling him that there might be a better, milder way; his inevitable accomplishment of his mission; our acceptance. Now, we'd think, he's ready to settle down. But there was always a further goal.

The first of these steps was his decision that he was at last ready for civil disobedience. Although Scott and I had known from the first that this was an ultimate aim, we'd nursed a hope that when it came right down to it, Gene wouldn't go that far. So when he wrote us of his decision, we tried again to oppose our reasoning to his. We kept questioning what we felt was a passion for going to prison. We said that losing one's fear of prison and death was wonderful, but having imprisonment as a goal disturbed us.

By summer, our irresistible force had given in to his immovable mountain, and we were resigned to his plans. Resigned is too mild a word. We had visited Polaris Action by this time and were beginning to understand. In one letter, I told my pupil-become-teacher that the thought of him was encouraging me at times to be more courageous in thought and deed than I might otherwise be.

In August, five months after arriving at New London, Gene was in jail. He and seven others had tried to swim to the submarine *Ethan Allen*. They had been stopped but not arrested and then had tried to reach the vessel by going through the main gates. This time, arrest had followed.

A telephone call from Gene the day before, and one from Marge Swann just after the arrest, kept us informed if not serene. Calls from local reporters who'd got the news from the wire services followed. This we'd been dreading, but found, to our relief, that the reporters were intelligent and objective, the stories written without slant or ridicule. One paper even quoted without comment such statements as this from a Polaris Action leaflet: "'So the pacifist actionists cannot stay away from the *Ethan Allen* just because they have been ordered to. Even if it means jail. They know that too many Germans were just obeying orders to look the other way. And they know that a Polaris submarine can cause more atrocities than 100 years of Auschwitz.'"

The papers also accurately printed Scott's and my comments:

" 'Young people are more direct,' said Keyes, explaining the difference in the actions of parents and sons." "Worried but proud," they described me, and quoted, " 'I respect his decision, but I'm not sure civil disobedience is the best way to fight armament. I wish he were safe at home or safe in college.' " . . .

We had every kind of reaction to his stand. Telephone calls, of course, accusing him of being a Communist. One caller became quite interested when we pointed out that it would be impossible for a pacifist to be a Communist, because he can never engage in violent revolution and because he always puts the individual's relation to God and conscience above his relation to the state, as the early Christians did. The man ended by requesting that we let him see some of our peace literature. Not all conversations ended on this friendly note, however. One man said flatly that anybody who did not obey his country's laws was a traitor.

Strangers wrote letters pro and con to the local newspapers. One man put it: "He is an admitted criminal who openly defies our laws when they interfere with his personal beliefs."

But when another answered, saying that though he did not share Gene's beliefs, he defended his right to fight for them, he received a call from the antagonistic letter writer apologizing for his own letter. . . .

Two and a half years passed . . . years in which he engaged continually in peace activity and also in the struggle for integration (which again brought jail). But his thoughts were being drawn more and more to one profound question—the question faced by every young man of his age—what Selective Service meant to him and what it meant to his nation. . . .

Gene studied, weighed and reweighed religious and pacifist writings; advice from the Central Committee for Conscientious Objectors; the Bible. He went into a retreat and faced himself and the meaning of life. It is not a simple deed at eighteen to probe the truth, to know oneself. But at last, convinced that he could in all honesty ask for it, he requested the conscientious-objector classification.

Yet he was not easy in his mind. Such a sentence as this one in an American Friends Service Committee pamphlet stayed in his thoughts: "We are convinced that our failures are due to our own unreadiness to live boldly by the faith we hold."

Was he really living boldly by his faith, Gene asked himself, to accept this easy way of being a legal conscientious objector? Didn't the objectors get tucked away in their own little cubby-holes of alternative service, so that most people didn't even know there were those who protested the draft? Shouldn't his goal be not simply to disengage *himself* from war but to ensure that his country, by ceasing to rely on force, regain its vision of the brotherhood of all men?

And time was so short, he kept fretting to us that summer. The world had no more than a few years to exist. He was absolutely convinced of this and was backed up in his opinion by hardheaded scientists and statesmen. A nuclear war probably wouldn't be started purposely, he answered us when we pointed out the caution of world leaders, who were more aware than he was of such perils. Statistically there was no doubt in the minds of many that if nuclear stockpiling and testing continued, chance would bring about accidental war.

In March, while studying at Pendle Hill, Gene went to Washington to testify against the bill to extend the induction provisions of the Universal Military Training and Service Act.

. . . He wished to "indicate my favoring of the idea of establishing an integral strategic *nonviolent* national defense system. . . . What is suggested is a basic reorientation of the defense posture of this nation."

He went on to clarify his stand:

"My responsibility as a citizen is to defend directly the integrity and institutions of the United States of America. My purpose is not to secure a special berth in the ship of state while others man its artillery. My purpose is equally to participate in the national defense, upon supplanting of the violent premises on which our national defense establishment is currently structured."

The clock kept ticking inexorably, and in December, Gene came home primed for action. He had now a clear and concrete plan of a way to challenge the draft law so that people would become aware it *could* be challenged. It was his belief that this law was now accepted as being as much a part of our government as the Bill of Rights. He felt most of us did not realize that whether the draft continued or was abolished lay in the hands not of some mysterious and far-off government, but in the hands of us, the people. Only we needed a shock to make us realize it, since years of legal protest by peace workers and others had wakened very few. It was as Mildred Olmsted, of the Women's International League for Peace and Freedom, has said: "I have often wondered why it is that a family which would make a great protest if the government took away their automobile or even their dog, says nothing when the government takes away their sons."

In keeping with the pacifists' way of explaining all actions beforehand, Gene wrote a letter to the two local papers and told them what he planned to do: "Christmas Eve reminds us of our duty to work for peace on earth, a world without war. . . . As a prayer for peace on earth, I will be holding a vigil on Christmas Eve in front of the office of the local draft board. If I can withstand the weather, I hope to witness for twelve hours, beginning at noon. In any event, at midnight Christmas Eve, I will be using my one-A draft card to light a candle."

To burn his draft card! The idea was as new and shocking to us when he first described it as it still is to most people. At that time, though Gene was not the first to do this, there had not been many, and the whole action seemed preposterous to us. . . .

He was dressed warmly and neatly, had on earmuffs and a dark-blue overcoat, and wore suspended from his shoulders a sign that read: "To Light This Candle with a Draft Card—A Prayer for Peace on Earth." The sign had been beautifully lettered by an artist friend. He was accompanied by his girl, who, for a large part of the day, kept vigil with him.

I was resigned and even, once again, as always seemed to happen when my worst fears were realized, proud.

All of us went there from time to time during the day to keep him company—our two younger sons and daughter and one son's girl, as well as Scott and I. Other friends unexpectedly came to accompany Gene for parts of the day. Even some strangers walked up and down with him now and again, not necessarily agreeing, but interested and eager to discuss. But, of course, Gene was the only one who kept vigil, and fasted, twelve long, cold hours.

At home, we were trying to go ahead with Christmas prepara-
tions—decorating the tree, wrapping presents. But we were
tense and absentminded and, as it grew late, were all at the
draft board again. This time, a crowd of about twenty-five was
there to watch. If any were unfriendly, they did not speak up.
TV cameramen and reporters were also waiting.

At midnight, there was a stir; the cameramen and others got
ready to snap the scene. Gene's girl began to play her part—
holding the candle while he got the draft card ready in a pair of
tongs. He took out a cigarette lighter, but a bitter wind kept
blowing out the flame.

I began praying again—Don't let this look ridiculous. It's so
important to him! Oh, let it light! And at last the card and the
candle were lit. The card burned quickly in the grip of the tongs.

I let go my breath. It was over. People crowded around. Some
were nervously laughing, and some were almost crying. I was
doing a little of both.

Scott went to Gene and patted his back, much as he used to
do when our son was little and succeeded in something he'd
been afraid to do, like climbing a high tree. I held him in my
arms a moment. We had no words. But he knew both of us were
close to him.

And so it has become. As we have watched him grow and
climb his high places, we no longer argue with him, no longer
call him foolish. We stand by our son, and we learn from him.

40. Michael Ferber:
"A Time to Say No" (1967)

As opposition to America's acts of war in Vietnam burgeoned in the
summer and fall of 1967, the Resistance—a national movement to oppose the war and American militarism through the refusal of conscription—settled on October 16 as the day on which it would seek the
illegal surrender of thousands of draft cards throughout the country.[1]
One part of this protest was a "Service of Conscience and Acceptance"
at Boston's Arlington Street (Unitarian) Church. At this service Michael
Ferber, a graduate student in English at Harvard who had been
"brought up in the basement of the Unitarian Church from the age of

two," gave a lay sermon, "A Time to Say No." For his role in the service, and particularly for the sermon, he was subsequently indicted for criminal conspiracy. At the service, Ferber said later, "at least fifty men burned their [draft] cards from William Ellery Channing's candlestick." Three or four times that number turned in their cards to clergymen who then forwarded them to the Justice Department.[2]

The following spring Ferber was tried, along with Dr. Benjamin Spock, William Sloane Coffin, Jr., Mitchell Goodman, and Marcus Raskin, for conspiring to "counsel, aid, and abet" young men who were prepared to refuse induction into the army. All except Raskin were found guilty in June 1968 and sentenced to two years in jail. Ferber was also fined $1,000; the three others who had been found guilty were fined $5,000 each. But the convictions were overturned on appeal the following year.

Michael Ferber had participated in New Left politics in high school and at Swarthmore College. He had applied for conscientious objector status but hadn't been able to make his draft board see the necessity of his position and had eventually decided to turn in his draft card, "partly to regain my own sense of dignity." This was, he said, for him and for many others, "the first large, perhaps existentially crucial act" of resistance, "but only the first act in a whole way of life, in the construction of a whole movement."[3]

Since his successful appeal Michael Ferber has completed his doctoral dissertation, "Religion and Politics in William Blake," and has joined the faculty of Yale University.

❀ "A Time to Say No" by Michael Ferber originally appeared in *The Liberal Context*, November 1967. It is reprinted here from the Appendix to Jessica Mitford, *The Trial of Dr. Spock* (New York: Alfred A. Knopf, 1969), pp. 259–263, by permission of Michael Ferber.

We are gathered in this church today in order to do something very simple: to say No. We have come from many different places and backgrounds and we have many different ideas about ourselves and the world, but we have come here to show that we are united to do one thing: to say No. Each of our acts of returning our draft cards is our personal No; when we put them in a single container or set fire to them from a single candle we express the simple basis of our unity.

But what I wish to speak about now is what goes beyond our saying No, for no matter how loudly we all say it, no matter what ceremony we perform around our saying it, we will not become a community among ourselves nor effective agents for changing our country if a negative is all we share. Albert Camus said that the rebel, who says No, is also one who says Yes, and that when he draws a line beyond which he will refuse to co-operate he is affirming the values on the other side of that line. For us who come here today, what is it that we affirm, what is it to which we can say Yes?

To be honest we have to admit that we in the Resistance still disagree about a great many things, whether we speak out about them or not. For example, here we all are in a church, and yet for some of us it is the first time we've been inside one for years. Here we are receiving the help of many clergymen, and yet some of us feel nothing but contempt for the organized religions that they represent. Some of us, therefore, feel a certain hypocrisy in being part of this service.

But it would not surprise me if many of the clergymen who are here today feel some of the same contempt for organized religion that our unreligious or anti-religious brothers feel. They know better than we do the long and bloody history of evils committed in the name of religion, the long history of compromise and Erastian subservience to political power, the long history of theological hair-splitting and the burning of heretics, and they feel more deeply than we do the hypocrisy of Sunday (or Saturday) morning. Perhaps the things that made some of us leave the church are the very things that made some of them become ministers, priests, and rabbis, the very things that bring them here today. Many of them will anger their superiors or their congregations by being here but they are here anyway.

There is a great tradition within the church and synagogue which has always struggled against the conservative and worldly forces that have always been in control. It is a radical tradition, a tradition of urgent impulse to go to the root of the religious dimension of human life. This tradition in modern times has tried to recall us to the best ways of living our lives: the way of love and compassion, the way of justice and respect, the way of facing other people as human beings and not as abstract representatives of something alien and evil. It tries to recall us to the reality behind religious ceremony and symbolism, and it will change the ceremony and symbolism when the reality changes.

As a part of this service we will break bread together. We do this, however, not because some churches happen to take Communion; we do this for one of the root reasons for Communion itself: that men around the world and for all time have found it good to eat together when they are sharing in something important.

The radical tradition is still alive; it is present here in this church. Those of us who disregard organized religion, I think, are making a mistake if they also disregard this tradition and its presence today. This tradition is something to which we can say Yes.

There is another disagreement among us, or if not a disagreement then a difference in attitude toward what we are doing today. It is a difference that cuts through the other differences, perhaps because it is a little inside each of us, and it leads to a mistake that we are liable to make no matter how else we agree or differ. In religious terms, it is to dwell too much on the possibility of the Apocalypse; in political terms, it is to dwell too much on the possibility of a Utopian society. We must not confuse the ceremony and symbolism of today's service with the reality that we are only a few hundred people with very little power. And we must not confuse the change inside each of us, important though that may be, with the change that we have yet to bring about in this country and the world. Neither the Revelation nor the Revolution is at hand, and to base our hopes and plans on them would be a tragic blunder.

Maybe all of us—Leftists or Liberals, Reformers or Revolutionaries, Radical Religionists or Hippies—maybe all of us are apocalyptarians, I don't know. Surely something else besides a cold rational calculation of sociological options has brought us here to this church. And surely we are in this church partly to celebrate the occasion of our noncooperation (and many of us will celebrate in a somewhat different way at parties with friends tonight). But let us not be deceived. The sun will rise tomorrow as it does every day, and when we get out of bed the world will be in pretty much the same mess it is in today. American bombers will continue to drop incendiary bombs on the Vietnamese people and American soldiers will continue to "pacify" their villages. The ghettos will continue to be rotten places to live in,

Black and Mexican farm workers will continue to get miserable wages. America's schools will continue to cripple the minds and hearts of its pupils. And the American Selective Service System will continue to send young men out to the slaughter.

Today is not the End. Today is the Beginning.

This is the Beginning because, very simply, we have to dig in for the long haul. It is not going to be easy to change this country. To change it is going to mean struggles and anguish day in and day out for years. It will mean incredible efforts at great human cost to gain a few inches of ground. It will mean people dedicating their lives and possibly losing them for a cause we can only partly define and whose outcome we can only guess at. We must say Yes to the long struggle ahead or this service will be a mockery.

We are brought to a third difference among us. Earlier today Nick Egleson spoke out against the kind of resistance whose primary motivation is moralistic and personal rather than political. He is saying that we must make ourselves relevant to the social and political condition of the world and must not just take a moral posture for our own soul's sake, even though that too is a risk.

To some extent this argument depends on terminology rather than fact. Today we have heard our situation described in religious terms, moral terms, political terms, legal terms, and psychological terms. Very few of us are at home in all these different modes of speech, and each of us habitually uses only one of them to talk and think in. But what is happening today should make it clear that these different modes of speech all overlap one another and they often all say the same essential things. Albert Camus, who struggled in a more serious Resistance than ours, believed that politics is an extension of morality, that the truly moral man is engaged in politics as a natural outcome of his beliefs.

To return to Nick's concern, the real difference is not between the moral man and the political man, but between the man whose moral thinking leads him to political action and the man whose moral thinking leads him no farther than to his own "sinlessness." It is the difference between the man who is willing to go dirty himself in the outside world and the man who wishes to stay "clean" and "pure."

Now this kind of "sinlessness" and "purity" is arrogant pride, and I think we must say No to it. The martyr who offers himself meekly as a lamb to the altar is a fool unless he has fully taken into account the consequences of his sacrifice not only to himself but to the rest of the world. We cannot honor him for his stigmata or his purple hearts unless he has helped the rest of us while he got them.

So then what are we to do? We must look at ourselves once more. We all have an impulse to purification and martyrdom and we should not be ashamed of it. But let us be certain that we have thought through the consequences of our action in the outside world, and that these consequences are what we want to bring about. Let us make sure we are ready to work hard and long with each other in the months to come, working to make if difficult and politically dangerous for the government to prosecute us, working to help anyone and everyone to find ways of avoiding the draft, to help disrupt the workings of the draft and the armed forces until the war is over. Let us make sure we can form a community. Let us make sure we can let others depend on us.

If we can [say] Yes to these things, and to the religious tradition that stands with us today, and to the fact that today marks not the End but a Beginning, and to the long hard dirty job ahead of us—if we can say Yes to all this, then let us come forward together to say No to the United States Government.

Then let our Yes be the loudest No our government ever heard.

41. Daniel Berrigan: *The Trial of the Catonsville Nine* (1970)

On May 17, 1968, seven Catholic men and two Catholic women entered a Selective Service office in Catonsville, Maryland, seized the files of 378 1-A registrants (those eligible for induction), and in a nearby parking lot poured homemade napalm on the captured documents and set them afire. Then they waited for the police. In October they were convicted in a Baltimore federal court of having destroyed government property; they were sentenced to terms in prison of from two to three and a half years. They were free, however, until their appeal was rejected by the Supreme Court in April 1970, whereupon two of the nine, Daniel and Philip Berrigan, went underground. They were captured by the FBI later that year.

Though they performed their action in Catonsville at a time when the American military involvement in Vietnam was near its peak, the group sought to protest not merely the war but what they saw as American imperialism around the world and the wholesale failure of American institutions. Their statement to the press read in part: "We, American citizens, have worked with the poor in the ghetto and abroad. . . . All of us identify with the victims of American oppression all over the world. . . . We submit voluntarily to their involuntary fate."[1]

The nine defendants did not contest the government's evidence that they had destroyed Selective Service records. Rather they believed that they were innocent because their act had been both a justified attempt to obstruct an immoral war and a selfless, prophetic testimony that could help to change the country's destructive course. It was, in short, not a criminal act but a potentially redemptive one. Through "the living theater of protest"[2] (which went on outside the court, in the form of teach-ins and demonstrations, as well as in their trial testimony and in their disobedient act itself) they sought to educate and to move a nationally significant audience.

This emphasis on their action's beneficent effects, however, was often subordinated to their sense that they had acted to end their own guilt, their personal complicity in their country's evils. This kind of innocence was of course beyond the reach of the court, and to some extent the defendants accepted the jury's legal verdict in advance, viewing the entire proceedings as part of the institutional machinery they had acted against. Indeed, they sometimes seemed to welcome a verdict of guilty, since acquittal could paradoxically blur the clarity of their witness. "The greatest good that can be extracted from that courtroom is conviction," Philip Berrigan wrote.[3]

Nonetheless, some of the defendants' testimony suggests a hope, however slim, that their act of nonviolent revolution might speak to something deep within the judge and jury (as well as many others) and win an acquittal that would itself be a powerful instrument of change. For Daniel Berrigan, in any case, the disobedient's two traditional concerns—his personal innocence and the constructive transformation of his society—were fused in a very Thoreauvian way, one that implied that the court's decision was ultimately inconsequential. The Catonsville raid, he said, was "an act beyond politics: a religious act, a liturgical act, an act of witness. If only a small number of men could offer this kind of witness, it would purify the world."[4]

By the time the appeals process had been exhausted, however, the Berrigans felt that "insanity still prevails." Thus, though they had originally believed in "the classical concept of civil disobedience, which involves a willingness to accept responsibility for one's illegal acts," the times now seemed to require an additional radical gesture, the evasion of the jail terms to which they had been sentenced. Daniel Berrigan now referred to the doctrine that disobedience should be followed by legal punishment as "a mythology . . . sedulously fostered by liberals," as a "principle [that] is obviously of interest to those in power."[5] Why should he act as though he too believed in his guilt?

Daniel Berrigan's play relies heavily on the language the participants actually used at the trial; it is condensed and adapted from the nearly nine hundred pages of trial transcript. It ran for 159 performances in New York in 1971.

Reprinted from Daniel Berrigan, *The Trial of the Catonsville Nine* (Boston: Beacon Press, 1970), pp. 28–31, 34–36, 46, 58–60, 81, 94–95. Copyright © 1970 by Daniel Berrigan, S.J. Reprinted by permission of Beacon Press.

DEFENSE
    . . . Father Berrigan, I ask you: did there come a time, then, when you began seriously to consider civil disobedience?
PHILIP BERRIGAN
    Yes   I came
    to the conclusion
    that I was in direct line
    with American democratic tradition
    in choosing civil disobedience
    in a serious fashion
    There have been times in our history
    when in order to get redress
    in order to get a voice   vox populi
    arising from the roots
    people have so acted

From the Boston Tea Party
through the abolitionist and anarchist movements
through World War I   and World War II
and right on
through the civil rights movement
we have a rich tradition
of civil disobedience

DEFENSE

Now, the action for which you are being tried here was not the first such action you were involved in. To state it briefly: seven months earlier, in October 1967, you along with the defendant Thomas Lewis and two others not present poured blood over Selective Service records in the Baltimore Customs House.

PHILIP BERRIGAN

We were prepared
for the blood pouring
because we had practiced civil disobedience
in Virginia
In fact my brother and myself
had practiced civil disobedience for years
by signing complicity statements
in support of draft resisters
So four of us took our own blood
and when the equipment for drawing our blood
broke down   we added animal blood
We attempted to anoint these files
with the Christian symbol of life and purification
which is blood

DEFENSE

Will you explain why, with a jail sentence staring you in the face, you felt impelled to act again at Catonsville?

PHILIP BERRIGAN

Neither at the Customs House   nor at Catonsville
do I wish my actions reduced
to a question   of acquittal or conviction
Rather I   and all of us
desire to communicate
with the bench   with the prosecution

with our country
We have already made it clear   our dissent runs counter
to more than the war   which is but one instance
of American power in the world
Latin America is another instance   So is the Near East
This trial is yet another
From those in power we have met
little understanding   much silence
much scorn and punishment
We have been accused of arrogance
But what of the fantastic arrogance   of our leaders
What of their crimes against the people   the poor and
   powerless
Still no court will try them   no jail will receive them
They live in righteousness   They will die in honor
For them we have one message   for those
in whose manicured hands   the power of the land lies
We say to them
Lead us   Lead us in justice
and there will be no need to break the law
Let the President do   what his predecessors failed to do
Let him obey the rich less   and the people more
Let him think less of the privileged
and more of the poor
Less of America and more of the world
Let lawmakers   judges   and lawyers
think less of the law   more of justice
less of legal ritual   more of human rights
To our bishops and superiors we say
Learn something about the gospel
and something about illegitimate power
When you do   you will liquidate your investments
take a house in the slums   or even
join us in jail
To lawyers we say
Defend draft resisters   ask no fees
insist on justice   risk contempt of court
go to jail with your clients
To the prosecution we say

Refuse to indict
opponents of the war
prefer to resign   practice in private
To Federal judges we say
Give anti-war people   suspended sentences
to work for justice and peace
or resign your posts
You men of power   I also have a dream
Federal Judges   District Attorneys   Marshals
Against the War in Vietnam
You men of power   you have told us
that your system is reformable
Reform it then
and we will help
with all our conviction and energy
in jail or out

.   .   .

DEFENSE
Would you explain your intent in acting in Catonsville, other
than destroying the files?
DAVID DARST
First of all to raise a cry
an outcry   at what was clearly a crime
an unnecessary suffering
a clear and wanton slaughter
Perhaps this is similar to the case
of a man in his home who sees a crime
someone is being attacked outside
His impulse   I think   his
basic human impulse
is to cry out   to call for help

.   .   .

That was one intention
an outcry that   hopefully
would stop the crime
I saw being perpetrated
Another intention was
to halt the machine of death
which I saw moving   and killing
In the same way perhaps

a person in Czechoslovakia
when tanks invade his country
throws bricks into the wheels
of the tanks
and sometimes a puny effort
stops a tank
This was my hope
to hinder this war
in a literal way
an actual physical way

DEFENSE

Do you have any other basis for the intent you have described?

DAVID DARST

An outcry against the fact
that our country can spend
eighty billions a year
chasing imaginary enemies
all around the world
I was living last year
in a poor ghetto district
I saw many little children
who did not have enough to eat
This is an astonishing thing
that our country
cannot command the energy
to give bread and milk
to children
Yet it can rain   fire and death
on people   ten thousand miles away
for reasons that are unclear
to thoughtful men

          ·   ·   ·

THOMAS LEWIS

          ·   ·   ·

I was aware too that
if I became involved in Catonsville
I would be summoned once more
for trial   This is the trial
and a greater sentence may follow
I was fully aware of this at the time

It was a very thoughtful time
In a sense   it was a choice
between life and death
It was a choice between
saving one's soul and losing it
I was saving my soul

.   .   .

I wasn't concerned with the law
I wasn't even thinking about the law
I was thinking of what those records meant
I wasn't concerned with the law
I was concerned with the lives
of innocent people
I went in there with the intent   of stopping
what the files justify
The young men
whose files we destroyed
have not yet been drafted   may not be drafted
may not be sent to Vietnam for cannon fodder
My intent in going there
was to save lives   A person
may break the law to save lives

.   .   .

MARJORIE MELVILLE
I did not want to bring
hurt upon myself
but there comes a moment
when you decide
that some things should not be
Then you have to act
to try to stop those things
On my return
I was very happy when I found
other people in this country
concerned as I was
I know that burning draft files
is not an effective way
to stop a war   but
who has found a way

of stopping this war
I have racked my brain
I have talked to all kinds of people
What can you do
They say yes   yes
but there is no answer
no stopping it
the horror continues

THOMAS MELVILLE

We wish to say lastly
why we went to Catonsville
Americans know
that their nation was born in blood
we have expanded our frontiers
and pacified the Indians
in blood

MARJORIE MELVILLE

The creature of our history
is our fatherland today
The history we create today
will form the minds and hearts
of our children tomorrow

THOMAS MELVILLE

I hear our President   confuse greatness with strength
riches with goodness   fear with respect
hopelessness and passivity with peace
The clichés of our leaders
pay tribute to property   and indifference to suffering
We long for a hand of friendship and succor
and that hand
clenches into a fist
I wonder how long we can endure

.   .   .

DEFENSE

What was the impact of the act of your brother Philip Berrigan
when he poured blood on draft files in Baltimore?

DANIEL BERRIGAN

I began to understand
one could not indefinitely obey the law

while social conditions deteriorated
structures of compassion breaking down
neighborhoods slowly rotting
the poor despairing   unrest
forever present in the land   especially among
the young people
who are our only hope   our only resource
My brother's action helped me realize
from the beginning   of our republic
good men had said no
acted outside the law
when conditions so demanded
And if a man did this
time might vindicate him   show his act to be lawful
a gift to society
a gift to history
and to the community
A few men
must have a long view
must leave history to itself
to interpret their lives   their repute

And so we stretch out our hands
to our brothers throughout the world
We who are priests to our fellow priests
All of us who act against the law
turn to the poor of the world   to the Vietnamese
to the victims   to the soldiers who kill and die
for the wrong reasons for no reason at all
because they were so ordered by the authorities
of that public order which is in effect
a massive institutionalized disorder
We say: killing is disorder
life and gentleness and community and unselfishness
is the only order we recognize
For the sake of that order
we risk our liberty   our good name
The time is past when good men may be silent

when obedience
can segregate men from public risk
when the poor can die without defense
How many indeed must die
before our voices are heard
how many must be tortured dislocated
starved maddened?
How long must the world's resources
be raped in the service of legalized murder?
When at what point will you say no to this war?
We have chosen to say
with the gift of our liberty
if necessary our lives:
the violence stops here
the death stops here
the suppression of the truth stops here
this war stops here
Redeem the times!
The times are inexpressibly evil
Christians pay conscious   indeed religious tribute
to Caesar and Mars
by the approval of overkill tactics   by brinkmanship
by nuclear liturgies   by racism   by support of genocide
They embrace their society with all their heart
and abandon the cross
They pay lip service to Christ
and military service to the powers of death
And yet   and yet   the times are inexhaustibly good
solaced by the courage and hope of many
The truth rules   Christ is not forsaken
In a time of death some men
the resisters   those who work hardily for social change
those who preach and embrace the truth
such men overcome death
their lives are bathed in the light of the resurrection
the truth has set them free
In the jaws of death
they proclaim their love of the brethren

We think of such men
in the world   in our nation   in the churches
and the stone in our breast is dissolved
we take heart once more

42. John William Ward: "To Whom Should I Write a Letter?" (1972)

John William Ward became president of Amherst College on July 1, 1971; he had been a professor of American history there for the preceding seven years. Since 1965, when he had taken part in teaching a course on the history of United States foreign policy and its bearing on this country's current military involvement in Southeast Asia, he had been opposed to the war. Twice he had taken part in peace marches in Washington. He had participated every Sunday for a year in a "peace vigil" sponsored by a local Quaker group on the Amherst town common.

On May 8, 1972, President Richard Nixon announced the mining of North Vietnam's harbors; in response, the Amherst Quakers began a program of civil disobedience at the gates of Westover Air Force Base. When a mass rally of students was called at Amherst College, President Ward was asked to speak at it. As he considered what he would say, he found himself "utterly frustrated by words and more words" and decided to commit civil disobedience himself as a symbolic gesture. On the day following his talk to the students (reprinted here), he and his wife, Barbara, were arrested for nonviolently obstructing access to the base, on a charge of disturbing the peace. Similar actions were performed, with a similar response from the Chicopee police, by some twenty-five members of the Amherst faculty and about three hundred students.

President Ward's lawbreaking was necessarily a matter of grave concern to Amherst's board of trustees, and at their June meeting they requested a private meeting with him. "The Board knew better than I," Ward has observed, "that it would be almost impossible to sustain the distinction I wished to make between myself as citizen and myself as President." But after "a strong and vigorous discussion"[1] the trustees voted unanimously that "while individual members of the Board of Trustees may or may not agree with President Ward's views with respect to the Vietnam War and differ as to the propriety of the particular means, passive civil disobedience, chosen by him to make his views as an individual known, the Trustees respect his right to make these personal decisions and the considerations of conscience which motivated his action. Their high regard for and confidence in him continue."[2]

Fellow Students:

I know you attend to what I say because I am president of the college. I thank you for that, but I want to speak to you in two voices. First, as president of Amherst College; second, in my own voice. I am tense and uneasy with the act of dividing myself in two: my hope, as president, has been not to lose myself in the role, the office, to retain a sense of my own self while still president. My personal unease is made worse because as I said at the start, I know you listen to me because I am the president. It is not Bill Ward you want to hear: you want to hear the president of Amherst College. So, let me begin first with the voice you want to hear, that of the president, and then speak as Bill Ward.

As president, I have a great affection for this place, this college. We know ourselves slenderly, but to the degree I know myself, that was one of the large reasons I was willing to say, yes, I would be president of it.

Let us begin where we are. Let us begin where we stand together. Let us make this place, Amherst College, as good and decent and humane a place as we can. I do not ask you to be more than human; I ask you simply to be human with one another. If we stand appalled at the cruelty and the indecency we see around us in the world, let us not give them a place here among us; let us not in our frustration turn ourselves into a likeness of what we despise and detest. I do not think we are going to save society this way, but we may find Amherst a better place to be together. That, you will recognize, is a sermon: the "doctrine," in the old style of preaching, is charity; unlike the old style of preaching, I leave the application of the doctrine to the imaginings of each of you.

Now let me make an application of the doctrine. I do not want you to miss it. As president, I am asking you not to let your wholly justifiable concern and your deep frustration turn you one against another or turn any of you against the College itself. Some may find that appeal sentimental. So far as it derives from sentiment, from feeling, it is. Some may find it naive and answer that insofar as the College is an institution in American society it is inevitably involved in all the wrongs of American society. I think not, but the argument is a long and subtle one and I do not want to stay with it now. I only want to say that I wish, as president, to keep the College safe, as in my slender power it is to keep it, from the dangers of the possible excess of passion. I will try to do that.

Night before last while I was in the Red Room, a student called my home and left word with my wife that he and other students hoped I would write a letter. Write a letter! To whom? One feels like a child throwing paper planes against a blank wall. I might write such a letter and you might cheer and, if the world goes on, you might think me a pleasant and sympathetic fellow. But the mines are laid [outside North Vietnam's harbors] and for the next few days we wait. God knows, I hope Nixon is right. God knows, I hope it works. Not for his sake, not even for the sake of the United States. For the sake of all those I have never seen. For mankind's sake.

We have lived with this bloody war for eighteen years. I was only ten years out of another war and most of you in this room were babies. Who has the strength to raise all the arguments again? I said on this campus three years ago that I think the "Vietnam War is a cruel and foolish mistake, that we got into it on a false ideological premise, that we are so hung up in our own cant that we cannot admit that we are wrong, that we are wasting lives because of a foolish pride." I still think that. To whom shall I say it in a letter? Voices louder than mine have been saying it for a long time. What are we protesting?

Let me say what I protest and what I, Bill Ward, self and citizen, propose to do. As I said when I took this office, I do not intend to disenfranchise myself or lose my rights as citizen because I am president.

Mr. Nixon promised us a solution through Vietnamization of the war. I find the policy repellent but, that aside, it has failed, so now we have the mining of harbors, the bombing of railheads, the interdiction of all supplies to North Vietnam. Mr. Nixon has ruled out withdrawal; the only way to negotiation again is through the application of greater and greater force; the next move lies in someone else's hands. What if the blockade fails? Mr. Kissinger in his press briefing is reported to have said that nuclear confrontation is an acceptable risk, preferable to the present land war in South Vietnam.

What I protest is not what has been done. What is done is done. No word of mine, no word of yours will change it. What I protest is what may come next. What I protest is there is no way to protest. I speak out of frustration and deep despair. John Dos Passos once wrote, "We only have words against/POWER SUPER-POWER," and *USA* ended in icy defeat. I do not think words will now change the minds of men in power who make these decisions. I do not. Since I do not, I do not care to write letters to the world. Instead, I will, for myself, join in the act of passive civil disobedience at Westover Air Force Base.

VII EPILOGUE

The rules of conscience . . . [are] entirely negative. They do not say what to do; they say what not to do. . . . They say: Beware of doing something that you will not be able to live with.

—*Hannah Arendt,* Crises of the Republic

43. Jeb Stuart Magruder: Testimony before the Senate Select Committee on Presidential Campaign Activities (1973)

Jeb Magruder joined the Nixon administration in 1969 and later became deputy director and chief of staff of the Committee for the Reelection of the President; in that capacity he became involved in the Watergate cover-up. During the hearings of the Senate Select Committee (the Ervin Committee) and his trial, he conceded that he had destroyed records and committed perjury. He pleaded guilty to charges of conspiring to obstruct justice and defraud the United States and served seven months of a ten-months-to-four-years sentence that was later reduced by Judge John J. Sirica.

His testimony is remarkable especially for its assertion that the dramatic public civil disobedience of opponents of the Vietnam war, especially that of William Sloane Coffin, had helped to make Magruder feel that lawbreaking could be justified. Magruder does not seem to have meant, however, that Coffin's activities were themselves acceptable; rather he believed that they contributed to the White House's feeling that since the opposition wasn't playing by the rules, the government didn't need to either. Later, Magruder said, he came to see clearly that he had been wrong: "two wrongs do not make a right." In short, he had been provoked by Coffin's challenge and misled by "a certain atmosphere" of indifference to legal restraints in the White House. His testimony tends to equate these two influences, admitting no distinctions between Coffin's exhortation to refuse the draft and the Watergate break-in and its concealment.

Reprinted from *The New York Times*, June 15, 1973, p. 19.

Q. [from Sen. Howard H. Baker, Jr.] Tell me more about why it was a reluctant decision [to go ahead with the Watergate break-in].

A. We knew it was illegal, probably inappropriate. We didn't think that much would come of it. We had at least 30 decisions we made that day about even greater sums of money than that $250,000.

Q. Did you have any [other] decision to make that day that involved any illegal action?

A. No, sir.

Q. Or any [other] clandestine activity?

A. No, sir.

Q. Did that stand out in your mind, why you made that decision reluctantly?

A. Yes, sir, I think so.

Q. Did you ever express any reservations about it?

A. Yes, sir.

Q. What did you say?

A. Well, that it was illegal and that it was inappropriate and that it may not work.

Q. To whom did you say that?

A. To Mr. Mitchell, Mr. LaRue, Mr. Strachan.

Q. What was Mr. Mitchell's reply?

A. I think he had similar reservations, sir. . . . But again, I think we have to, in all honesty, say that we thought there may be some information that could be very helpful to us and because of a certain atmosphere that had developed in my working at the White House, I was not as concerned about its illegality as I should have been at that time.

Q. I still can't quite come to grips with why you all had an expressed reservation about this and you still went ahead with it.

A. I knew you would get to this line' of questioning, so why don't I give you what I think is the appropriate response here.

I had worked for some two years, three years, really, in the White House and at that time I was mainly engaged in the activities trying to generate some support for the President. During that time we had worked primarily relating to the war situation and worked with anti-war groups.

Now I had gone to college, as an example, under—and had a course in ethics as an example under William Sloane Coffin, whom I respect greatly. I have great regard for him. He was quoted the other day as saying, well, I guess Mr. Magruder failed my course in ethics. And I think he is correct.

During this whole time we were in the White House and during this time we were directly employed with trying to succeed with the President's policies we saw continuing violations of the law done by men like William Sloane Coffin. He tells me my ethics are bad. Yet he was indicted for criminal charges. He recommended on the Washington Monument grounds that students burn their draft cards and that we have mass demonstrations, shut down the city of Washington.

Now, here are ethical, legitimate people whom I respected. I respect Mr. Coffin tremendously. He was a very close friend of mine. I saw people I was very close to breaking the law without any regard for any other person's pattern of behavior or belief.

So consequently, when these subjects came up although I was aware they were illegal we had become somewhat inured to using some activities that would help us in accomplishing what we thought was a cause, a legitimate cause.

Now, that is absolutely incorrect; two wrongs do not make a right.

For the past year, I have obviously had to consider that and I understand completely that that was an absolute, incorrect decision. But that is basically, I think, the reason why that decision was made, because of that atmosphere that had occurred and to all of us who had worked in the White House, there was that feeling of resentment and of frustration at being unable to deal with issues on a legal basis.

I fully accept the responsibility of having made an absolutely disastrous decision, or at least having participated. I didn't make the decision, but certainly participated in it.

Q. A decision really that is going to affect history that was made in almost a casual way.

A. Yes, sir. . . . Now, I think to be fair [about the cover-up], Senator, I think you have to realize that I felt, and I can't speak for the others, that the President had no knowledge of this plan and consequently if it had gotten out that people like Mr. Mitchell and others had been involved at that point in time, I honestly thought that his re-election would be probably negated.

Q. Did it ever occur to you that there might be other alternatives, that one of them might be to report this directly to the President or to the F.B.I. and make a clean breast of it at that moment, that that might have less effect on the election, rather than more effect—

A. As I said, we did indicate at one point that we might possibly do that up to a certain point. I think it was felt that if it ever reached Mr. Mitchell before the election, the President would lose the election. Since he was not involved, to my knowledge, I thought that was the best decision. I did not think it was a right decision, but I thought it was the best decision. . . .

Senator [Sam J.] Ervin: I was very much impressed with your testimony about the climate that prevailed in the White House and afterwards in the Committee to Re-elect the President. As a matter of fact, was there not a fear there of Americans that dissented from policies of Government? You spoke about your former professor—

A. The Reverend Coffin. Yes.

Q. He just came down and demonstrated. There were a great many demonstrations, weren't there?

A. He did quite a bit more than demonstrate.

Q. He was supposed to try to frustrate the draft.

A. He did, and he participated in many activities that were considered illegal.

Q. You were disturbed at the demonstrations, weren't you, the people at the White House?

A. Yes, sir. We were.

Q. The reason I asked the question, I have had to spend my time fighting such laws and legislative proposals as no-knock laws, preventive detention laws, the claim that there was an inherent right of the President to bug anybody suspected of domestic subversion, and things of that kind. And I just could not understand why people got so fearful.

A. I would characterize that at least my reaction was stronger after three years of working in that atmosphere than it had been before.

Q. I am familiar with that kind of atmosphere. I came up here during Joe McCarthy days when Joe McCarthy saw a Communist hiding under every rose bush and I have been here fighting the no-knock laws and preventive detention laws and indiscriminate bugging by people who've found subversives hiding under every bed. In this nation, we have had a very unfortunate fear. And this fear went to the extent of deploring the exercise of personal rights for those who wanted to assemble and petition the Government for redress of grievances.

Some of it happened before you got into the White House and I am not blaming you, because even under a Democratic Administration, I had an investigation here where they became so afraid of people that they used military intelligence to spy on civilians whose only offense was that they were dissatisfied with the policies of the Government and assembled and petitioned for relief.

Now, I think that all grew out of this complement of fear, did it not, the whole Watergate incident?

A. I think from my own personal standpoint, I did lose some respect for the legal process simply because I did not see it working as I had hoped it would when I came here.

Mr. [Fred D.] Thompson [chief minority counsel]: Since we are talking about your motivation and your frame of mind at that time, I feel like I should ask this question: Were you concerned about legitimate demonstrations, or were there more serious things going on in the country at that time? Up until that time had there been bombings of public buildings, for example?

A. Well, I think it goes much deeper than that, not only were there bombings of public buildings, we had death threats against Mr. Mitchell's life. We had continuous demonstrations in front of our headquarters.

Q. Had there been a series of break-ins of F.B.I. offices, for example?

A. Yes, sir, many.

Q. Was it your opinion at the time there were plans afoot to make some attempt to overthrow the Government by illegal and improper means?

A. I would not go so far as to say overthrow the Government. I think we had some concern about them overthrowing our convention as they did the Democratic party convention in 1968. . . .

44. William Sloane Coffin, Jr.: "Not Yet a Good Man" (1973)

Before his cordial encounter with Jeb Magruder at Williams, William Sloane Coffin, Jr., had chosen work that forms an unlikely professional background for a leading radical activist. His undergraduate career at Yale was interrupted by a four-year stint in the army as a liaison officer, first with the French army and then with the Russian; his divinity schooling was completed only after three years' work on Russian affairs with the CIA. Ordained a Presbyterian minister in 1956 at the age of thirty-four, he served as chaplain for a year at Andover, performed a similar service at Williams, and then (in 1958) moved on to Yale.

In his third year in New Haven the Reverend Dr. Coffin became a national figure through his participation in the Freedom Rides that helped to end segregation in public facilities throughout the South. In May of 1961, as part of an integrated group that also included (among others) Ralph Abernathy and Fred Shuttlesworth, he was arrested and briefly jailed in Montgomery, Alabama, for seeking to be served at a segregated lunch counter. (The charges were breach of the peace and unlawful assembly.) In 1963 he was arrested again, this time in an interfaith, interracial drive that ultimately succeeded in desegregating an all-white amusement park near Baltimore. These commitments, despite the lawbreaking they involved, had broad support at Yale.

Four years later Coffin's dramatic, persistent support of Vietnam draft resisters placed him in a more complicated position. Yale's president, Kingman Brewster, Jr., defended Coffin's right to dissent as a member of a "free university," but he also characterized Coffin's public speeches as "strident" and publicly disavowed Coffin's position on the draft. Speaking to a large gathering of Yale parents in the fall of 1967, Brewster said that he found it "especially distasteful when those who urge the resistance are too old to be able to share fully the personal and moral consequences of refusing to serve. . . . The chaplain's effort to gain spot news coverage seems to be unworthy of the true trial of conscience, which touches most of your sons and preoccupies so many."[1] Brewster also insisted on the importance and difficulty of the issues, however, and implied that Coffin was contributing something special to education at Yale. Coffin's response was a courteous one: "I am grateful for a president with whom one can disagree profoundly and still remain friends."[2]

Three months later Coffin was indicted (with Benjamin Spock, Michael Ferber, Mitchell Goodman, and Marcus Raskin); he was convicted and sentenced to two years in jail. After the Court of Appeals ruled that the judge's improper instructions to the jury made a new trial necessary, the government dropped its charges against him.

The Reverend Dr. Coffin resigned his position at Yale in 1975 and is now senior minister of the Riverside Church in New York. He has been at work on his autobiography and has traveled widely on behalf of a program that strives to alleviate world hunger.

I was very fond of Jeb Magruder when we were together at Williams College. It was in 1958, his senior year and my first year as teacher and college chaplain. He and two classmates used to take my wife and me to dinner. He babysat for our daughter. Although we never saw each other after his graduation, for several years we corresponded.

During his time at Williams I worried about Jeb. I used to say to him: "You're a nice guy, Jeb, but not yet a good man. You have lots of charm but little inner strength. And if you don't stand for something you're apt to fall for anything."

When I saw him again on television testifying before Senator Ervin's committee, I was again drawn to him. While I do not excuse his conduct, I want to say something in explanation, for his testimony said as much about his education and American society as it did about Jeb himself.

In the 1950's students were agreeing their way through life. There was no civil rights movement to speak of and of course no antiwar movement. At Williams, as at so many exclusive colleges, there were few blacks, no Chicanos, no women and altogether too many fraternities which tended to promote an elitist team spirit, and breed a mistrust of healthy criticism. Professors everywhere were morally asleep. For the most part they represented the bland leading the bland. Education was for making a living, not a life, to be traded upon rather than to be used to create a better world.

Jeb was very gregarious. He wanted to be liked. He had a much greater sense of himself when he was with others than when alone. As a natural winner, he conformed easily to the American success ethic of the day—popularity, power, money.

As his ethics teacher, I wish now I had stressed the errors and illusions that stem from the fear of being a loser in this particular game plan. I wish I had pointed out the paradox of winners being losers, and losers winners. I wish I had stressed the importance of solitude. I wish I had emphasized that it is the individual consciences of history which, as opposed to the mass mind, best represent the universal conscience of mankind.

Maybe these emphases would have helped Jeb to develop individual convictions. Certainly it would have helped his understanding of civil disobedience, for many of the great consciences of history—Moses, Jeremiah, Jesus, Socrates, Thoreau, Gandhi —many we today regard as heroes were notorious lawbreakers in their time.

I was shocked to hear Jeb lump all lawbreakers together. He should have known—and the Senators pressing him should have reminded a listening nation—that Martin Luther King and many in the antiwar movement were protesting what they considered to be illegal laws whose constitutionality could be tested only by a refusal to obey them. There is an enormous difference between trying to keep the nation under the law and trying to keep it under Nixon, between being a loyal servant of the Constitution and being a loyal servant only of the man who hires you.

If there are differences in ends so there are differences in means. Whatever Dr. King and Dr. Spock did they did openly. All America could see and judge. Jeb operated behind closed doors. Most of the people in the civil rights and antiwar movements were careful not to infringe on the civil liberties of other citizens. Jeb and his friends deliberately violated these liberties. When the Supreme Court declared against him, Dr. King went from Georgia to Alabama to take his punishment. The draft resisters who went to jail accepted theirs. But Jeb's crowd, far from accepting punishment, tried only to conceal their crimes. Dr. King and those who followed him disobeyed the law to protect it. It is a sad and savage irony if Government officials learn from the practitioners of civil disobedience that law is made to be circumvented.

Teaching is at best a precarious business; the rational mind is no match for an irrational will that needs to place popularity and power above truth. Nevertheless all of us who taught him, and American society as a whole, could have done better by Jeb. Now we have the opportunity to learn from him the ancient lesson that to do evil in this world you don't have to be evil— just a nice guy, not yet a good man.

Notes

General Introduction

1. Harrop A. Freeman, "A Remonstrance for Conscience," *University of Pennsylvania Law Review* 106 (1958):813, 815.

2. John G. Richardson, *Obedience to Human Law Considered in the Light of Divine Truth* (Lawrence, Mass.: H. A. Cooke, 1852), p. 13.

3. William G. McLoughlin, *New England Dissent 1630–1833: The Baptists and the Separation of Church and State*, 2 vols. (Cambridge: Harvard University Press, 1971), vol. 1, p. 169.

4. William G. McLoughlin, "Massive Civil Disobedience as a Baptist Tactic in 1773," *American Quarterly* 21 (Winter 1969):713.

5. Ibid., p. 711.

6. Ibid., passim.

7. For two later arguments on behalf of this kind of civil disobedience, see Henry Grew, *Christian Loyalty* (Hartford, Conn.: Hudson & Goodwin, 1810); and Daniel Sharp, *Obedience to Magistrates Inculcated* (Boston, 1840). Sharp specifically limits the right of disobedience to cases in which religious worship is interfered with by statute.

8. McLoughlin, "Massive Civil Disobedience," p. 717.

9. Henry David Thoreau, "Civil Disobedience," in *Thoreau: People, Principles, and Politics*, ed. Milton Meltzer (New York: Hill & Wang, 1963), pp. 40–41.

10. Quoted in Leon Friedman, *The Wise Minority* (New York: Dial Press, 1971), p. 198n.

11. Richard Hofstadter, "Reflections on Violence in the United States," in *American Violence: A Documentary History*, ed. Richard Hofstadter and Michael Wallace (New York: Vintage Books, 1971), p. 34.

12. This point is expanded in the introduction to Part III.

13. Quoted in John A. Pollard, *John Greenleaf Whittier: Friend of Man* (Boston: Houghton Mifflin, 1949), p. 600.

14. Quoted in William R. Hutchison, *The Transcendentalist Ministers* (Boston: Beacon Press, 1965), p. 140.

15. Quoted in Ronald V. Wells, *Three Christian Transcendentalists: James Marsh, Caleb Sprague Henry, Frederic Henry Hedge* (New York: Columbia University Press, 1943), p. 215.

16. See the selection from Phillips in Part III.

17. Harold Schwartz, "Fugitive Slave Days in Boston," *New England Quarterly* 27 (1954):193.

18. Pollard, *John Greenleaf Whittier*, pp. 600–601; italics added. Nathaniel Hall's sermon in Part III gives a fuller version of this doctrine.

19. "Testimony of A. Philip Randolph . . . before the Senate Armed Services Committee Wednesday, March 31, 1948," in *Black Protest Thought in the Twentieth Century*, ed. August Meier, Elliott Rudwick, and Francis L. Broderick (Indianapolis: Bobbs-Merrill, 1971), p. 277.

20. Martin Luther King, Jr., *Stride toward Freedom* (New York: Harper & Row, 1958), p. 85.

21. Tom Wicker, "The Malaise beyond Dissent," *New York Times*, March 12, 1967, sec. 4, p. 13.

1. Edward Hart and others: *The Flushing Remonstrance*

1. Haynes Trébor, *The Flushing Remonstrance: The Origin of Religious Freedom in America* (Flushing, N.Y., 1957), p. 18. See also Harrop A. Freeman, "A Remonstrance for Conscience," *University of Pennsylvania Law Review* 106 (1958):806–830.

2. Quoted in Trébor, *Flushing Remonstrance*, p. 12.

2. Jonathan Mayhew: "Discourse Concerning Unlimited Submission and Non-Resistance to the Higher Powers"

1. Charles W. Akers, *Called unto Liberty: A Life of Jonathan Mayhew, 1720–1766* (Cambridge: Harvard University Press, 1964), p. 165.

2. Bernard Bailyn, ed., *Pamphlets of the American Revolution, 1750–1776* (Cambridge: Belknap Press of Harvard University Press, 1965), vol. 1, p. 209. Bailyn's characterization is by no means altogether complimentary, however; he calls Mayhew's attack on the hierarchy of the Anglican church "flagrant provocation, heedless defiance, of the spiritual arm of what was, after all, a singularly indulgent state" (p. 207).

3. Sermon of March 1749, pp. 2–3. The manuscript (HM 8047) is in The Huntington Library, San Marino, California, and is quoted by permission.

4. Isaac Backus: "An Appeal to the Public for Religious Liberty"

1. William G. McLoughlin, ed., *Isaac Backus on Church, State, and Calvinism: Pamphlets, 1754–1789* (Cambridge: Belknap Press of Harvard University Press, 1968), pp. 10–13.

2. Ibid., p. 305.

3. William Henry Allison, "Isaac Backus," *Dictionary of American Biography* (New York, 1958), vol. 1, p. 469; McLoughlin, *Isaac Backus*, pp. 6–7.

5. William Lloyd Garrison: "Review of Gerrit Smith's Letters" and "Trial of Rev. Mr. Cheever"

1. Louis Ruchames, ed., *The Letters of William Lloyd Garrison* (Cambridge: Belknap Press of Harvard University Press, 1971), vol. 2, p. 46n.

2. Carleton Mabee, *Black Freedom: The Nonviolent Abolitionists from 1830 through the Civil War* (New York: Macmillan, 1970), p. 56.

3. Walter M. Merrill, ed., *The Letters of William Lloyd Garrison* (Cambridge: Belknap Press of Harvard University Press, 1971), vol. 1, p. 576n.

6. William Ellery Channing: "Lecture on War"

1. John White Chadwick, *William Ellery Channing: Minister of Religion* (Boston: Houghton Mifflin, 1903), p. 407.

2. Quoted in Jack Mendelsohn, *Channing: The Reluctant Radical* (Boston: Little, Brown, 1971), p. 211.

3. William Francis Channing to Thomas Wentworth Higginson, January 24, 1879, quoted by Higginson in *The Independent*, no. 2790 (May, 22, 1902), p. 1236.

7. John Pierpont: *A Discourse on the Covenant with Judas*

1. William R. Hutchison, *The Transcendentalist Ministers: Church Reform in the New England Renaissance* (Boston: Beacon Press, 1965), p. 118.

2. Nathaniel Hall, *A Discourse on the Life and Character of Rev. John Pierpont* (Boston: Walker, Fuller, 1866); Octavius Brooks Frothingham, *Boston Unitarianism, 1820–1850* (New York: Putnam, 1890), pp. 184–186.

8. John Greenleaf Whittier: "Massachusetts to Virginia"

1. Edward Wagenknecht, *John Greenleaf Whittier: A Portrait in Paradox* (New York: Oxford University Press, 1967), p. 146. For discussion of the stresses on Whittier's absolute pacifism and its occasional waverings, see Wagenknecht's chapter "The Almost Perfect Pacifist," pp. 144–156; and Albert Mordell, *Quaker Militant: John Greenleaf Whittier* (Cambridge, Mass.: Riverside Press, 1933), p. 161.

2. Quoted in Whitman Bennett, *Whittier: Bard of Freedom* (Chapel Hill: University of North Carolina Press, 1941), p. 186.

3. Quoted in Mordell, *Quaker Militant*, pp. 160–161.

9. James Russell Lowell: "On the Capture of Fugitive Slaves near Washington"

1. Martin Duberman, *James Russell Lowell* (Boston: Houghton Mifflin, 1966), p. 83.

2. Ibid., pp. 75–83; and *The Anti-Slavery Papers of James Russell Lowell* (New York: Negro Universities Press, 1969 [1902]), vol. 2, p. 79.

3. *Anti-Slavery Papers*, vol. 2, p. 186.

10. Francis Wayland: *The Duty of Obedience to the Civil Magistrate*

1. See Theodore Collier, "Francis Wayland," in *Dictionary of American Biography* (New York, 1958), vol. 10, pp. 558–560. A staunchly contrary view of Wayland's contributions to American higher education may be found in Samuel Eliot Morison, *Three Centuries of Harvard* (Cambridge: Harvard University Press, 1936), pp. 286–288.

2. Edward H. Madden, *Civil Disobedience and Moral Law in Nineteenth-Century American Philosophy* (Seattle: University of Washington Press, 1968), p. 17.

3. William G. McLoughlin, *New England Dissent 1630–1833: The Baptists and the Separation of Church and State*, 2 vols. (Cambridge: Harvard University Press, 1971), vol. 2, p. 1274.

4. See John H. Schroeder, *Mr. Polk's War: American Opposition and Dissent, 1846–1848* (Madison: University of Wisconsin Press, 1973), pp. 110–111.

11. Henry David Thoreau: "Resistance to Civil Government"

1. See William G. McLoughlin, "Massive Civil Disobedience as a Baptist Tactic in 1773," *American Quarterly* 21 (Winter 1969):727.

2. Henry David Thoreau, *Writings of Henry David Thoreau* (Cambridge, Mass.: Riverside Press, 1894), vol. 10, p. 154.

Introduction to Part III: Disobedience to the Fugitive Slave Law of 1850

1. Daniel Webster to William Henry Furness, February 15, 1850, quoted in George Ticknor Curtis, *Life of Daniel Webster* (New York: D. Appleton, 1870), vol. 2, pp. 401–402. Furness, a Unitarian minister in Philadelphia, was one of many who insisted on a more rapid rate of progress and who drew more radical conclusions than did Webster from the premise that God's plan was ultimately opposed to slavery. Several of his sermons in the 1850s advocated civil disobedience in response to the Fugitive Slave Law.

2. See John H. Schroeder, *Mr. Polk's War: American Opposition and Dissent, 1846–1848* (Madison: University of Wisconsin Press, 1973), p. 91n.

3. An earlier statute had been in effect since 1793, but it had been enforced only desultorily and indeed had been practically nullified in several northern states both by the passage of "personal liberty laws" and by considerable popular disobedience. See, for example, Larry Gara, *The Liberty Line* (Lexington: University Press of Kentucky, 1967), pp. 117–118.

4. Ralph Waldo Emerson, *Miscellanies*, vol. 11 of *Works of Ralph Waldo Emerson* (Cambridge, Mass., 1904), p. 219.

5. Samuel J. May, *Some Recollections of Our Antislavery Conflict* (Boston: Fields, Osgood, 1869), p. 349.

6. Gara, *Liberty Line*, p. 102.

7. William C. Cochran, *The Western Reserve and the Fugitive Slave Law* (Cleveland, 1920), p. 99.

8. Quoted in the *Liberator*, 20 (April 5, 1850):55. Among the signers were three members of the faculty of Andover Theological Seminary and some eminent representatives of Harvard, including Jared Sparks, its president, and George Ticknor. Webster received similar testimonials from other northern groups. See *Correspondence between Mr. Webster and His New Hampshire Neighbors* (Washington, D.C., 1850); *Letter from the Citizens of Newburyport, Mass., to Mr. Webster* (Washington, D.C., 1850).

9. Allan Nevins, *Ordeal of the Union* (New York: Scribner, 1947), vol. 1, says (p. 400): "Even in the Northeast the clergy was largely on the side of the Compromise and of adherence to national mandates."

10. See *Mr. Webster's Speeches at Buffalo, Syracuse, and Albany*, (New York: Mirror office, 1851), esp. p. 18.

11. Quoted in Samuel Gilman Brown, ed., *The Works of Rufus Choate* (Boston: Little, Brown, 1862), vol. 1, pp. 172–173.

12. This and the following quotations are from *Proceedings of the Constitutional Meeting at Faneuil Hall* (Boston, 1850).

13. See Harold Schwartz, "Fugitive Slave Days in Boston," *New England Quarterly* 27 (1954):191–212; and Stanley W. Campbell, *The Slave Catchers: Enforcement of the Fugitive Slave Law, 1850–1860* (Chapel Hill: University of North Carolina Press, 1970), esp. chaps. 3–7.

14. Quoted in Albert Mordell, *Quaker Militant: John Greenleaf Whittier* (Cambridge, Mass.: Riverside Press, 1933), pp. 160–161.

15. Theodore Parker, *The Function and Place of Conscience, in Relation to the Laws of Men* (Boston: Crosby & Nichols, 1850), p. 25.

16. Richard Hofstadter and Michael Wallace, eds., *American Violence: A Documentary History* (New York: Vintage Books, 1971), pp. 84–89.

17. See Nevins, *Ordeal of the Union*, vol. 1, pp. 407, 410.

18. Robert F. Lucid, ed., *The Journal of Richard Henry Dana, Jr.* (Cambridge: Harvard University Press, 1968), vol. 2, p. 628 (May 26, 1854). Dana attributes the change to the passage of the Kansas-Nebraska Act. See also Campbell, *Slave Catchers*, pp. 49–50.

12. Lewis Hayden, William C. Nell, and others: "Declaration of Sentiments of the Colored Citizens of Boston, on the Fugitive Slave Bill"

1. Benjamin Quarles, *Black Abolitionists* (New York: Oxford University Press, 1970), pp. 199–218.

2. Ibid., pp. 149–150.

3. Carleton Mabee, *Black Freedom: The Nonviolent Abolitionists from 1830 through the Civil War* (New York: Macmillan, 1970), chap. 11.

4. Ibid., p. 165.

5. Ibid., p. 197.

6. Mrs. Stowe's actual debt to Henson seems to have been minimal. See her *Key to Uncle Tom's Cabin* (Boston: John P. Jewett, 1853), pp. 26–27, and Robin W. Winks, Introduction to *An Autobiography of the Reverend Josiah Henson* (Reading, Mass.: Addison-Wesley, 1969), pp. v–xxx.

7. Quarles, *Black Abolitionists*, p. 26.

8. Mabee, *Black Freedom*, pp. 64, 258.

13. Theodore Parker: *The Function and Place of Conscience, in Relation to the Laws of Men*

1. Henry Steele Commager, ed., *Theodore Parker: An Anthology* (Boston: Beacon Press, 1960), p. 9.

2. Parker, "Transcendentalism," quoted in ibid., p. 91.

14. Samuel Willard: *The Grand Issue*

1. Samuel J. May, *Some Recollections of Our Antislavery Conflict* (Boston: Fields, Osgood, 1869), p. 366.

2. See Charles E. Park, "Samuel Willard," in *Heralds of a Liberal Faith*, ed. Samuel A. Eliot (Boston: American Unitarian Association, 1910), vol. 2, pp. 90–94; *Christian Examiner* 50 (May 1851):516.

15. Nathaniel Hall: *The Limits of Civil Obedience*

1. The phrase is from George W. Briggs, "Sermon," in *A Memorial of the Reverend Nathaniel Hall* (Boston: Ebenezer Clapp, 1876), p. 42.

2. Ibid., p. 25. See also Charles A. Humphreys, "Nathaniel Hall," in *Heralds of a Liberal Faith*, ed. Samuel A. Eliot (Boston: American Unitarian Association, 1910), vol. 3, pp. 154–157; and Octavius Brooks Frothingham, *Boston Unitarianism, 1820–1850* (New York: Putnam, 1890), pp. 189–205.

16. Daniel Foster: *Our Nation's Sins and the Christian's Duty*

1. Walter Harding, *The Days of Henry Thoreau* (New York: Alfred A. Knopf, 1965), p. 322.

2. Daniel Foster, *Farewell Sermon* (Springfield, Mass.: George W. Wilson, 1850).

3. Ibid., pp. 12, 11.

4. Foster, *Our Nation's Sins and the Christian's Duty* (Boston: White & Potter, 1851), p. 30.

5. Ibid., pp. 7, 13, 14, 15, 21.

17. Charles Beecher: *The Duty of Disobedience to Wicked Laws*

1. Lyman Beecher Stowe, *Saints, Sinners, and Beechers* (Indianapolis: Bobbs-Merrill, 1934), pp. 338–340. See Robert Merideth, *The Politics of the Universe: Edward Beecher, Abolition, and Orthodoxy* (Nashville: Vanderbilt University Press, 1968), pp. 213–224. Merideth suggests that other issues, including political ones, may have had as much to do with the trial as the ostensible ones did.

18. Gerrit Smith: *The True Office of Civil Government*

1. Carleton Mabee, *Black Freedom: The Nonviolent Abolitionists from 1830 through the Civil War* (New York: Macmillan, 1970), p. 318.

2. Ibid., p. 327. The idea that slaveowners should be compensated for giving up their slaves was anathema to many abolitionists, since the proposed payments seemed to legitimize the ownership of persons as property.

19. Thomas Treadwell Stone: *An Address before the Salem Female Anti-Slavery Society*

1. Nicholas P. Gilman, "Thomas Treadwell Stone," in *Heralds of a Liberal Faith*, ed. Samuel A. Eliot (Boston: American Unitarian Association, 1910), vol. 3, pp. 358–361.

20. Joshua Giddings: *Speeches in Congress*

1. Jane H. Pease and William H. Pease, *Bound with Them in Chains: A Biographical History of the Antislavery Movement* (Westport, Conn.: Greenwood Press, 1972), p. 250.

2. Ibid., p. 257.

3. Ibid., p. 266.

4. Quoted in James Brewer Stewart, *Joshua R. Giddings and the Tactics of Radical Politics* (Cleveland: Press of the Case Western Reserve University, 1970), p. 269.

21. Wendell Phillips: Speech at the Melodeon on the First Anniversary of the Rendition of Thomas Sims

1. See Carleton Mabee, *Black Freedom: The Nonviolent Abolitionists from 1830 through the Civil War* (New York: Macmillan, 1970), pp. 318, 321; and Oscar Sherwin, *Prophet of Liberty: The Life and Times of Wendell Phillips* (New York: Bookman Associates, 1958), p. 335.

22. Harriet Beecher Stowe: *Uncle Tom's Cabin*

1. William R. Taylor, "The Plantation Novel and the Sentimental Tradition," in *Intellectual History in America*, ed. Cushing Strout (New York: Harper & Row, 1968), vol. 1, pp. 225–228; and Barbara M. Cross, "Harriet Beecher Stowe," in *Notable American Women, 1607–1950: A Biographical Dictionary*, ed. Edward T. James (Cambridge: Belknap Press of Harvard University Press, 1971), vol. 3, pp. 396–399.

2. Cross, "Harriet Beecher Stowe," p. 397.

3. Ibid., p. 398.

4. Ibid., p. 399.

5. Quoted in Oscar Sherwin, *Prophet of Liberty: The Life and Times of Wendell Phillips* (New York: Bookman Associates, 1958), p. 278.

23. Thomas Wentworth Higginson: *Massachusetts in Mourning*

1. Quoted in Tilden G. Edelstein, *Strange Enthusiasm: A Life of Thomas Wentworth Higginson* (New Haven: Yale University Press, 1968), p. 105.

2. Ibid., passim, esp., p. 205; Carleton Mabee, *Black Freedom: The Nonviolent Abolitionists from 1830 through the Civil War* (New York: Macmillan, 1970), p. 318.

25. Lydia Maria Child: *The Duty of Disobedience to the Fugitive Slave Act*

1. Jane H. Pease and William H. Pease, *Bound with Them in Chains: A Biographical History of the Antislavery Movement* (Westport, Conn.: Greenwood Press, 1972), p. 44.

2. See the excellent article on Mrs. Child by Louis Filler in *Notable American Women, 1607–1950: A Biographical Dictionary*, ed. Edward T. James (Cambridge: Belknap Press of Harvard University Press, 1971), vol. 3, pp. 330–333, which also includes a comprehensive bibliographical note.

3. The full text of the *Address* and the names of the signers are given in Benjamin R. Curtis, ed., *A Memoir of Benjamin Robbins Curtis* (Boston: Little, Brown, 1879), vol. 1, pp. 328–336.

26. Elizabeth Cady Stanton, Lucretia Mott, and others: "Declaration of Sentiments and Resolutions of the First Woman's Rights Convention"

1. Elizabeth Cady Stanton, Susan B. Anthony, and Matilda Joslyn Gage, eds., *History of Woman Suffrage* (New York: Fowler & Wells, 1881), vol. 1, pp. 73–74.

2. See Robert E. Riegel, *American Women: A Story of Social Change* (Rutherford, N.J.: Fairleigh Dickinson University Press, 1970), p. 223.

27. Susan B. Anthony: Statement to the Court

1. The language of the Fourteenth Amendment, on which this argument was based, is as follows: "All persons born or naturalized in the United States, and subject to the jurisdiction thereof, are citizens of the United States and of the State wherein they reside. No State shall make or enforce any law which shall abridge the privileges or immunities of citizens of the United States. . . ."

2. Two quite different favorable outcomes were regarded as possible by the suffragists: first, that the NWSA's constitutional argument might be upheld in the Supreme Court, as it had been by a number of constitutional lawyers and a few members of Congress (see Ida Husted Harper, *Life and Work of Susan B. Anthony* [Indianapolis: Hollenbeck, 1898], p. 429); and second, as Susan Anthony urged, that juries would "fail to return verdicts of 'guilty' against honest, law-abiding, tax-paying United States citizens for offering their votes at our elections" (Elizabeth Cady Stanton, Susan B. Anthony, and Matilda Joslyn Gage, eds., *History of Woman Suffrage* [New York: Fowler & Wells, 1881], vol. 2, p. 646).

3. Harper, *Life and Work*, p. 433n.

4. Stanton et al., eds., *History of Woman Suffrage*, vol. 2, p. 690.

5. Harper, *Life and Work*, p. 432. Susan Anthony candidly expressed her long-standing determination to vote even before she received an encouraging legal opinion from her chief counsel, Judge Henry R. Selden (Stanton et al., eds., *History of Woman Suffrage*, vol. 2, p. 654).

6. Stanton et al., eds., *History of Woman Suffrage*, p. 646.

7. In the last years before the Civil War, as an agent for the American Anti-Slavery Society, Susan Anthony had exhorted her audience to "overthrow this government, commit its blood-stained Constitution to the flames, blot out every vestige of that guilty bargain of the fathers" (quoted in Alma Lutz, "Susan Brownell Anthony," in *Notable American Women, 1607–1950: A Biographical Dictionary*, ed. Edward T. James [Cambridge: Belknap Press of Harvard University Press, 1971], vol. 1, p. 53).

28. Abby Smith: Speeches and Letters

1. See Elizabeth George Speare, "Abby Hadassah and Julia Evelina Smith," in *Notable American Women, 1607–1950: A Biographical Dictionary*, ed. Edward T. James (Cambridge: Belknap Press of Harvard Uni-

versity Press, 1971), vol. 3, pp. 302–304; and Mary Wilhelmine Williams, "Abby Hadassah Smith," in *Dictionary of American Biography*, vol. 9, pp. 233–234.

2. Julia Smith, *Abby Smith and Her Cows, with a Report of the Law Case Decided Contrary to Law* (Hartford, Conn., 1877), p. 8.

3. Elizabeth Cady Stanton, Susan B. Anthony, and Matilda Joslyn Gage, eds., *History of Woman Suffrage* (New York: Fowler & Wells, 1881), vol. 3, p. 98.

29. Militant Suffragists Picket President Wilson

1. Eleanor Flexner, *Century of Struggle: The Woman's Rights Movement in the United States*, rev. ed. (Cambridge: Belknap Press of Harvard University Press, 1975), pp. 271–279.

2. Doris Stevens, *Jailed for Freedom* (New York: Boni & Liveright, 1920), p. 66.

3. Ibid., pp. 64–65.

4. Ibid., p. 124.

5. Doris Stevens, a leading militant who became one of the movement's historians, prophesied that "when all suffrage controversy has died away it will be the little army of women with their purple, white and gold banners, going to prison for their political freedom, that will be remembered. They dramatized to victory the long suffrage fight in America" (*Jailed for Freedom*, p. 63). Her claims for the decisiveness of the militants' tactics are almost certainly exaggerated, however, omitting as they do a number of other influences, especially the immense activity of the NAWSA once it had been revivified by the leadership of Carrie Chapman Catt. See Flexner, *Century of Struggle*, pp. 286–303, 319–337.

6. Flexner, *Century of Struggle*, p. 295.

7. Ibid., p. 297.

30. A. Philip Randolph vs. Wayne Morse

1. Lerone Bennett, Jr., *Confrontation: Black and White* (Chicago: Johnson Publishing Co., 1965), p. 179. Bennett observes (p. 186) that the March on Washington Movement was "the first Negro mass movement that was not based on black nationalism."

2. Quoted in Jervis Anderson, *A. Philip Randolph: A Biographical Portrait* (New York: Harcourt Brace Jovanovich, 1973), p. 259.

3. Ibid., pp. 276–278. For a sympathetic exposition of the army's viewpoint, see Hanson W. Baldwin, "Segregation in the Army," *New York Times*, August 8, 1948, p. 51.

4. Bennett, *Confrontation*, p. 179; Anderson, *A. Philip Randolph*, p. 261.

5. Anderson, *A. Philip Randolph*, pp. 106–108.

6. Quoted in "Randolph Tells Philosophy behind 'March' Movement," *Chicago Defender*, June 19, 1943, p. 13.

7. Quoted in "Randolph Tells Technique of Civil Disobedience," *Chicago Defender*, June 26, 1943, p. 13.

8. See Anderson, *A. Philip Randolph*, pp. 279–280, and *Congressional Record*, vol. 94, pp. 4314–4317. In 1940 Thurgood Marshall had advised Secretary of War Henry L. Stimson that "Negroes who were refused the right to serve in all branches would prefer to go to jail" (Joseph P. Lash, *Eleanor and Franklin* [New York: Norton, 1971], p. 529).

9. *Congressional Record*, vol. 94, p. 4312.

10. Quoted in ibid., p. 4317.

11. Ibid. Later White again said publicly that the NAACP wouldn't support civil disobedience but would "continue to campaign against segregation and discrimination within the framework of the U.S. Constitution" and would help to organize demonstrations against a Jim Crow army (*New York Times*, August 8, 1948, sec. 1, p. 18).

12. The text of Randolph's prepared statement to the committee may be found in August Meier, Elliott Rudwick, and Francis L. Broderick, eds., *Black Protest Thought in the Twentieth Century* (Indianapolis: Bobbs-Merrill, 1971), pp. 274–280.

31. Martin Luther King, Jr.: Three Statements on Civil Disobedience

1. Quoted in *New York Times*, February 22, 1956, p. 1.

2. Martin Luther King, Jr., *Why We Can't Wait* (New York: Harper & Row, 1964), pp. 68–69.

3. Ibid., pp. 26–27.

4. David L. Lewis, *King: A Critical Biography* (New York: Praeger, 1970), p. 387.

5. Martin Luther King, Jr., "Showdown for Non-violence," *Look*, April 16, 1968, p. 24.

6. Quoted in Charles Fager, *Uncertain Resurrection: The Poor People's Washington Campaign* (Grand Rapids, Mich.: William B. Eerdmans, 1969), p. 18.

32. Stokely Carmichael: "Black Power"

1. *New York Times*, August 5, 1966, p. 10.

2. Ibid., March 14, 1967, p. 39; May 1, 1967, p. 12.

3. Quoted in ibid., October 30, 1966, sec. 1, p. 63.

4. Quoted in ibid., August 18, 1967, p. 17; see also ibid., August 4, 1967, p. 6. Nonetheless, in 1968 Carmichael agreed to march nonviolently with Martin Luther King in the Poor People's Campaign. But his emphases since then have been pan-Africanist or revolutionary or both. For much of the past several years he has lived in Guinea (West Africa).

33. John Haynes Holmes: "A Statement to My People on the Eve of War"

1. Quoted in Ray H. Abrams, *Preachers Present Arms* (New York: Round Table Press, 1933), p. 193. This denominational belligerence

precipitated Holmes's withdrawal from his Unitarian affiliation and his
church's change of identity from the Unitarian Church of the Messiah
to the nondenominational Community Church of New York. On the
surveillance of the Secret Service, see Abrams, *Preachers Present Arms*,
p. 200. I have drawn also on Holmes's autobiography, *I Speak for Myself* (New York: Harper & Row, 1959), and on Carl Hermann Voss, ed.,
A Summons unto Men: An Anthology of the Writings of John Haynes Holmes
(New York: Simon & Schuster, 1971). Holmes was one of the most
widely known radicals in the United States and is mentioned or discussed in many scholarly studies. A particularly suggestive (and critical) discussion of his pacifism may be found in Charles Chatfield, *For
Peace and Justice: Pacifism in America, 1914–1941* (Knoxville: University of
Tennessee Press, 1971), pp. 63–66. For information on the fate of other
pacifist clergymen during the war, see Abrams, *Preachers Present Arms*,
chap. 11.

2. Quoted in *New York Times*, April 3, 1917, p. 13.

3. John Haynes Holmes, "A Statement to My People on the Eve of
War," *The Messiah Pulpit*, May 1917, p. 14.

4. Ibid., p. 9.

34. Carl Haessler, Maurice Hess, and Roger Baldwin: Statements by Conscientious Objectors

1. Lillian Schlissel, ed., *Conscience in America: A Documentary History
of Conscientious Objection in America, 1757–1967* (New York: Dutton,
1968), pp. 128–132; Norman M. Thomas, *The Conscientious Objector in
America* (New York: B. W. Huebsch, 1923), pp. 14–23.

2. Schlissel, ed., *Conscience in America*, p. 130; Staughton Lynd, *Nonviolence in America: A Documentary History* (Indianapolis: Bobbs-Merrill,
1966), p. 173.

35. Albert Einstein: The Two Percent Speech

1. Otto Nathan and Heinz Norden, eds., *Einstein on Peace* (New
York: Simon & Schuster, 1960), p. 92.

2. Ibid., p. 208.

3. Ibid., p. 169.

4. Ibid., p. 123.

5. Quoted in *The Nation*, 133 (September 2, 1931):239.

6. Nathan and Norden, eds., *Einstein on Peace*, p. 172.

7. Ibid., p. 233.

8. Ibid., pp. 226–233.

9. Ibid., pp. 235–236.

10. Ibid., p. 461. For a detailed, explicit critique by Einstein of his
earlier advocacy of war resistance, see ibid., pp. 230, 461–462.

36. Jessie Wallace Hughan: *The Beginnings of War Resistance*

1. *New York Times*, April 11, 1955, p. 23.

2. Ibid., June 9, 1922, p. 17.

3. Their actions were taken even though Miss Hughan had her principal's support. See Howard K. Beale, *Are American Teachers Free?* (New York: Octagon Books, 1972), pp. 35, 51, 585.

4. Other names on the list, which was prepared by the Military Intelligence Service and referred to by the Service's spokesman as "a Who's Who in Pacifism and Radicalism," included Jane Addams, Scott Nearing, John Haynes Holmes, Norman Thomas, Roger Baldwin, Eugene Debs, and Charles Beard. Beard was one of several of the group who vehemently denied having been pacifists after the initiation of hostilities. Miss Hughan's public comment was more tranquil: "I am glad to appear on any list that begins with Jane Addams' name." See *New York Times*, January 25, 1919, pp. 1, 4; January 26, 1919, sec. 1, p. 8.

5. Lawrence S. Wittner, *Rebels against War: The American Peace Movement, 1941–1960* (New York: Columbia University Press, 1969), pp. 40–41.

37. Leon Thomson, Donald Benedict, David Dellinger, and others: *Why We Refused to Register*

1. Leon Thomson et al., *Why We Refused to Register* (New York, [1941?]), pp. 11–12. See also Staughton Lynd, *Nonviolence in America: A Documentary History* (Indianapolis: Bobbs-Merrill, 1966), p. 296.

38. Albert Bigelow: "Why I Am Sailing into the Pacific Bomb-Test Area"

1. Albert Bigelow, *The Voyage of the "Golden Rule": An Experiment with Truth* (New York: Doubleday, 1959), esp. pp. 23–25, 91–115; Albert Bigelow, personal communication, November 19, 1976, and January 21, 1977. Bigelow's crew members were William Huntington, George Willoughby, and Orion Sherwood.

39. Charlotte E. Keyes: "'Suppose They Gave a War and No One Came'"

1. Charlotte E. Keyes, personal communication, August 24, 1976. Further information about Gene Keyes's concept of resistance may be found in Alice Lynd, ed., *We Won't Go: Personal Accounts of War Objectors* (Boston: Beacon Press, 1968), pp. 15–32.

2. Charlotte E. Keyes, personal communication, October 11, 1976.

40. Michael Ferber: "A Time to Say No"

1. Jessica Mitford, *The Trial of Dr. Spock* (New York: Alfred A. Knopf, 1969), p. 27. See Miss Mitford's book generally, esp. pp. 18–29. On the Resistance see also Alice Lynd, ed., *We Won't Go: Personal Accounts of War Objectors* (Boston: Beacon Press, 1968), pp. 238–243, and Michael Ferber and Staughton Lynd, *The Resistance* (Boston: Beacon Press, 1971).

2. Quoted in Mitford, *Trial of Dr. Spock*, pp. 18–19, 28; Michael Ferber, personal communication, August 3, 1976.

3. Quoted in Mitford, *Trial of Dr. Spock*, pp. 20, 26.

41. Daniel Berrigan: *The Trial of the Catonsville Nine*

1. Quoted in Francine du Plessix Gray, *Divine Disobedience: Profiles in Catholic Radicalism* (New York: Alfred A. Knopf, 1970), p. 133.
2. Ibid., p. 226.
3. Quoted in ibid., p. 207.
4. Ibid., p. 57. The words are recalled by Francine Gray from an oral statement by Fr. Berrigan.
5. Paraphrased in *New York Times*, August 10, 1970, p. 34; quoted in ibid., August 16, 1970, sec. 2, p. 3.

42. John William Ward: "To Whom Should I Write a Letter?"

1. John William Ward, personal communication, August 5, 1976.
2. Minutes of June 1972 meeting of Amherst College Board of Trustees.

44. William Sloane Coffin, Jr.: "Not Yet a Good Man"

1. Quoted in *New York Times*, October 29, 1967, sec. 1, p. 15. On numerous occasions, however, Coffin had virtually courted arrest.
2. Ibid. The *Yale Daily News* was less generous to the president than the chaplain was, criticizing Brewster for his "vilification" of Coffin (*New York Times*, October 31, 1967, p. 12).

Index

CIVIL DISOBEDIENCE
IN AMERICA

Designed by R. E. Rosenbaum.
Composed by G & S Typesetters, Inc.
in 10 point VIP Palatino, 2 points leaded,
with display lines in Palatino bold.
Printed offset by Thomson–Shore, Inc.
Warren's No. 66 text, 50 pound basis.
Bound by John H. Dekker and Sons, Inc.
in Joanna book cloth
and stamped in All Purpose foil.

Library of Congress Cataloging in Publication Data
(For library cataloging purposes only)

Main entry under title:
Civil disobedience in America.

Includes bibliographical references and index.
1. Government, Resistance to—Addresses, essays, lectures. 2. Political science—United States—History—Addresses, essays, lectures. I. Weber, David R.,
1943–
JC328.3.C55   323.6'5   77–90914
ISBN 0–8014–1005–3